D1084060

Man in Community

Volumes in This Series

I. *Christian Social Ethics in a Changing World*
II. *Responsible Government in a Revolutionary Age*
III. *Economic Growth in World Perspective*
IV. *Man in Community*

Man in Community

Christian Concern for the Human in Changing Society

Edited by EGBERT DE VRIES

ASSOCIATION PRESS · NEW YORK
SCM PRESS · BLOOMSBURY STREET · LONDON

Man in Community

Published by Association Press, 291 Broadway, New York, N. Y. 10007
and
SCM Press, Bloomsbury Street, London

First Printing April 1966
Second Printing June 1966
Third Printing May 1967

Library of Congress catalog card number: 66–11797

Publisher's stock number: 1605

72

PRINTED IN THE UNITED STATES OF AMERICA

PREFACE

In 1962, the Central Committee of the World Council of Churches authorized the Department on Church and Society to begin preparations for a world conference to be held in 1966. The theme that was finally selected was "Christians in the Technical and Social Revolutions of Our Time." The department was also requested to undertake such preparatory studies as would help the conference in considering the central issues for Christian social ethics in contemporary society. In 1963, the Working Committee of the department recommended the preparation of four books of essays on the following subjects:

I. *Christian Social Ethics in a Changing World*
II. *Responsible Government in a Revolutionary Age*
III. *Economic Growth in World Perspective*
IV. *Man in Community*

We are pleased to commend these books to Christians around the world, and we invite them to share with us their reactions and opinions on the issues raised therein. Although the books are primarily intended as preparatory reading for the 1966 conference, it is hoped that they will also be used for discussion in local and regional groups around the world, after the conference as well as before.

Not since the Oxford World Conference on Church, Community and State, in 1937, has there been a similar world-wide effort to rethink Christian social responsibility. The study volumes for that conference dealt largely with the theological issues of social ethics within the context of the churches' encounter with the challenges of that time. Since then, new technical and social revolutions have overtaken societies all over the world, and new issues of social ethics have arisen as the churches have responded to them. The first of the present volumes deals with the theological problems of social ethics as such, while the others concentrate on relating theological insights to the actual problems of Christian responsibility in the contemporary situation of world political, economic and social change.

These symposia do not pretend to represent the full range of viewpoints held within the ecumenical fellowship on these questions. This is impossible in the space of four volumes on such large themes. The aim is rather to reveal the wide range of attitudes and opinions held, giving special attention to new and challenging points of view.

The responsibility for the structure and contents of these volumes is shared by the international editorial committees, which met in 1963 and 1964 to prepare the outline of each book and to review the first drafts of the contributions; by the chairman or editorial conveners of these committees, who have since become the editors of the books; and by the staff of the Department on Church and Society, who necessarily had to undertake the large part of the detailed editorial work and correspondence. Each writer remains responsible for the content of his contribution.

We are grateful to all those who have contributed to the volumes and to those who have commented on the essays in draft form. We acknowledge with appreciation the contribution of the

Church and Society staff—Professor Mauricio Lopez, the Reverend Thomas Okuma and, in particular, Miss Margaret Sinclair, one of the early workers in the Universal Christian Council for Life and Work, who forsook her retirement for three months to assist us in preparing the manuscripts for publication. We depended throughout on our secretarial staff, Miss Audrey Smith, Miss Christa Stalschus and Miss Judith Brown, who typed the many drafts of these manuscripts.

M. M. THOMAS, *Chairman,*
Working Committee
Department on Church and Society

PAUL ABRECHT, *Executive Secretary*
Department on Church and Society

World Council of Churches
Division of Studies

CONTRIBUTORS TO THIS VOLUME

Egbert de Vries Rector of the Institute of Social Studies, The Hague; formerly staff member of the Department of Agricultural Faculty in the University of Indonesia (1940-1946); economic adviser and chief of Agricultural Division, International Bank (1950-1956); chairman of the Working Committee on Church and Society of the World Council of Churches (1955-1961). Author: *Agriculture and Prosperity in Pasuruan, East Java,* 1931; *The Earth Pays,* 1949; *Man in Rapid Social Change,* 1961. (Netherlands Reformed Church)

Masao Takenaka Professor, Christian social ethics and sociology of religion, and dean of School of Theology, Doshisha University; chairman of the Committee of the Witness of Laity of the EACC; chairman of Political Commission of WSCF. (United Church of Christ)

André Dumas Professor of ethics at the Faculty of Theology in Paris. Author of *Der Krieg in Algerien; Le contrôle des naissantes; Opinions protestantes; La soumission chrétienne* (L'éthique interhumaine des épitres du Nouveau Testament et notre temps); *Une théologie de la reconciliation: Dietrich Bonhoeffer;* co-author of *L'homme marxiste et l'homme chrétien.* (Église Reformée de France)

(Mrs.) Kiyoko Takeda Cho Professor, history of modern Japanese thought, International Christian University; director, Committee on Asian Cultural Studies. (United Church of Christ in Japan)

David W. Barry Executive director, New York City Mission Society; pioneer revising the role and the strategy of the church in relation to modern urban problems. Co-author (with Everett C. Parker and Dallas Smythe) of the Television Radio Audience and Religion. (United Presbyterian Church in the U. S. A.)

Orlando Fals Borda Professor of sociology and dean of the Faculty of Sociology at the National University of Colombia; ex-director general of the Ministry of Agriculture of Colombia. Author of *Peasant Society in the Colombian Andes; Education in Colombia; Community Development in Colombia; Rural Housing in Brazil,* etc.; co-author with a Colombian Roman Catholic priest of a study of violence in the rural areas of Colombia. (Presbyterian)

Monica H. Wilson Professor, social anthropology, School of African Studies, University of Cape Town. Author of *Reaction to Conquest*—a sociological study of the conflict of European and African culture in the Transkei; *The Analysis of Social Change,* based on observations in Central Africa (with Godfrey Wilson); *Good Company, Rituals of Kinship Among the Nyakyusa, Communal Rituals of the Nyakyusa,* on a people of Tanzania; *Langa,* a study of the process of urbanization in Cape Town (with Archie Mafeje); and other publications. (Church of the Province of S. Africa—Anglican)

Helmut Begemann Superintendent in the Westfalian Landeskirche. Author of *Strukturwandel der Familie* (Hamburg, 1960). (Evangelical Church in Germany)

Daisuke Kitagawa Executive secretary, Division of Domestic Mission, Home Department; formerly on the staff of the WCC Department on Church and Society, 1956-1960; secretary for racial and ethnic relation, 1960-1962. Author of *Race Relations and Christian Mission* and *The Pastor and the Race Issue.* (Protestant Episcopal Church)

Dietrich von Oppen University professor; author of *Das personale Zeitalter, Verbraucher und Genossenschaft* (Zur Soziologie und

Sozialgeschichte der deutschen Konsumgenossenschaften). (Evangelical Church in Germany)

Julio R. Sabanes Methodist pastor and professor at the Union Theological Seminary in Buenos Aires. (Methodist)

James M. Gustafson Chairman, Department of Religious Studies, professor of Christian ethics, Yale University. Author of *Treasure in Earthen Vessels: The Church as a Human Community*. (United Church of Christ, U. S. A.)

Margaret Mead Anthropologist; associate curator of ethnology 1942-1964, curator of ethnology since 1964, The American Museum of Natural History. Author of many books; world famous for her anthropological studies, her latest book being *Continuities in Cultural Evolution,* 1964. Member of the WCC Working Committee on Church and Society. (Episcopalian)

Richard Kaufmann Feature editor of *Süddeutsche Zeitung* and *Westermann's Monatshefte*. Science editor of the weekly paper *Christ und Welt*. His book *Der Menschenmacher* was first published as a series of articles in *Christ und Welt*. Translator of published works from English into German, among them *Parkinson's Law*. His publications include the novel *Der Himmel zahlt keine Zinsen* (1950); *Gebrannte Kinder*—a sociological study on postwar youth; and *Der Menschenmacher*—a book on the challenge of modern biology to man and society. (Evangelical Church in Germany)

Erna M. Hoch Born in a Swiss family with a tradition of theological studies and missionary work (Basel Mission, Malabar coast in India). Medical doctor and psychiatrist. From 1956-1961, director of Nur Manzil Psychiatric Centre, Lucknow, under the auspices of Methodist Church of Southern Asia and Methodist Board of Missions, New York. Since 1961, private research, unofficial and honorary services as an adviser to Ministry of Health, Government of India. In 1964, short-term consultant with World Health Organization for India (Mental Health). At present visiting professor (Mental Health) at Institute of Social Sciences, Kashi Vidyapith, Varanasi, India. (Evangelical Reformed Church of the City of Basle)

Marvin P. Halverson Secretary, Foundation for the Arts, Religion and Culture, Inc.; formerly executive director, Department of Worship and the Arts, National Council of Churches in the U. S. A.; also formerly director of studies and dean of students, The Chicago Theological Seminary, Chicago, Ill.; editor, *Hand-*

book of Christian Theology; editor, *Religious Drama 1* and *Religious Drama 3;* author, *Great Religious Paintings;* author of numerous articles and reviews in various periodicals. (United Church of Christ, U. S. A.)

Heinz Flügel Born in São Paulo in 1907. Author, *Mythen und Mysterien* (Poems, 1930); *Der Hahnenschrei,* a collection of radio plays; *Zweifel—Schwermut—Genialität* (1952); *Zwischen Gott und Gottlosigkeit* (1957), a collection of essays about modern culture and world of faith; in 1960, was awarded the essay-prize by the Foundation for the Promotion of Literature; latest published works include *Herausforderung durch das Wort* (1962) (critical essays on modern literature); *Konturen des Tragischen,* February, 1965 (tragic figures in world literature); especially known for his radio broadcasts on subjects related to modern man and literature. Presently on the staff of the Evangelical Academy, Tutzing. (Evangelical Church in Germany)

Arend Th. van Leeuwen Director of Kerk en Wereld, ecumenical lay training center in Holland; missionary and student of Islamic thought and culture; teacher at the missionary college at Oegstgeest (Holland). Author of *Ghazali as Apologist of Islam* (Leiden, 1947); *Hendrik Kraemer, Pionier der Ökumene* (Basel, 1962); *Christianity in World History* (London, 1964). (Netherlands Reformed Church)

C. I. Itty B.A. physics from Madras Christian College; M.A. in psychology, Madras University; graduate work for one year, Union Theological Seminary, N. Y.; 1950-1952, traveling secretary, SCM of India; 1952-1953, secretary, SCM, Indonesia; 1953-1954, secretary, YMCA, Indonesia; 1957-1960, assistant general secretary, SCM, in India; 1960-1963, assistant secretary, Youth Department, WCC; associate secretary, WCC, Laity Department. (Orthodox Syrian Church of the East)

Charles C. West Professor of Christian ethics, Princeton Theological Seminary; formerly assistant director of the Ecumenical Institute at Céligny, Switzerland. Author of *Communism and the Theologians; Outside the Camp,* a study of the church in mission; co-editor with Robert Mackie of *The Sufficiency of God: Essays in Honor of Dr. W. A. Visser't Hooft;* and, with David Paton, of *The Missionary Church in East and West.* (Presbyterian)

Father Paul Verghese Associate general secretary of the WCC since May 1962; director of Division of Ecumenical Action; former personal secretary to Emperor Haile Selassie of Ethiopia; chief adviser to Welfare Foundation, and executive secretary to the Ethiopian Government's committee for the distribution of relief aid; honorary lecturer in religion at the University College, Addis Ababa; from 1954-1957, general secretary. Orthodox Christian Student Movement in India; 1955-1957, honorary associate secretary of the Indian SCM; former newspaper reporter, postmaster and associate secretary of the Indian Post and Telegraph Union for Travancore and Cochin; STM from Yale Divinity School; 1961, ordained a priest of the Syrian Orthodox Church. (Syrian Orthodox Church)

CONTENTS

PART II

Society and Tension

PART III

Christian Bases of Man in Community

FOREWORD

by Egbert de Vries

Man in community is not a new theme in ecumenical circles; it was one of the featured topics at the 1937 Oxford conference on Church, Community and State. Yet only in recent years have the churches managed to overcome two handicaps which have obstructed more creative thinking on this subject: first, the tendency to defend an unrealistic Christendom conception of social and cultural institutions; and second, the difficulty in accepting the views of social scientists for fear of their hidden ideological or philosophical assumptions which were assumed to be in conflict with the Christian faith.

We have made much progress in overcoming both these handicaps in recent years, and *Man in Community* is some reflection of this. Sociologists, anthropologists, psychologists, natural scientists, students of culture and theologians have collaborated in preparing these chapters. It is clear that they are looking beyond traditional Christian attitudes on Church and Community. What they have to say constitutes a new stage in Christian reflection on the problems of divining the patterns of human living for our time.

A book on man and community is a presumption. Everything human relates to man and community and the selection of specific issues is arbitrary. We chose to limit ourselves to those topics which were of special concern to the churches today.

The two essays in Part I point to the issues confronting the church as it evaluates the changes which occur in European and Asian society in the transition from tradition to modernity. Of course, the words "tradition" and "modernity" are themselves subject to debate.

Part II focuses on specific areas of tensions in contemporary society: the questioning of ideologies, the meaning of the urban revolution and the racial crisis. Against this background Part III discusses the Christian bases of man in community. Is there a specific Christian contribution to the renewal of community? What is its biblical and theological basis?

The contributions to Part IV explore the meaning of man and community from the perspective of science and culture. Three branches of the human sciences are represented: anthropology, biology and psychiatry. There are also two essays on modern culture and community. The first is a search for wholeness in art, work and leisure, and the second is an interpretation of the constructive social analysis in modern literature.

Throughout the volume there is a recognition of the problem of the secular in contemporary society. Part V brings this into focus through four essays inquiring into the attitude of Christians to a secular society. All agree on the reality of the secularization process, but differ substantially in their interpretation.

Many readers will be struck by the diversity of views in this volume. Two contradictory emphases in particular stand out: the stress on the threats to a truly human society which are inherent in the new social and technical developments, and the note of hope in the new human possibilities apparent in the revolutionary changes of our time.

These differing attitudes only emphasize the need for continuing dialogue within and outside the church about man in modern community. This is the presupposition of a faithful response by Christians. It is in this spirit that we offer this collection of essays.

PART I

MAN IN A CHANGING WORLD

I

FROM TRADITION TO MODERNITY

by EGBERT DE VRIES (Holland)

IT is a platitude that man and community are on the road from tradition to modernity. The dynamics of today's world make for change, irresistible and pervasive. No society can any longer remain traditional: all people and all communities are undergoing rapid change. No society—with the exception of a few very small and isolated communities—wants to resist change or has the power to exclude it. The essays in this volume, as in the others, are related to these processes of change and development.

The fact that "modern society" itself is involved in these processes and consequently is only a step in the direction of the society of the future is less easily grasped. But in what direction is society moving? Can we extrapolate from the past? Can we learn from recent and present-day processes? Do we have a lodestar to guide us? Do we have in mind a structure for the society of the future? All these questions are relevant, and answers are being sought and offered from all perspectives.

For the social scientist, the analysis of ongoing processes is a challenging task, but to project the future, let alone draw up a blueprint for a future society, is for him out of bounds.

In the realm of social ethics, human behavior is tested against certain principles, and the philosopher has the right to develop new norms to deal with new situations as the occasion arises. Should we perhaps leave it to the statesman to devise methods of social control or to give guidance in the realizing of new structures? And what about the theologian who is primarily concerned with the relation of God to man and of men to one another?

At the center of the analysis is man-himself, subject and object of the social processes. But can man-himself be identified? Can man consider himself as a being with spontaneity, capable of new impulses, both responsive and responsible? Is he an entity, even if a changing entity? Or is he a cluster of functions, emanating from a cluster of hidden potentials?

In large measure, the processes of man and community on the road to modernity have made these questions obvious and relevant. Men and society change under the impact of forces which can in turn become tools in the hands of man-himself, to be used within a framework of rules and regulations, or of structures, which man can change.

Gone are the days when these rules and structures were believed to follow directly from revelation—or are there some rules and structures which are immune from human decisions and choice? Gone also are the days when these norms were believed to be inherent in the *"harmonie-pre-établi,"* the ordained, if hidden, natural order, to be discovered rather than established.

Psychological and social research has shown that almost anything is possible, although perhaps not everything can be realized in the long run or on a large scale. But man is pliable, his mind can be molded, he can be influenced in many different ways, even unconsciously. And social structures, small and large, can exist and develop simultaneously in fundamentally different directions.

Is it possible, then, to discern a pattern in the recent developments from the past to the present? Is it possible to test this pattern against the gospel? These seem to be among the important questions for the churches. Only a few introductory remarks are appropriate at this point.

One cannot avoid a confession of faith in discussing these matters. It is of primary importance to make this the starting point. The supreme reality of God in the past, the present and the future, and his relation to persons and human community in the revelation of his love and power, and his purpose for man and society—all these are matters of faith.

Science and Change

In many respects modernity makes freedom possible: freedom of choice and therefore freedom to realize in human life and in the structures and functions of society a living relation to God; but also, freedom to organize human relations in the interests of certain groups or ideologies. Modernity has to a large extent done away with the sacral approach: the belief that some system of norms and structures captures in human, temporary forms the essence of eternal, spiritual powers. It is the essence of paganism and yet it has pervaded the churches and many social institutions. Its transformation into spirituality is possible only through God's revelation in history and in the present. But autonomous man with his relentless protest against fixed norms has used the results of scientific research to uncover the relativity and therefore the implausibility of the sacral interpretation. By attempting to identify the sacral and the spiritual, whether interpreted as faith, religion, customs or ethics, science has at the same time reduced the "field of operation" of God in history.

Modern medicine provides an example. In the pre-technical age, disease was seen as a punishment for disobedience to God or the rules of society, or as the effect of "the evil eye," an act of hate or spite, or an attempted murder by a fellowman. The discovery of sources of infection revealed illness in many cases to be the effect of the fight of the human organism against microbes or poisonous material. What then remains of faith? Where is God? What is the value of prayer? In the first excitement aroused by medical discoveries, the sacral ceremonies connected with the problems of health were transformed into secular rules of hygiene and the prescription of drugs. This provided liberation from the bonds of sacrality and eliminated untold misery, pain and grief.

Nevertheless the mysteries of health and illness, of life and death, are not solved by microscopes, experiments on mice and the synthetic production of miracle-drugs. And modern medicine has again concentrated its attention on the unity of mind and body, of person, family and community.

Yet in recent years, biological research has been probing into the secrets of the life processes, and at present nearly all the chemical compounds produced in the living organism can be made synthetically in laboratories and factories. When the first, simple attempt succeeded in the early part of the nineteenth century (urea), it looked like a victory over God. Would our faith be shaken if the life-process itself could be synthesized? Again, the application of biological research has enriched our lives, and without the science of genetics and plant and animal physiology we should all starve. Crop failure and famine are no longer considered a punishment of man by God, but a neglect of man for men.

The same is true of our increasing capacity to recombine the energy resources of the atom. The question is not whether mankind is entitled to use this power, but rather how will he use it?

In the fields of physics ("matter" and "antimatter") and cosmogony ("creation" and "self-perpetuation") wholly new concepts have been developed. Everywhere such secularization is taken for granted, and sacral notions are being thrown out. At no point, however, do responsible scientists find a *"reductio ad infinitum"* of spiritual realities.

Secularization in the natural sciences is one thing. But does it have the same liberating effect in the social field? It is not self-evident that methods of analysis and experiment can be transferred from one field to another. It was not until the middle of the nineteenth century that the methods of natural science were applied to the social sciences.

The deterministic, secular schools in sociology, political science and cultural anthropology had little trouble applying "natural science methodology" to the various social sciences. In psychology, they met with the medical and anthropological approaches. And the results again were gratifying to the analytical mind to say the least.

Yet a word of caution is in order. We are troubled when research probes into the mind of man. I for one feel uneasy when I see pictures of scientists peeking into the brains of their fellowmen, and discovering ways to change important expressions of man's personality structure. But here again we fear the way in which this knowledge might be used, rather than the discovery itself. We know all too well that mass propaganda in the ideological field and mass advertisement in the service of commercial interests are on the prowl, trying to mold us in their image. And we distrust our own capacity to discern, analyze, choose, be responsible in our reactions. However, we should not forget that in matters of human relations, of social functions and structures, the measure of freedom of choice is generally much larger than physics, biology or chemistry.

Also the relation between object and subject in the research is often at least a shade different. This is borne out by the well-known facts of the effect of research attention given to the object, and the reciprocal relation between observer and observee.

And in action the interrelationships of hierarchy and order, of love and care, of exchange (buying-selling), of cooperation, mutuality and reciprocity, which are operative during the process, are generally much more important than the design or blueprint for organizational arrangements.

Out of the depths of personality creative forces evolve in these social relationships, and there should be scope for flexibility—that is, uncertainty—in order to leave room for creativity.

Patterns of Change

Traditional society is characterized by *rhythm,* rather than by innovation. Living organisms are indeed built for rhythm—daily, seasonal and annual processes, birth, growing-up, aging, the succession of generations. Agriculture, which is the main occupation, symbolizes these rhythmic processes. Modern society is characterized by a continuous flow of processes, as symbolized by industry, and it fits people into these processes.

Rhythm brings periodic movements of acceleration and deceleration of labor and rest. Continuity demands acceleration of the total process and resists deceleration. Quantification and precision are its corollaries, and these require standardization and a degree of uniformity.

Modernity therefore implies new ways of production, new types of social relationships, and a new awareness of the environment by the human person.

In industrial production—in the office as well as the factory or mine—the requirements of the process force individuals to comply with strict rules. Disregard of these regulations endangers not only productivity but often the safety, health and lives of fellowmen. They have a high ethical value, as exemplified for "the man in the street" by traffic regulations in a modern city.

The dangers are obvious. The sociologists and psychologists have found convincing evidence that man may become a slave of his industrial environment, just as when he toiled on the land he may have been a slave of traditional social structures or a victim of nature. The situation of small man in large society may be as difficult as that of small man in small community, although the underlying forces are different. In traditional society, the enslavement of man—if not a corollary of war—was the result of the limitations and vagaries of nature and the subsequent "survival of the fortunate." There was a thin line and a precarious balance between a plentiful harvest and famine. Society often became highly stratified, with little social mobility, although as a whole it promised a degree of shelter for the orphan, the widow and the beggar.

In modern society, standardization, the repetitious movements of mechanized equipment, and the need for continuity require punctuality and unremitting attention. There is a thin line and a precarious balance between rapid progress in the firm and demotion to even more monotonous work and perhaps unemployment. Social mobility is high, but the competition for the top jobs is fierce. As a whole, modern society provides a degree of security through social institutions and laws or regulations. In a bureaucracy depersonalization has reached a point where the "bureaucrat" is in essence a standardized tool.

From the Christian point of view has man "gained the whole world but lost his soul"? Or has he rather been liberated from superstition, magic and suffering? Is modernity the outcome of a revolt against God-ordained social structures and beliefs? Or is it the result of activities of "man set free"?

These are not pseudo-questions. True, the friction between traditional values and new needs has always existed as exemplified by the clashes between herdsmen and agriculturists from Cain and Abel on, or between city and land (apparent in the words of the Old Testament prophets). But today these age-old problems have taken on a worldwide and perhaps decisive importance for the future of mankind.

No one can any longer escape the impact of modern science, technology, mass production and mass communication. The use of atomic energy, the action of chemical compounds on nature, mass propaganda, all these have become matters of life and death—biologically, socially and ethically. Indeed, the *enlargement* of scale is another trademark of modernity. It is obvious in production, but even more pervasive in communications. Take, for example, the use of spying and communication satellites, which know no boundaries.

The interdependence of national societies, small communities, families and persons in this interdependent whole is staggering for traditionally minded people, those who still think in late eighteenth and nineteenth century categories, for which the rational thought and choice of the individual was considered to be the motor and yardstick of development. The type of modernity characterized by individualism has proved to be merely transitional. Mass society requires a swing back to group decisions, to binding regulations, to conformity in consumption patterns and in behavior, to teamwork. In this sense it may seem to resemble pre-industrialized rural society, but it is essentially different. Genuine person-to-person relationships are restricted to one part of life—that within the family; they are no longer decisive in social life. Our present age is characterized by a functionalization of life. Decisions, or at least coercive influences, emanate from a wide variety of functions. This thorough functionalization favors efficiency and productivity, speeds up decisions and is indispensable in view of mechanization. But it exposes man to pressures from conflicting spheres of power and interest.

The daily life of a city dweller in any metropolitan area in the world provides a very simple illustration. Every day he lives in many societies, each with its own code; and perhaps during a small part of that day, or of the week, in a religious community. He has to accommodate himself to a rapid succession of codes of behavior and ethical values. The reaction of "older" and "younger" generations to these changes differs significantly. Older people are often bewildered, they become unbalanced and develop nervous tensions, but young people enjoy themselves. According to Teilhard de Chardin, this is part of a rapid human evolution—a further development of the mind of man so that he observes and learns more quickly and can thus grasp opportunities for progress and survival, where people or communities which reacted more slowly would perish. *Dynamism* is therefore a prerequisite for survival. If real freedom is seen as the freedom of choice and the freedom to change, our modern world offers a vast array of completely new possibilities. And yet a society which is made up of a wide network of multidimensional interrelations and of intercommunications with feedback and other "modern" social techniques, makes man dependent upon others, as never before—or as was never apparent except in an emergency.

As the links between man and his fellows have become all-important, the community has again come to exert pressing claims upon him. In preindustrial societies this claim was laid primarily in relation to nature in the common fight against the weather, wild animals, plague and disease: here there was no room for choice. In the intermediate individualist, rationalist, early stages of industrialization, a certain class was able to liberate itself from these chains. But the laboring class merely exchanged for the dangers of nature the perils involved in the daily struggle for bread and the threat of unemployment. In modern society no one can escape the process of *"socialization,"* but much larger groups have had some freedom of choice. However, if some solution commensurate with human dignity is to be found for those who today are without choice or chance—the permanently unemployed, the school drop-outs—everyone will have to make some sacrifice of freedom, even in the most mundane matters (such as levels of taxation influencing choice of consumption). This changing situation has made the progressive liberals of the recent past into backward-looking conservatives. Is there any need for the Christian to identify himself with this liberalism in the name of freedom?

I should like to consider these characteristics of modernity as we live it today as spiritually and ethically neutral. But they must be judged by the room which they provide for certain spiritual values, for example, *creativity, opportunity to serve* and *freedom.* A Christian derives these values from the gospel: from the revelation of God as Creator, of his Son who came to serve, and of the Spirit, who sets us free.

Traditional society—by definition—leaves very little room for *creativity.* It has, of course, its great cultural, religious heroes and leaders, its famous emperors and soldiers. In order to function, these had to innovate, to search, to venture. In traditional society, these great figures are the molders of the past and therefore the strength and pride of the present. But they rarely are builders of the future.

In modern, dynamic society, greatness is always forward-looking, innovative. And through mechanization and communication, its impact may be tremendous. Is then, historically speaking, the golden time for spontaneity, for creativity, for innovation, *on the threshold between* tradition and modernity? Is it the moment when the shackles of the past have been thrown off, but the assembly line of the future is still under construction?

Christianity and Change

The Christian church was born in such a period between periods —"in the fullness of time"—and this means that of necessity it is always looking for an expression of spontaneity and creativity in its own community. Churches cannot be the place for refuge from the onslaught of modernity. And since it is out of the whole personality that creativity is born, the church must be concerned that the integrity and dignity of the human personality is held as the highest value of modern industrial society.

Creativity flourished through Christianity in the first centuries of the Christian era, in the Renaissance and Reformation, also in the first century of Islam. Thereafter, it has been secularized and has become a steady, organized flow; and thus it runs the danger of shutting out "real" creativity.

Christians might also express creativity through service. *Opportunities to serve* exist in any society. They are remarkably frequent in any changing society. The variety of service has grown with the needs, and human response is often much more direct in the exchange of service than in any other form of contact (in thought, in art, in authority, to mention a few). No wonder, that people have found service to their fellowmen an unfailing bond with them. Real service is understood, its sincerity is "felt by intuition." Fake service—an act of self-aggrandizement, or source of satisfying the need for importance—is sensed and rejected.

For Christians, this is a reason to rejoice. It means that modern society has developed a sense of "discovering Jesus Christ in disguise" as the Servant. The Christian cannot expect an easy life, if he dares to follow Christ, serving fellowmen. It is no coincidence that in periods of social change, in stress and strain, the churches have found their great opportunity in service. Service unites as no other human relation, and this is exemplified in the ecumenical movement. We can safely predict that the faster the world moves toward modernity, the richer the possibilities for service.

Freedom of action or service as the gift of the Spirit, does not automatically follow from the inherited capacity of man. Rather it is the fruit of suffering and sacrifice and victory over enslavement, which is more the "natural" condition of man as a social animal.

Freedom must therefore be preserved and protected against coercion and conformity. Real freedom is the fruit of love, rather than a sign of independence. And only in this way can freedom be the ferment of interdependence. Otherwise cohesion and interdependence become tyranny and (mutual) oppression. Freedom can therefore be maintained only by constant vigilance; it never can be taken for granted. It is an external truth, but specifically more true in modern society, that freedom can best be promoted by the defense of freedom of others. Thus freedom is unthinkable without responsibility for society and people. As a gift of the Spirit, freedom pervades, corrects and cleanses relationships. Thus, it has a social function, indispensable in the complexities of modern life.

At the roots of these values in modern society stands the human personality as an integrated whole. And this is the *mystery of our existence.*

To our surprise, we find that the human personality can adapt itself to changes in the environment in a remarkable way, including those engineered by collective action. In many cases, this is not accompanied by a sense of being lost or lonely. In many others it is, although on the surface people's behavior appears to be well adapted. The resilience of the human body and mind to noise, toil, monotony, instruction, propaganda, advertising, is remarkable. We find the jet plane commonplace and will soon be adjusted to supersonic speed, although our grandfathers found the railroad a dangerous experiment with vulnerable bodies.

The engineers predict that modernity is only at its beginning and our grandchildren—more likely already our children—will undergo even more drastic changes in their environment and systems of communication.

It is our common responsibility to find openings for creativity, service and freedom. It is grace, given to Christians, to realize them in a period of change from tradition to modernity.

2

BETWEEN THE OLD AND THE NEW WORLDS

by MASAO TAKENAKA (Japan)

SEVERAL factors contribute to the complexity and the peculiarity of the issues which arise in the process of transition from the traditional to modern society in Asia.

First of all, in contrast to what happened in the West, the process has occurred within a relatively short period in history. In the West the transition began about the time of the Reformation and covered a period of over four hundred years, in the course of which the peoples of the West have adjusted themselves to it. We record such revolutionary events as the Reformation, the industrial revolution, the Declaration of Independence, the French revolution, the enlightenment, the civil war and the proletarian revolution. Within this period religious, industrial, economic, cultural and political changes came about.

In Asia the transition from the traditional to the modern is of more recent date. In Japan modernization began at the Meiji restoration period in 1868, but the reform was mainly external, and the actual democratization of Japanese society did not begin until after the Second World War, when many Asian countries attained political independence. This historical time factor is an important element in our study, because a social change which is rapid and sudden may lead to confusion and frustration.

Second, the change has been not only sudden but simultaneous. With the declaration of political independence, the people of Asia have experienced all at once a reformation, an industrial revolution, a proletarian revolution and a French revolution. They are confronted with the problem caused by the lack of balance in the development of various fields and with the vital responsibility of establishing the right priorities among the different elements which demand change. After the Meiji period, the Japanese government gave priority to building up their national power, while limiting democratic freedom among the people. In the postwar period, the government's urgent concern was to raise the standard of living through economic expansion, while paying less attention to the cultivation of the quality of personal resources.

Third, we notice in Asia a harmonious coexistence of traditional cultures and modern technology. It evokes a sense of wonder to find, on the roof top of a supermodern industrial firm in Tokyo, a small Shinto shrine before which the employees meet every morning for a brief ceremony. Many taxi drivers in Osaka hang a Shinto talisman in their cars to ensure their safety. In an ordinary rural Japanese home it is not unusual to find a Buddhist family shrine on top of the television set. The harmonious attitude toward other religions, ideologies and ways of life has been greatly influenced and nurtured by the impact of nature, which has always been of fundamental importance in Asian life. Rather than fight against nature, the dominant attitude has been to live with and according to nature.

This harmonious attitude was extended to the realm of thought and human relations, creating an atmosphere of coexistence and tolerance. This means that in the process of transition we encounter a carry-over of the traditional element of culture into a new setting. Deep down in the minds of ordinary Japanese, for example, there is a primitive religious mentality, and their human relationships are quite often based on a feudalistic pattern. Yet they not only wear modern clothes but live in a modern organization, receiving the constant impact of advanced, supermodern technology. Thus Asia today reveals a peculiar coexistence and harmony of primitive, feudalistic, modern and supermodern elements.

Fourth, in many of the Asian countries the people experienced colonial control, by western powers and by Japan, during the Second World War. The impact of western dominance cannot easily be forgotten and removed. Having gained political independence, Asian nations live in interdependence with other nations of the world. Today this degree of interdependence has been accelerated by the impact of commercial and technological developments. The end of colonialism does not mean the isolation of the Asian countries from the rest of the world. It means the demand for a new type of interdependence and world solidarity.

Over one hundred years ago (1853) three steamships arrived for the first time at the port of Uraga, near Tokyo. Their arrival shocked the people of Japan, who were enjoying a long sleep, having cut themselves off from the rest of the world. From that time on, social change in all realms of society proceeded with great speed and soon the problem of maintaining harmony and coexistence, in a diverse cultural climate yet in an interdependent world, arose. It is in this setting that we should examine the specific issues which emerge from the process of transition from a traditional to a modern society.

From a Vertical Society to a Horizontal Community

One of the decisive trends in the process of transition is the breakdown of the feudalistic, hierarchical structure and the rise of the masses to demand their individual rights and freedom. In the early process of modernization in the West we can distinguish a strong emphasis on individualism. There, an effort was made to safeguard individual dignity as the basic unit of society. Later, however, trends in the opposite direction were discernible—stressing the fulfillment of individual desires without considering the welfare of the whole community. We recognize here the difficulty encountered in the process of modernization in the West—the trend from a vertical, feudal society to that of an atomized, disintegrated community.

In Asia the breakdown of the feudalistic society provides an opportunity to establish an interpersonal, horizontal community. But in reality there is a trend toward one of two extremes—either to individualism or to the new form of hierarchical relationship.

In 1866, Hiromichi Kozaki, a distinguished leader of the Christian church in Japan, wrote a provocative book called *Seikyo Shinron* (The New Thesis on Religion and Politics). In it he made a violent attack on Confucianism, which was the basic ethical foundation of the old society. According to Kozaki, Confucianism is a quite distinct way of governing society with the aim of bringing peace to the nations. He examined the means of achieving this end, depicting the five basic Confucian codes as these rules of government. The Confucian ethics divide society sharply into two groups, not according to functions, but to status, which demands loyalty from those who are governed and gives those who govern the right to order. Thus, the five codes state that the subject must give absolute loyalty to the emperor; the son must give filial obedience to his parents; the wife must follow the husband; the young must obey their elders; and friends must trust each other.

It was Kozaki's contention that except for that among friends, all these relationships are hierarchically defined, toward a vertical human relationship in which the lower accepts the orders of his superior and obeys his commands. Thus, the feudal structure of society is a closely organized society in which vertical relationships predominate. Kozaki diagnosed the need for a radical change in this situation and advocated the transformation of the traditional structure into an interpersonal, horizontal relationship as exemplified by the Christian faith. But in the course of modernization during the last eighty years, between the Meiji restoration of 1868 and the end of the Second World War, the trend was less toward extreme individualism than toward a resurgence of the spirit of the old, traditional society in the new dress of a modern setting. Japanese nationalism first took the form of the civil liberty movement in the early 1880's, but after the Imperial Edict of Education in

1890 it became increasingly authoritative in character. The Imperial Edict became the cornerstone of Japanese society; it took the Confucian moral teachings and adapted them in such a way as to strengthen the national power within the hierarchical structure. Japan quickly accepted western technology and industrialization, but changed little in the international orientation of life until 1945, when the absolute divinity of the emperor was first challenged. This shows that technological development does not necessarily introduce a new perspective, but that it is often used as a means of supporting a traditional, established system of values.

The Increase of Conformity

In a traditional society the people are required to give loyalty to a higher authority. It is a society which operates by commandments from the top to the lower strata. In modern Asian society, despite much discussion and inclination toward individualization, matured selfhood has been a slow and struggling process. One of the difficulties in this process of transition is that a technologically organized life demands a readiness to adjust. To use David Riesman's terminology in his book, *The Lonely Crowd,* we see an increasing trend among the people to assume an "other directed" pattern of personality. At work one must obey the production schedule; in the home, one becomes a passive recipient of the TV program. Rather than develop the power of self-determination, people become sensitive in modern society to the evaluation and stimulation of others, especially to the demand to organize. Here we see that the traditional Asian attitude of adjustment to natural environment strengthens the trend to social conformity. A harmonious attitude toward nature tends to be transformed into social relationships which strengthen attitudes of conformity.

There are three characteristic ways in which human relations develop in this situation. One is an attitude of conformity, observed in the external life of organization. Another is an extreme attitude of conflict and antagonism which is occasionally manifested at a moment of crisis as the result of an underlying dissatisfaction. A third is to criticize and talk about others without personal confrontation. There is a decisive lack of genuine personal dialogue.

Here we see the key question, whether the impact of technology increases a sense of conformity or whether it opens up opportunities to develop interpersonal horizontal relationships. In countries where the traditional culture has been strongly rooted and where the harmonious attitude toward the natural environment has been predominant, technology and organization may strengthen attitudes of conformity and adjustment. On the other hand, technology may bring about a change not only in people's external working conditions but in the human relationships of an industrial society.

For example, the development of the labor union movement may create new opportunities when it cultivates a horizontal and interpersonal society, raising the status of workers and promoting mutual dialogue among people who have different functions and specialized gifts and abilities. The labor union movement may help the workers to recover their dignity and self-identity and may bring people into a horizontal relationship wtih other components of industrial society. On the other hand, within organizations in industrial society, including labor unions, the feudalistic spirit of conformity and the harmonious attitude toward nature still survive in a way which creates a new form of vertical control and passive adjustment. Union members tend to lack a positive attitude in participating in the democratic process within the union. They would rather support an undemocratic boss because in the old society they were accustomed to be subordinate to orders from above.

Many of the social changes in Japan took place not at the grassroots level, but from the top to the bottom by order of those who were in positions of control. The Meiji restoration of 1868 was not a revolution from below, but a restoration of the sovereignty of the emperor, who initiated reforms for the benefit of the people. Again, in the postwar setting, it was the occupation forces who introduced many revolutionary policies, such as land reform, the establishment of labor unions and the dissolution of the financial oligarchy. These reforms were directed from the office of the general headquarters of the supreme commander rather than coming from the people themselves. Many labor unions sprang up like mushrooms after rain. To members of the unions, the right to organize was given from above rather than being personally acquired after struggle. Thus the changes took place quickly, without causing much damage. But we must not forget the underlying problems of mutual adjustment. We acknowledge especially the importance of labor education and the cultivation of the workers in order to bring about healthy and responsible industrial relations.

Division and Cooperation

Technological development and scientific advance imply specialization. As science develops, the fields of discipline which investigate particular phenomena narrow. Advance in scientific investigation leads to the fragmentation and disintegration of life. We experience this today in our universities, which add an increasing number of new courses and of specialists every year. Technology is the application of scientific study to practical operations. As science develops specialized fields of study to increase technological progress, a greater division of labor inevitably takes place, which in turn necessitates a greater number of specialists with technological knowledge and competence in each particular field of operation. This leads to a disintegration of organic life, separating specialists from each other according to their respective fields.

In a traditional society other factors have tended to divide people—language, religion, caste, place of birth, education; and though people increasingly migrate from rural to urban areas, they still tend, in the cities, to form associations according to the prefecture from which they come. There is a strong sense of identification with a particular group. In the modern setting society puts much emphasis on education. People are classified according to their university rather than to their ability or qualifications. In industrial companies and large organizations associations are formed by those who graduated from the same university, for the purpose of mutual help. In many instances, a person's promotion depends on the "school family" to which he belongs. Divisions according to school families and local circles disintegrate society.

The sudden change from a feudalistic to an industrial and technological society does not give adequate time in which to develop and exercise selfhood. Instead, technology may increase the group divisions which already existed. In the industrial society the forms of divisions are admittedly different from those of the pre-industrial and feudal society, yet a similar mentality and attitude of group divisions tends to be carried over into the technological society. For example, in the past if a person were ill he was treated in hospital by a doctor and an attendant nurse. But today the treatment of the sick involves many specialists: chemists, social caseworkers, psychotherapists, machinists, computer operators, and so on. In a highly developed industrial organization the division of labor is much more highly intensified. Here we see the danger of carrying over into the modern industrial society the feudalistic group identity—widening the cleavage and division not according to a person's place of birth but according to his specialized function.

Yet at another level, technology forces people to cooperate. Technicians and engineers must work as a team. Of necessity people are brought together to cooperate, respecting each other's gifts and functions. Here we find a new opportunity to experiment, to open up a new dimension in the horizontal interpersonal relationship of people who have skills and responsibilities. Technological and industrial development requires a new type of joint human effort different from both the old paternalistic and the modern totalitarian pattern. It also differs radically from the isolated individualistic structure, since in a technical society every factory worker is involved in the process of production. Each person is essential, since the work of the group cannot be accomplished unless all contribute to the whole process.

Thus the process of transition introduces another important possibility, that of bringing a new type of solidarity and joint action into the functional interaction of people. They need to gain an understanding of the whole before they can begin their particular job. They must visualize the whole, seeing the relationship of all its parts, if they are to help create the final product. In the face of the trend toward disintegration, people long to find a foundation for a responsible human community.

Verses in the Epistle to the Ephesians which use the image of the body, have relevance here. The writer speaks neither to the conformed, nor to the isolated individual. He recognizes unity in diversity, each bringing gifts for joint action. The secret of organic life rests, not upon human resources, but on the reconciling power of Christ who "has broken down the dividing wall of hostility" (Ephesians 2 : 14). He has abolished in his flesh the old commandments and ordinances in order that he may create in himself one new man in place of two, reconciling both to God and to his neighbors. This body, the new community in Christ, helps to develop a sensitivity of partnership in solidarity: "We are to grow up in every way into him who is the head, into Christ, from whom the whole body joined and knit together by every joint with which it is supplied, when each part is working properly, makes bodily growth and upbuilds itself in love" (Ephesians 4 : 15–16). Maturity is characterized as the interrelatedness of each part in solidarity as an organic whole.[1] But it is worth remembering that the image of the body refers to the growth of the Christian community, however small it may have been, not only existed in a particular geographical and social setting, but had a mission to provide, in its everyday life, a foretaste of the coming kingdom. The image of the functioning body not only refers to the growth of a matured Christian community, but shows the pattern of the coming society, to be seen in the reality of Christian community, which is the first-fruit of the new humanity.

Toward the Provisional Telos

A man who lives during a period of transition searches for knowledge of the future. He realizes that the foundations of the

[1] Paul Lehman defines maturity as "the integrity in and through interrelatedness which makes it possible for each individual member of an organic whole to be himself." PAUL LEHMAN: *Ethics in a Christian Context,* 1963, p. 55.

past have been shaken and that his present existence is dissatisfying and ambiguous. He acts when he discovers something to hope for in the future. Man is a historical being living not only in the memory of the past but in anticipation of the future. A man in the midtwentieth century is not likely to think of the future in a rosy, idealistic way, as did the utopian thinkers of the eighteenth century; he is much more of a realist, if not a pessimist: he acknowledges the relativity of the present world.

In Asia, as they struggled for political independence, men and women looked toward the future with hope. Now that independence has been gained, however, apathy and uncertainty about the future have crept in. Confronted with the difficult and painful process of national development, there is a temptation to fall into social amnesia, to forget one's social responsibility and to be concerned with immediate private gain and pleasure. During the period of nationalism in Japan, the people had a sense of mission and of vocation in performing their work; national education and propaganda helped them to see a vision for the future. One must have a focus in life to understand history, and history here means personal identification in a common destiny. In times of rapid social change men and women are like travelers, leaving an old rural home and moving into the city. It is not an individual transition, but a social movement from an old to a new place. One is bound to ask seriously whither this earthly pilgrimage leads. In a time of transition people search for the meaning of the future. When the old religions and the classical ideologies are swept away, people are uncertain as to the direction of future society. One must develop a framework of the future city. In short, in times of social change, man becomes teleological. In this connection we can understand why the Communist movement and some of the new religions, like Sokagakkai, have great appeal in Japan. Despite their limitations they indicate the direction in which people should move. They present a social and "this-worldly" *telos,* something anticipated here and now as a common goal, and not the individualistic or spiritualized *telos*. It is easy to criticize the irrelevant and faulty promises contained in these quasi-religious movements, but the challenge to the Christian is to define the Christian *telos* in such times of social change as we are experiencing today. Criticizing others is not much help unless we present a positive alternative.

In Christian thinking about the future we must confess that we have been timid in considering where we are going, in relevant and realistic terms. In the eighteenth and nineteenth centuries we find several Christian social thinkers who thought of the *telos* as a realizable social structure. They were teleologists, but they were also idealists in identifying the kingdom of God with the highest social order which will be manifested in this world. They thought of the future but considered it in an idealistic way, projecting a rosy future kingdom which would come to fulfillment in the world. In spite of their diversity of thought, we find this common characteristic in the social thinkers of the eighteenth and nineteenth centuries, from Robert Owen to Walter Rauschenbusch. They anticipated the future ideal society as the kingdom of God on earth.

Against this rather worldly idealistic trend, the theological tendencies in this century are much more cautious. If, during the previous century, the predominant thinking in Christian ethics was expressed through the teleological form, the social thought of the midtwentieth century is expressed through contextual ethics. This difference is partly due to the impact of the "theology of crisis" and to the reaction against the former liberal and idealistic theology. Christian theologians have been emphasizing the moral ambiguity of men, and their ethical perplexity in modern society, in a way which helps to restore a balanced perspective. Therefore, one of the major trends in Protestant social ethics is described as "situational ethics." Instead of projecting the ideal social goal or depicting the absolute categorical commandment such as that given in the Sermon on the Mount, Protestant social thinkers consider the immediate and concrete ethical response within a particular given situation; we have become more realistic. This is relevant because, in dealing with social policies, we must think in terms, not of what is best, but of what is possible in highly complex, given situations.

Yet at the same time we cannot base ethics wholly on given social situations. If we accept contextual ethics without the constructive and positive framework of an ethical structure, we shall be in a dangerous position. Here I suggest three of the temptations or limitations to which we shall be exposed:

a. One characteristic of contextual ethics is that it tries to deal with ethical issues within their concrete context. There is no other relevant way with which, I admit, to deal with them, but it has its danger: it tends to deal with ethical responses individually, fragmentarily and to lack insight into the ethical and moral implication of the problem as a whole. We may call this the individualization trend in contextual ethics. We must guard against this temptation diligently in the Protestant church, which has strongly emphasized the strength of the individual rather than the concept of being a part of the whole. In a world, furthermore, which has become increasingly interdependent, we must break through the individualistic trend in contextual ethics. The content of the Christian gospel and the context of the present-day world urge us to think more seriously of the reality of world interdependence.

b. Then there is the conservative element in contextual ethics. We appreciate the concreteness and the realistic emphasis gained by recent developments in Christian ethics, but there is a temptation to be caught up in the dilemma of a given situation, adapting ourselves to it rather than developing creatively a new framework to replace the old foundation. In being realistic we are inclined to cynical judgment, protesting against man's sinfulness, finiteness and moral ambiguity. We need to recover a prophetic insight, in order not only to analyze a situation but to see its construction with relevance to the future. A prophet not only judges, but sees a vision—the vision of deliverance from captivity and of entering the "new Jerusalem."

c. Third, we must be aware of the element of subjectivism in contextual ethics. By taking a given situation seriously, contextual ethics leads us to make relevant personal decisions in concrete realities. This does not mean that we can make any decision primarily on the basis of the given situation. Ethical choices are made not only in the light of a realistic understanding of the situation, but also in that of the ultimate concern. In times of social change, Christians must interpret the social situations and make decisions in the light of the biblical drama of redemption. Instead of proclaiming an ideal society created by human ability, we should discern the signs of the times in the light of God's design in the world. We have been given, in the coming of Jesus Christ, the vision of the final goal of history. In this event we affirm the victory of the redeeming power of God over principalities and powers. Through the testimony of the Bible we have received the vision and promise of the new city which will come at the end of history. Living between two eras, Christians always look to the future. They are not idealists or dreamers who talk of the future in an irrelevant way. No one has a definite blueprint for the future society, but Christians possess a power in the gospel which provides a provisional *telos* in the light of the ultimate *telos*. This provisional *telos* must be thought of in terms not of an individual's purpose but of a common goal. The Bible expresses this thought in the image of a common life, the city of God. "Behold, the dwelling of God is with men. He will dwell with them, and they shall be his people, and God himself will be with them; he will wipe away every tear from their eyes, and death shall be no more, neither shall there be mourning nor crying for pain any more, for the former things have passed away" (Revelation 21 : 3–4).

In our ecumenical thinking, therefore, on church and society, we are entering a new stage. Between Oxford, 1937, and Amsterdam, 1948, the emphasis of Christian teachings was on the social issues of that period, yet the common framework of thinking was not clearly expressed. At Amsterdam, the concept of responsible society came into existence and provided a basic perspective. Someone has referred to the concept of responsible society as the middle axiom, presenting a general guide in the light of Christian perspectives. Since Evanston, 1954, in meeting the challenges of the revolutionary world, we have developed the study on the common Christian responsibility toward the areas of rapid social change.

It has helped Christians to gain a practical understanding of the changing world and to make relevant decisions. We are now at another stage—that of the provisional social *telos*. As we build up definite knowledge of the changing world and begin to interpret and analyze the actual situation, we need to think together about the common provisional direction and pattern of future society in the light of the biblical revelation. We may not necessarily think of the kind of society required for the year 3000, but we should direct our attention to thinking out of the provisional social goal which we want, not only in our own national and local community, but in our interdependent world.

Search for the Ground of Hope

In the period of transition from the old to the modern society, people are confronted with three social issues, uncertainty, rebellion and indifference.

Since the traditional norm is not applicable in a new society, people become uncertain as to the foundation of moral life. In the feudalistic period, the Confucian teaching and the Buddhistic attitude to life provided the basic framework of society. In the nationalistic period, the moral teaching as described in the Emperor's edict on education was the basis for the national way of life. But today, there is widespread ambiguity in defining the center of moral life. In this period of transition confusion and uncertainty prevail. A small group may take a negative and critical attitude, rebelling against the existing order and institutions. Dissatisfied and frustrated, their reactions are negative, and they do not play their part in developing a common framework of realistic participation in the modern world. Social injustice should certainly be met by critical protest, but there is a lack of the constructive realism that is required if we are to grapple with the development of a new society with the cooperation of different interest groups.

Perhaps the most widespread attitude is that of indifference to the affairs of society, both because people are not accustomed to participate constructively in a complex social situation and because of the impact of mass media. People are concerned with immediate individual interests and tend to forget their common social responsibilities. We forget our common humanity and put our individual private interests first. A worker, let us say, tries to get more overtime for himself in competition with his fellow worker, but is indifferent to his responsibility in the coming union election. Or a student, in a highly competitive system of entrance examinations, forgets to think of the ultimate question of the meaning of life; he is interested only in getting a better grade than his classmates in the next examination. Or a lawyer is deeply concerned with a local political deal in his Rotary Club, but forgets his role as a lawyer in the improvement of the inadequate minimum-wage law of his city. Or a churchman is occupied with installing a new stained-glass window memorial, but forgets his role in the racial struggle in his own community.

In the complex jungle of modern society, there is a tendency to apathy and resignation. It expresses itself in various ways. In Thailand a common saying is *"Maipen rai,"* "Never mind"; in Indonesia people often say *"Tida magapa,"* "Ask not why"; in Japan, *"Shikataga nai,"* "There is no other way," expresses a feeling of resignation. It is not the heroic reformer with idealistic vision to make sweeping changes that we need, but a vital spiritual force to awaken men and women from their social amnesia. We need the power of anamnesis, a re-awareness of self-hood in the human community and the recognition of one's responsibility in our interdependent world.

Marxists have charged religion with being "the opiate of the people." We should not ignore or cover up this charge. In history certain religions have quieted the conscience of the oppressed, but it is unfair to historic reality if we do not point out that this is only half the picture. There have been a number of occasions when religion was not an opiate but the driving force of a new civilization. The Christian gospel does not individualize man; it stimulates him to see his personal responsibility toward his neighbors in the community, not because he has something to give them, but because he has encountered the eternal God who became man to share the burden of all men. The Christian faith does not lead man to retire behind an individual religious wall, but sends him out into society, where the horizontal relationship is acute. The gospel proclaims that God became man to overcome man's sin and death by participating in man's suffering and struggle. When the people of God accept this vision of the gospel, they become the creative and driving force in history, functioning as the salt of the earth, the mustard seed in the field and the leaven in the bread. Man has irreplaceable and irreducible hope in Jesus Christ. It is the hope with which one can continually present a Christian witness in the midst of our struggling world. This hope is based on the historic event: God became man in order that man may become true man.

PART II

SOCIETY AND TENSION

3

THE IDEOLOGICAL FACTOR IN THE WEST

by André Dumas (France)

Myth, Order and Ideology

There are two characteristics of our society today: on the one hand, it is increasingly possible to analyze it economically, geographically and historically—that is, to examine the forces which explain and determine man as far as his external liberty is concerned; on the other hand, society can be ordered in accordance with the findings of the "ideologists"—that is, it can be oriented in accordance with men's inward allegiance to and interpretation of history. Ideas are thus pursued as if they were only the secondary (and often mystifying) results of the material realities from which they spring, and at the same time *exalted* as if, by obtaining a global understanding and commitment, man could at last participate actively in molding the society of the future. This is an age in which we are very skeptical about ideals, but at the same time we avidly swallow compelling ideas. We object to idealism because it presupposes the existence of absolute models which do not exist in fact, dividing human life into a law that is not applied and a fact that is not justified. Idealism differs from prophecy in that it presupposes a permanent divorce between values and history. The criterion of idealism is separation, its aim is purity, its nostalgia is for the unrealizable, and its setting is the bad conscience. However, one must not draw the conclusion that contemporary anti-idealism is tantamount to pure pragmatism. On the contrary, scientific social analysis today aims at discovering a new collective "cogito" which will provide, on the basis of experimental evidence, the meaning of the whole and in which the individual will be a part. Thus, Karl Mannheim writes, the social observer seeks "to submit the whole structure of his conscience and his thought to a total sociological analysis." [1] The ideological function has become the cement which holds together the changing societies of our time.

In the primitive societies myths were used in order to explain, unite and regenerate the social reality when it was in danger of becoming obscure or dispersed, or exhausting itself as it was separated more and more from its origins. In the classical societies an order existed that was both cosmological and theological, which human society had to reproduce, thus preserving it from wastage and excess. But contemporary societies are no longer concerned about their mythical origins. Critical science has reduced them to the level of legends. Nor do our societies believe in an unchangeable classical order which would indicate man's rightful place and task. Formerly the universe was regarded as finite, reflecting its order in man. Today we seek in man's own mind for order, in order to project it onto an infinite universe. Deprived of original myths and guides-to-the-universe, our contemporary societies nevertheless need a worldwide image to inform them about the direction and convergence of their respective projects. Between Descartes and Hegel, it was possible to believe that the human mind could do without any world view apart from the mechanical reconstitution of the universe solely by the power of scientific hypothesis. That was the age of reflection which paid little attention to others or society. It was the time when the human mind worked in creative solitude, in a setting that had no soul and no life in which the "engineering" power of the human technician had free play. Man felt no need to substitute ordering ideologies for the Aristotelian view of the world, which had been shattered at the

[1] KARL MANNHEIM: *"Idéologie et Utopie,"* p. 74, French translation, Rivière, Paris, 1956.

beginning of the seventeenth century by physics and reflective philosophy. The ideological vacuum did not last long. The social indifference manifested by minds as different as Pascal and Descartes was succeeded, from the beginning of the eighteenth century (in a picturesque and impulsive way) and from the beginning of the nineteenth century (in a scientific and systematic way) by the renaissance of worldwide conceptions. The ideologies superseded the original myths and the cosmic order, after the brief interim of intellectual individualism.

These contemporary ideologies are more interested in the birth of a future than in returning to origins, or in preserving stability. In them history plays an eminently positive role; whereas in the mythical universe history is losing force all the time, and in the classic universe it is an accidental setting, a temptation both to the soul (perdition) and to the mind (distraction). The contemporary ideologies do not have this pejorative view of history. Even the atheist ideologies regard history as the biblical truth of the time which is running toward an eschatological consummation; history is therefore awaiting its consummation; it is not in terror of its own fragility. The future will reveal the lack of variety in the present. The purpose and meaning of history are to be found in the future, not in the past nor in some transcendent explanation. It is a paradox that this biblical idea of the-transcendent-that-is-coming (as opposed to "the-transcendent-that-was-in-the-past" or to "the-transcendent-which-exists-outside-this-world") has received greater prominence in the secularized ideologies of the contemporary world than in the classic view of Christendom, which has too often confirmed Nietzsche's opinion that "Christianity is a Platonism for the people." For this alone the ideologies merit positive appreciation by Christians. They do not claim ideals whose perfection dominates existing social forces; they present themselves in terms of forces which are already at work in history, forces which are moving toward an end that will deliver history from its ambiguity, by revealing the mystery which it unconsciously conceals within it. The ideologies, therefore, are not objects of thought, they are methods of thought. They would like merely to express the facts which have become a collective explanation and will. Unlike the myths, therefore, the ideologies are based on a scientific interpretation; and unlike the classical ontologies (which gave precedence to *being* and *nature* before consciousness) the ideologies are based on a human awareness which has power to organize. Here one already sees how difficult it will be to define their status, because they want to participate both in the objectivity of science and in the subjectivity of the human enterprise. Owing to their desire to draw upon both sources, the ideologies will be menaced, on the one hand, by the determinism of the certified facts and, on the other hand, by the freedom of choice. The ideologies therefore present a tremendous problem: *who* is entitled to interpret world history, if that history contains the germ of an evolution which gives it meaning? Placing themselves on the same plane as faith in a divine purpose within and for history, the ideologies will present a tremendous challenge to that faith.

Second, the ideologies are markedly collective in character. They are contemporary with the rise of the masses. They appeared when solitary reflectiveness (inaugurated by the seventeenth century) exploded through its encounter with the vast revolutionary movements whereby history took possession of the individual consciousness in France, in the U.S.S.R., in China and in Cuba in 1789, 1917, 1949 and 1959. Here again one can trace the thought of the Bible, which speaks collectively of "the people," of "the church of God," which never isolates the individual from his environment (of which he is always the firstfruit or the survival), and never thinks of the individual as indifferent or isolated. By giving positive meaning to the masses, therefore, the ideologies consider "the crowd" as the real potential of nations. The ideologies do not believe that collective awareness crushes the individual; they believe that it develops the personality. Classical Christianity has always regarded this teaching about the masses with suspicion, and has always stressed the pejorative sense of the word implied in Saint Augustine's "massa peccati"—the "menial lump" mentioned in Romans 9 : 21, which, however, in Romans 11 : 16 becomes "holy" throughout. The contemporary ideologies are conceived in order to find a positive meaning in the modern existence of the masses, crowded increasingly into the urban agglomerations, harnessed to mass production, forced into mass consumption and influenced by the mass communications. Here ideology is opposed to the two usual consequences of the mass: the tyranny of incommunicable, charismatic power, or the defense of the wishes of the individual. Indeed, an ideology may lose strength in two ways: either when authoritarianism is absolute, or when private life gains definite ascendancy over public life. But neither of these situations has much chance of developing in our contemporary societies, despite the repeated affirmations that the ideologies are on the decline; it would be truer to say that they are being modified. Admittedly, our societies do not favor absolute power to the extent of becoming disinterested in the methods by which the masses identify themselves with their projects. The extension of the word "democratic" to all countries (socialistic or capitalistic, countries with one-party government or with several parties, industrial or traditional countries, monarchies or parliamentary countries) is a universal sign of this concession to the will of the masses to assert itself and assume power.

Moreover, the growing importance of joint decisions shows that no contemporary society can allow its citizens to revert to the position of the isolated pioneer, nor even of the free artisan. If necessary, it is private happiness which plays the role of an ideological stimulus; but the ideology (whether tacit or avowed) will always be there in order to coordinate the adherence of society to the general aims.

The ideological function seems, therefore, to be a constant in contemporary societies. It springs from the desire to let the masses participate in creating their own future, at a time when that future is no longer dictated either by convincing myths or by a respected order. The ideologists play the difficult role fulfilled, in ancient times, by the priests and, in more recent times, by philosophers. It is their task to explain the latent meaning within the history that is to be made. They have to explain the social symbols which are sometimes in danger of becoming devouring idols. In fact, they must propose a mobilization of the collective energies, and their proposal may always be a mistake or—what is even more serious—a lie. The ideological function seems inevitable and essential in order to strengthen the social fabric, to avoid the tyranny of monopoly, or withdrawal into the private sphere; and therefore the exercise of this function in contemporary societies is a dangerous occupation.

Ideologies, which are at the same time the products of social conditioning and an awakening in view of commitments in thought and action, thus constitute the main challenges to the Christian faith in the contemporary societies—as the myths were in the societies of antiquity, and as the philosophies were in the classical societies. The ideologies bear a strange resemblance to religious faith because, like faith, they are growing up, moving toward the collective future of history, guiding it toward a central point which may be a mystery or a meaning, and asking man to help, through his own consecration, to hasten the time when the ideological scheme will become an idealized experience. There was far less resemblance between the archaic myths, or the theories of the philosophers, and the substance of faith, than is apparent in history. But this very similarity means that the ideologies are formidable competitors with faith. Do they not manifest a constant tendency not merely to question faith but to replace it, at a time when the evidence of de-Christianization coincides with the speeding-up of history and with the rise of the masses? With their similarity to religious faith, the ideologies often try to replace the very content of faith, either in the extreme form of total ideologies—like Marxism—or in the diluted form of an ideological ethos.

I shall examine these two forms one after the other before dealing with the relations between the Christian faith and the ideological function in contemporary societies.

Ideology and Marxism

Ideology is a comparatively recent word. It was popularized through a work by Antoine Destutt de Tracy, published between

1803 and 1815 and entitled "Eléments d'idéologie," which was consulted by Marx in 1844. Following the tradition of Locke and Condillac, Destutt de Tracy studied the formation of ideas, regarding them like plants which grow up in man's logical nature. Ideology classifies ideas in relation to their characteristics and in relation to their etymology. The ideologists therefore believe that a sensualistic naturalism and a rational optimism can be taught as the bases of liberty. In their view ideology has an essentially positive meaning. It is rooted in man's rational nature and provides a sound basis for his action in history. It is the abstract and collective expression of the observations carried out concerning the functioning of the human mind.[2]

Very soon, however, the word "ideology" assumed a pejorative meaning. Napoleon, who was attacked by the ideologists, cast the word in their teeth as an insult. In his view it denoted idle, subversive speculations, inventions divorced from reality which really concealed a thirst for power. "It is to ideology, that sinister metaphysic, that all the misfortunes of France must be attributed," he stated to the Conseil d'État in 1812. Most important of all, ideology is connected with another tradition in philosophy far older than that of Locke or Condillac—namely, the tradition of Bacon. According to Bacon, science is constantly menaced by ideas (idols). Bacon draws a distinction between the "idola tribus," illusions inherent in the human mind, the "idola specus," errors peculiar to individuals, the "idola fori," false concepts derived from current language, and the "idola theatri," the speculations of the philosophers. Ideology thus denotes the speculative idolatry which impedes true scientific knowledge. In the eighteenth century these misleading idols were called "prejudices." The Age of Enlightenment served to unmask them and to disclose the interests which lay beneath them. Even before Marx encountered it, therefore, ideology had acquired a pejorative sense, for two reasons: Napo-

---

[2] See ANDRÉ LALANDE: *Vocabulaire de la Philosophie,* I, 336, 4me édition, Paris, 1938.
CHARLES WACKENHEIM: *La faillité de la réligion d'après Karl Marx,* p. 271, Puf, Paris, 1963.
H. BARTH: *Wahrheit und Ideologie.*

leonic power had accused it of being an abstraction; and the critical, material tradition of Helvetius and Holbach had branded it as a delusion and an oppression.

Marx was aware of both these attacks on ideology. He proceeded to take up his own battle against the idealism of Kant and especially Hegel, whom he accused of putting the cart before the horse, taking effects for causes by locating in the *transcendent,* the metaphysical and in the realm of ideas the basis for explaining economy and need, which can be explained only in what is *immanent.* Ideology was to become the typical example of mystifying, roundabout thinking. Ideological thinking meant inconsistency, secondhand thinking which claimed to stimulate reality whereas in fact it merely reflected it in order to conceal it. Stendhal also attacked the ideologists because they wanted to classify ideas apart from the human consciousness: "An ideological treatise is an insolence," he wrote. "You don't think that my reasoning is good?" From a different point of view Marx also attacked ideology for its insolent, incapable externality, which claimed to explain and justify history without reference to political economy.

In his first works, Marx did not use the word ideology. He speaks of theories characteristic of the imaginary ideas which the ruling classes use to clothe and conceal their real interests. I quote a single passage which appeared in the "Gazette Rhénane" in May, 1842: "As the real position of these gentlemen in the modern state does not correspond in any way to the idea that they have of their own position, as they live in a world that is *outside the real world,* so that their *imagination* takes the place of their heads and their hearts, since they find no satisfaction in practice they are forced to turn to theory, but to *the theory of the transcendent,* namely *religion.* This . . . becomes more or less consciously only a cloak of holiness concealing aspirations which are extremely secular and quite imaginary. . . . To the requirements of practice they oppose a mystical-religious theory which is the pure product of their own imagination; to what is humanly reasonable they oppose sacred entities superior to man; and to the true sanctuary of ideas they oppose points of view which are vulgar, arbitrary and impious." [3]

The "theories" (which Marx was soon to call "ideologies") are therefore the fantastic product (partly deliberate, partly unconscious) of a *contradiction* between what is real and its idealistic justification in the minds of those who profit by it, but refuse to evaluate it in terms of the reality of their own needs. Theories are like Noah's cloak thrown over the needs of this life by people who are walking backwards toward an imaginary life "beyond."

In this passage written in 1842, however, Marx still speaks of "the sacred sanctuary of ideas" and opposes it positively to the utilitarian vulgarity of the theories. In the best tradition of eighteenth-century France and of German idealism, he martials the "humanly reasonable" ideas against the suprahuman entities. The great turning point toward historic materialism had not yet been taken. At that time Marx would still have been glad to be called a humanistic idealist, inspired by Hegel's "phenomenology of the mind" in his fight against conservative supranaturalism.

It was in 1845 that Marxism became the science of the materialist approach to history, when Marx replaced the word "theory" by the word "ideology" in his famous work *"L'idéologie allemande—Critique de la philosophie allemande la plus récente dans ses représentants Feuerbach, B. Bauer et Stirner et du socialisme allemand dans ses divers prophètes."* [4] "Ideology" is the pathology of human knowledge which strays away from the real processes of life (the development of productive energy, relationships within production, the division of labor) and finally opposes human ideas to the conditions of human society. The ideologist thus reflects the maladjustment of man. The people who are really producing wealth no longer enjoy the product of their work. The workers no longer regard the social force as their own power, but as a foreign force which enslaves them. Ideology conceals the economic and material origin of this enslavement; it even justifies this enslavement at three levels, which are dealt with in Marx's later writings: the level of money (the economic fetish which interposes a screen between the

[3] MEGA I, 1, pp. 198–199.
[4] First published in full in 1932.

producer and the consumer), the level of the state (the political fetish which interposes a screen between the citizen and the self-administration of his communal life), and the level of religion (the metaphysical fetish which interposes a screen between man and his own possibilities). Man is thus prevented by the illusory ideologies from perceiving the real production on which his own position depends and which creates a good environment for him, if he knows how to realize it.

Furthermore, Marx does not deny that this real productivity also includes ideas which thus escape the condemnation of the ideologies. Marxism will always protest that it is not a purely economic theory, as one might be led to think from the famous polemical phrase: "It is not conscience which determines life, it is life which determines conscience." [5] Indeed life, if it is summed up in the processes of production, explicitly includes in those processes the material products, and also "the principles, ideas and categories," which correspond to human social relations, because (like those relations) they are "the transient outcome of history." [6] It would therefore be wrong to exclude from human nature man's capacity to produce ideas, which are destined in their turn to influence society. Engels reacted against this materialistic view, which defaces the whole of human reality. He recognized the power of ideas and their reactions; at the same time he tried not to deny the materialistic assumptions of Marxist theory. "The reflection of all the real struggles in the minds of those who participated in them—political, legal and philosophical theories, religious concepts and their development into systems of dogma—also influence the course of the historic struggles. . . . An ideological point of view reacts in its turn upon the economic basis and may modify it to a certain extent." [7]

We now have the *two different concepts of ideology* contained in Marxism, which make it so difficult to analyze:

---

[5] MEGA I, 5, p. 15.

[6] MEGA I, 6, pp. 179–180.

[7] Letters to Joseph Bloch and Conrad Schmidt: "Etudes philosophiques," pp. 128 and 135, *éditions sociales,* Paris.

I. First, the function of ideology is criticized in class societies. There, ideology is the reflection of the interests of the dominant class, protecting the privileges of material and spiritual production. Ideology covers up the economic divergences, whereby one class makes use of the ethical universality of ideas in order to camouflage its own selfish interests. A classless society should therefore be able to do without any arsenal of ideology, because in a classless society man can clearly perceive where he is going. The function of ideology should be eliminated in a classless society, together with its three classical products—money, the state and religion. The ideological mystification of a divided society should be superseded by a creative infrastructure in a classless society. Thus the immanence of work would replace the transcendence of ideas. Philosophy would be put into practice and carried into effect by the proletariat. In the Manifesto, Marx clearly affirms that in any case communism could not present itself as a new ideology: "The theoretical concepts of the Communists are not based on ideas or principles invented or discovered by these or those reformers. They are merely the general expressions of the actual conditions within an existing class-struggle, a movement of history which is taking place before our very eyes." By abolishing class divisions in society, Marxism ought therefore to abolish the ideological products of the false mentality—the hypostatized, mystifying projections of real life.

II. However, Marxism presents itself as an essential, true ideology. The Communist parties in power attribute a decisive function to the ideological struggle. Ideology is therefore no longer the inverted reflection of the real world (as Marx originally regarded it); it is the instrument whereby the proletariat awakens to its unifying role in history. It is the responsibility of the Communist party to promote this awakening by raising the ideological level of the masses. There is a change here in the essential meaning of the word "ideology"; it is no longer a mystifying reflection. It is becoming the description of aims to be attained on the communal road toward essential freedom. Marxism justifies the maintenance of the ideological function in the societies which are moving toward communism, by explaining that ideology is no longer used there to disguise individual interests, which are opposed to the main stream of economic development, because the infrastructure of private interest has been suppressed. Within the interaction between basis and superstructure (as Engels expresses it) ideology does not reflect the basis inversely: it helps it to develop its potentialities more and more. The basic antagonism between ideology and reality disappears, giving place to an emulation which tends toward concord. It is only a tendency, for since Communist society has not yet fully realized its theoretical objectives, it still needs ideological stimulus. Theory still has precedence over practice, but there is no longer any contradiction between the idea and the real. Since ideology now reflects the real basis of society, it participates in its truth, while anticipating its experience. "In this function theory becomes ideology again, not in the form of false conscience, but as a deliberate distance and dissociation from, even opposition to, repressive reality. By this very fact, ideology becomes a political factor of the first importance. For the Communist states the struggle on the ideological front becomes a struggle for survival." [8]

This justification for maintaining ideology in a society which is theoretically moving toward the suppression of "screens" and mediations between man and his self-transformation through work presents difficult problems. In actual fact the proletariat should abolish the temporary function of ideology by transforming reality. In actual fact ideology has not been eliminated, any more than the state. It has become stronger the longer Communist society lasts. This compels one to ask: "Instead of being the temporary corrective of an evolving society, has not ideology merely become an instrument of coercion in the hands of those who hold the political power?" "Just because Marxist analysis reveals economic discrepancies and ideological camouflage, is it not completely disarmed when this camouflage is used by a state which theoretically fully expresses the needs of all?" One must believe in the perma-

8 Herbert Marcuse: *Le Marxisme soviétique,* p. 170, Gallimard (French translation).

nent value of the proletariat, as the agent and instrument which carries out the immanent meaning of universal history, in order to be immune from all doubt concerning the nature of the proletarian state, and the fundamental impossibility of that state becoming in its turn an ideology which oppresses the individual worker.

Where can Marxism find the guarantee that its own ideology will not also reflect the interests, if not of a class at any rate of a country which is unique, despite its claims to universality? And how can it guarantee that as it advances into the future, the Communist party may not become divorced from the realities of the force of production, thus divorcing theory from practice in the same way as it accuses the class societies of doing? By what signs can one recognize the disappearance of ideology in favor of the productive relationship between man and his instruments? In what sense is this disappearance linked with the disappearance of the state, of money and of religion? Is it a consequence of their disappearance, the final vestige of the class society? Or should ideology disappear before the state, money and religion, thus manifesting that the new society is sufficiently clear about itself to dispense with authoritarian teaching carried out by strengthening the Communist party?

This evolution of the function of ideology within Marxism reveals two points:

1. As a method, Marxism is an aspiration to harmonize word and action (as in the biblical concept of God's Word). This harmony is destroyed by idealism, which creates a divorce between the ideal and reality. To paraphrase Marx's famous phrase about religion, Marxism (as an anti-ideological method) is the expression of man's real distress due to being separated from himself, and his protest against that distress.

2. As an achievement, Marxism is a movement in which the transcendent is replaced by the future. In Marxism, ethics disappear in history, and freedom becomes comprehension of historical necessity. The persistence of the ideological struggle is an indication that the Communist "Parousia" is delayed. But then, if the

end of history is replaced by an indefinite dialectic of progress in history, ideology serves the purpose of measuring the distance between the aims and the reality. This re-establishes a transcendence situated in the future which (like everything transcendent) in its turn becomes an unattainable goal, that is, an ideal.

After having promised the end of ideological mediation, therefore, Marxism becomes merely one of the prospects of the industrial society. It has changed from a complete ideology into an ideological ethos, which is so characteristic of the situation in the West today.

The Ideological Ethos of the West

Karl Mannheim draws a distinction between ideology and utopia, defining the former as the conservative justification of the *status quo* and the latter as a creative outlook which transcends the social reality and wants to change it. In his view, ideology is the formation of a system interested in benefiting power; whereas utopia is an invitation to stop regarding the form of that power as inevitable. In this sense ideology would not constitute a real alternative, but would always be an idealization either of the present or of the future, an idealization which would consolidate the existing power. The utopia which reveals itself as different from the present and from its logical future, would arouse the aspirations of the masses to a possible change of the structures. After the decline of the ideologies, is it possible that the contemporary world will return to the utopias?

The question is a serious one, for the ideologies (including the most totalitarian of them—Marxism) have not realized their ambition to change the quality of history. In the advanced industrial societies of the West the ideologies have reduced their global promises to the dimensions of a quantitative improvement of society. The political parties no longer mobilize the masses to take decisions on radical alternatives. They have become families which survive by virtue of people's attachment to a certain tradition and the electoral machinery which seeks to enlist the support of people by taking care not to frighten them. To a large extent, therefore, the ideological programs belong to the past. Their present electoral strategy consists in trying to capture the votes of the *center*—the decisive voice in the affluent society of the West, which has no major collective ideology.

Unlike a total ideology, an ideological ethos recognizes its own inability to establish a reality which is perfectly coherent. As Jeanne Hersch writes, in a total ideology "instead of being proposed to everyone as an endless task, the cohesion of plans for living becomes the affair of a body of doctrine, through which it explains itself and through which it is carried out." [9] In an ideological ethos the overall aim is still to nationalize and direct the social struggle; but the objections involved in the project are recognized at the same time as the project itself. What was a struggle for radical liberation develops into an adaptation to fresh obstacles and a reflection on the contradictions that exist within the great ideological movements. There are manifestations of such adaptations and reflections in the West today. I shall proceed to analyze them on the basis of their principal motivations.

1. *The first ideology of the industrial societies is economic growth.* The slice of cake to be distributed to each person must be increased; the pitiless technical competition, national and international, must be maintained; more leisure must be offered—rather than liberation in work—in order to counteract the bad effects of modern work. Thus a pragmatic socialization takes shape which absorbs the isolated elements that lag behind. This "productivist" ideology combines national power with private prosperity. It tries to avoid the anarchy of personal profit and also the apathy of an overcentralized bureaucracy. It makes use of the methods of flexible or concerted planning. It becomes the common good of the industrial societies because, in face of the menace of worldwide nuclear warfare, their political régimes have decided to transpose their doctrinal competition to the level of their economic expansion. The race for the moon has superseded the crusading spirit.

---

[9] Jeanne Hersch: *Idéologie et Réalités,* p. 14, Paris, 1956.

This change is a good one, for the pragmatic pursuit of greater affluence is less destructive than the terrorism of superior thinking.

However, there are serious internal and external limits to the ideology of growth. First, growth creates disparities and inequalities, which are on the increase. There is a growing disparity between those who produce the output and those who have to beg for a few crumbs. On the worldwide level, growth is widening the gulf between the industrial countries and the underdeveloped countries. Within the industrial countries the gap is widening between the skilled workers and the unskilled; this gap is less apparent, but it is widening just as much. Expansion does not create homogeneity; rather it produces tensions which are very difficult to overcome, because they seem to be due to rational causes. The disparity between the different standards of living creates bitterness and violence among the underprivileged. And there is no worldwide demonstration or denunciation on their behalf, like the protest made by Marxism against private capitalism on behalf of the industrial proletariat. The weaker sectors are vegetating. Confronted by the ideology of growth they feel incapable of establishing their right to humanity except on the fact of their poverty. They are the lame horses of industrial society, and bear no resemblance to the "reserve army" of industry, as Engels called the unemployed workers of the nineteenth century. They do not constitute a labor force, for they cannot work. They see themselves not as a potential majority but as a forgotten minority, until the day when, in certain situations, their mass exclusion from the fruits of expansion makes them attack the affluent societies. Their stagnation, in strong contrast with the rapid progress in the other sectors, is the outer limit of "productivist" ideology—the living obstacle to its universal application.

Moreover, growth is an *indefinite* objective. It does not constitute a value in itself, as competition may have been in a system of free enterprise, or justice in socialism. Admittedly the planners for growth like to recognize its formal side. Whether they are Communists or neo-capitalists, they associate other criteria with expansion: the degree of social participation, the priority of creation over consumption, the priority of public solidarity over private interest, the priority of international aid over national egoism. But these ulterior values added on to the original objective of growth, with its different incitements, are in grave danger of remaining theoretical. They are desirable, optional correctives, not objectives assigned and desired by the collectivity. They are the moral luxury permitted by economic growth, not a basic program. This is clear from the difficulty experienced in trying to integrate collective utopias into the "productivist" societies, as soon as state compulsion slackens in favor of private affluence.

The ideology of growth is therefore a contradictory phenomenon. On the one hand, it is the realization of the economic and political plans which preceded it. Its aim is to abolish the poverty which is due to scarcity, and to promote freedom which is rendered possible through abundance and choice. On the other hand, it takes away all justification from the people who happen to be excluded from growth, not as the result of exploitation but owing to bad luck at the start. And growth has no qualitative aim. It is the rule of means which have no collective ends. Having partially solved the question of needs, its lack of any meaning apart from material prosperity is all the more apparent. To quote Karl Mannheim again, growth is an ideology which conserves technical power without stimulating society to utopian aims.

2. *The second ideology of western societies is security.* The hazards of life are diminished through provision and foresight. Society tries to become its own providence, deliberately planning certain characteristics for the future. This increase in the degree of awareness and collective organization is clearly an advance in social thought. By extending the field of action, society widens its responsibilities. In this way our societies are trying to substitute prevention for cure, competence for improvization, and education for dissatisfaction. This security represents a high degree of respect for human personality, by safeguarding people against the machinations of the "manager" and protecting them within a network of institutions. The more definite and calculable this security becomes, the more certain and reliable this policy becomes, and

less and less arbitrary. It is less brilliant, but also more serviceable. Instead of deploring the phenomenon of technocracy, we should pay tribute to it for the fact that human government benefits from a good administration of affairs.

Security is also a paradoxical phenomenon. It is the major claim made by industrial societies, but it does not supply them with an equivalent amount of affection. Two deep needs seem to be in conflict here: on the one hand, *the daily* round of little disciplines which are indispensable to the functioning of modern social security; and, on the other hand, the need for *adventure,* the myth of movement and "getting away from it all" fed by the press, culture and personal desires. There is a tension between this continual practice of strict adjustment and the dream of carefree spontaneity. In our industrial societies this tension expresses itself especially among young people; they have to force themselves to enter the system of skilled workers, and at the same time they are longing for a life that is extravagantly rich in affection. They imagine that they are living a life full of poetry, whereas in reality they are destined merely for security. But it is not only the young people who feel this tension. The whole culture in the social-security societies manifests this thirst for what is interesting, unpredictable and uncontrollable. The security of the imagination is undermined by novels, plays and films. On the other hand, in the societies which offer no economic security, the chaos of experience is transfigured into a controlled, legitimate contemplation by the classic arts. When society provides for all real needs, the artist becomes unrealistic or surrealistic. He turns from the concrete to the abstract, from harmony to discord, from the security of what he knows to the insecurity of what he invents.

Social security, the constant ideology of our societies, is thus accompanied by a deliberate inward insecurity. The public life organized by man bores him as a private person. It does nothing to feed his imagination. The western world (which increasingly includes Soviet society) is not solving the tension between efficiency and affectivity. That is why the industrial societies are so affluent materially and at the same time so frustrating psychologically. The ideology of security does not automatically bring happiness. There is a paradox here, manifest especially in the outbursts of youth and in modern art, but it exists everywhere and it prevents the ideology of security from resulting in a utopia of hope. That is why the advanced industrial societies no longer venture to extol social hope to the same extent as their technical progress.

3. *Lastly, the contemporary ideologies are internationalized.* Expansion and security are universal phenomena. Not only do the social techniques and models tend to be similar everywhere, but so do the young people and the different cultures. Internationalism, which was formerly the utopia and the ideology of the great revolutionary movements, has become a fact in contemporary society. Marxism finds a strange confirmation: the mode of production is becoming uniform, even if politics are different. The divergence is more and more taking place between the North and the South, and less and less between East and West. Internationalism is a phenomenon which levels out the ideological differences and creates similar standards of living everywhere.

However, this internationalism is paradoxical also. The special forms of nationalism are springing up again on every hand, and not only as expressions of chauvinist egoism. The people and the nations belonging to the common universe of technology are afraid to go forward toward a future that has no past, toward a project that has no memory, in other words, a civilization that has no culture. Our time may thus be said to be experimenting in interdependence and celebrating independence; on the one hand, it is moving toward a world market and, on the other hand, it is tending to establish national or continental conclaves. The ideology of internationalism does not result in an international utopia. The image of the world is therefore much more confused than at the time when nationalism and internationalism constituted two clearly opposed views.

Thus the ideological climates of the West seem to be complex phenomena in which one project conflicts with another, in which the aims cast a shadow: growth creates disparity and insignificance; security creates the longing for adventure; internationalism revives loyalty to the special traditions of the past. The West has no total ideology affirming the radical need for liberty, as Marxism had. This explains the relativization of the ideological ethos in a society which nevertheless aspires to an awareness of its collective future. Paradoxically we are experiencing the exact opposite of utopian socialism which preceded the Marxist régime, and which believed in its aims without having the means. We have the means, but we have lost the aims. Partially realized, socialist ideology has become a technique of indefinite growth, of progressive security and definite internationalism. But it lacks the collective will which animated socialist utopianism. Instead of denouncing the worship of ideology, we must therefore revive people's belief in utopias, if we want to tackle our situation in the West.

Christian Faith and Ideology

Faith is not an ideology—that is, the expression of a social group with its own causes and its own interests. Faith is a response to a call which comes from elsewhere; it is an act which does not express a situation, but which replies to a call through obedience. An ideology is a rational system of collective needs. On the other hand, faith is a personal commitment, a venture at a turning point in history. For instance, Abraham's faith was not an ideology corresponding to the transient needs of the Children of Israel at that time. It was a personal decision taken by the "father of that people" (Ab-ham). Faith is the acceptance of a vocation; it is not the deduction of an interpretation. Faith and ideology, therefore, are not on the same level of knowledge and action. This can be seen more clearly if one compares their final stages: faith never turns into sight; it is always eschatological, otherwise it would no longer be faith. Ideology, on the contrary, has to manifest itself in collective expressions, otherwise it would have to be classified among the abstract categories of the ideal.

A clear distinction must therefore be drawn between *faith* (which is a personal response and an eschatological expectation) and *ideology* (which is a collective symbolization and a history program). However, they must not be systematically opposed to one another. They are rather two spheres which should preserve each other; for the secular ideologies warn faith not to merge with the spiritual armament of a particular group (social, national or cultural), not to deteriorate into a Christian ideology side by side with the other social ideologies. When faith becomes confused in this way with the collective stimulus of a human group, it loses its savor, its universality, its risk and its promise. It is then obliged to play the role of a competitor, and this alienates the members of the other groups from it. It then replaces the kingdom by Christian civilization, the gospel by the social principles of Christianity, the Holy Spirit by spiritual values, and vocation by planning.

Parallel with this, faith warns the ideologies not to set themselves up as faiths to be worshiped, involving personal obedience and promises of eschatological transformation. The ideologies must remain methods of rational interpretation and historic change. When an ideology yields to the temptation to become a faith, it replaces analyses with the *credo,* its principles by a *message,* its aim by a *vocation,* and its impersonal method by *the cult of personality*. An ideology then becomes corrupt, because it is attempting to be a challenge instead of an explanation.

An ideology therefore represents the degradation of faith into the abstract; and faith represents the personalized degradation of ideology. However, it is not so easy to distinguish between faith and ideology in actual life. The function of ideology is part of our contemporary societies. It acts as a running-belt between the aims of society and the masses. Its role is positive, if it symbolizes a collective project of which it has become actively aware. Its role is negative, however, if the symbol becomes an idol, a schema imposed by power, a collective unawareness serving a false aim. It is difficult to discern between these two aspects of the ideological function. We often have illusions about its positive side, or else we only perceive its dangers. Both aspects do exist, both in the total ideologies and in the ideological climates. We must therefore be constantly on our guard, and this means supporting symbols as well as criticizing idols. The Christian faith is not opposed to ideologies, but to *idols*. Like Marxism, the Christian faith aspires to act as it speaks, both collectively and personally. In order to do this it supports itself, not on an idealized sublimation of needs, but on a concrete continuation of the incarnation. The Christian faith is faith not in the idea, nor in what is real, but in God's act in human history, in the commitment of God's action in the evolution of the world.

4

THE IDEOLOGICAL SPECTRUM IN ASIA

by Kiyoko Takeda Cho (Japan)

Wherever human beings believe in some idea, hold to some value concept, or seek to change social and political systems, there are bound to be conflicts of ideas and ideologies. Particularly since the Second World War, Asia has been undergoing rapid changes: from a stagnant to a dynamic society, from colonial status to independence, from hierarchical and autocratic regimes to liberalism and democracy, from a feudalistic system to capitalism, and so on. The conflict of ideas and ideologies in Asia today arises from the very changes for which all its people are striving with such enthusiasm. Hence we must ask, What is the nature and direction of these changes?—for it is these which determine the nature of the conflict of ideas and ideologies.

In this essay I shall discuss the conflict in terms of the struggle for "independence" and "modernization" and the question of "pacifism"—three axes around which all the conflicting ideas and ideologies move according to their logic and value concept.

Independence

"Independence" has been the common goal of Asians for the past one hundred years and remains so today. Yukichi Fukuzawa, one of the most outstanding intellectual leaders in modern Japan, has said, "When a person is independent, a nation is independent." For Fukuzawa, an independent person and an independent nation were indivisible and interdependent. In other words, when a person can secure his own independence, a nation can secure its independence from colonial rule. This thesis has become a slogan for modern Japan, even though very often the balance between the two poles was lost by overemphasis on either nationalism or individualism. Fukuzawa wrote in his famous book, *The Encouragement of Learning,* that "Heaven has not created man above man nor man below man. . . . To be independent is to govern oneself and not to be dependent upon others." "Independence" in the sense of self-support, self-government, self-determination and self-respect has two connotations: on the one hand, the spiritual [1] and intellectual independence of dehumanized Asian men and women; on the other, a more ideological meaning—the social, political and economic independence of individuals from the traditional hierarchical and semi-feudalistic social system and also the freedom of nation from foreign rule. For Fukuzawa the spiritual and mental independence of man and the political independence of the nation are one, for only when independent men participate in nation-building can the nation itself attain independence.

Jawaharlal Nehru, in his autobiography,[2] quotes C. F. Andrews as an echo of the cry of the Indian people: "The only way of self-recovery was through some vital upheaval from within. The explosive force needed for such an upheaval must be generated within the soul of India itself. It could not come through loans and gifts and grants and concessions and proclamations from without. . . . Therefore, it was with the intense joy of mental and spiritual deliverance from an intolerable burden, that I watched the actual outbreak of such an inner explosive force, as that which actually occurred when Mahatma Gandhi spoke to the heart of India the mantra—'Be free! Be slaves no more!' and the heart of India

[1] In Fukuzawa this element was weak.
[2] Pp. 66–67.

responded. In sudden movement her fetters began to be loosened, and the pathway of freedom was opened."

Lu Hsün, and outstanding modern Chinese intellectual of whom Mao Tse-tung has written, "Lu Hsün is the greatest saint of New China," resisted western and all other outside influences and sought for a truly independent spirit in the slavish and stagnant mind of the Chinese people. He said: "Only the independent spirit of the people is respectable and only when it is exalted will there be true progress in China." [3]

In postwar Asia, "nationalism" has been a popular slogan in the struggle to obtain political, economic and intellectual (or spiritual) independence from western domination. However, the meaning or nature of nationalism differs according to the national and historical situation. In Japan, in the years between the Meiji Restoration (1868) and the end of the Second World War (1945), "nationalism" connoted the family-state ideology of the emperor system in which the unity of the independent person and the independent nation was lost—the independent nation with wealth and power was exalted at the expense of the independent person. After the war, nationalism was extremely unpopular in Japan, but in all other parts of Asia it became the slogan for independence. However, more recently nationalism has been revived in two forms: the old imperial family-state ideology with its respect for traditional culture, and a new nationalism similar to that of other Asian peoples, with an emphasis on political and economic independence.

The first type is being fostered by reactionary politicians and extreme rightists who are attacking the leftists, including political and labor leaders, and intellectuals.[4] Some intellectuals are also reaffirming the old nationalism and interpreting the Great Asian War

[3] He also said: "The other side of a despot is a slave. When he holds power, he behaves as an almighty and when he loses power, he shows himself to be slavish." For Lu Hsün, it was essential for oneself to know that he himself is slavish and to be courageous enough to face this reality.

[4] Inejiro Asanuma, one of the leaders of the Socialist Party was murdered a few years ago by a rightist, and the family of the publisher of a novel which dealt humorously with the imperial household has been attacked by extreme rightists. Such events have encouraged revival of a kind of mood of "taboo."

(Second World War in Asia) as a struggle for independence from western pressure. A large monthly intellectual magazine has been publishing for over a year installments of an essay which strongly criticizes the discussion of responsibility for the war which was carried on rather widely during the postwar period among progressive intellectuals. The author claims that the war started one hundred years ago at the very beginning of modern Japan and that it still continues today. Criticism of American military attacks on North Vietnam expressed by the liberal intellectuals is supported by those whose nationalism is anti-western or anti-American, rejected by those whose nationalism is anti-Communist.

The new type of nationalism is rather strong among some liberal and Marxist intellectuals. In 1963 a very interesting play, "A Japanese Called Otto" was written by Junji Kinoshita, a popular writer, and performed by a famous drama group. The hero of the play is a Japanese communist spy, Hotsumi Ozaki, who was caught and executed by the Japanese government in 1944. In this drama, Ozaki is pictured as a man caught in the conflict between nationalism and internationalism—loyalty to his nation and loyalty to the international Comintern. This drama was very popular among intellectuals and young people because it presents the common problem of intellectuals, including Communists, today. They have begun to recognize the challenge of both the new nationalisms in Asia and Africa as they strive for political, economic and cultural independence, and also of certain international ideologies. The conflict between communist China and the U.S.S.R. has encouraged a diversified interpretation of Marxism: supporters of communist China are generally found in the Communist party, of the U.S.S.R. in the Socialist party; although the spirit of Asian nationalism leads Japan to back China against the western pressure of the U.S.S.R.

There is also a third form of nationalism today—the sincere search for a healthy combination of personal and national independence, as expressed in Fukuzawa's thesis. This is known as "Kokuminshugi," people's or democratic nationalism. There is in Japan today a kind of "history boom," a critical study and reevaluation of traditional culture and thought in an effort to root democratic nationalism in the cultural soil of this country. In such studies we find criticism not only of the family-state ideology where individual freedom was neglected, but also of the kind of individualism or humanism which was an irresponsible escapism and utopianism refusing to participate in efforts to reform social and national life.

This inquiry into the idea of "independence" of the individual and of the nation, is bringing about a very interesting diversity in the interpretation of certain ideas or ideologies. Nationalism, democratic liberalism, humanism and Marxism can never be given a single stereotyped interpretation. In this dynamically changing Asia, all these ideas are seeking to determine the course of history and in the process of functioning within the historical reality they inevitably become diversified. The division among the Marxists is not only a reflection of the split between China and the U.S.S.R. Many Marxists who criticized the totalitarian nature of the Communist party or who sought for the meaning of humanism or freedom in Marxian ideology have been expelled from the party, and have organized several groups, among them "Zengakuren," the National Federation of Student Organizations, which is openly critical of the Communist party because of its servile obedience to the direction of foreign communist authorities, and which contains some anarchistic elements which to some extent express a mood of individualism as against authoritarianism. The younger generation puts great value upon its own experience, and is skeptical of any pre-established ideas, philosophies, ideologies, systems, or powers. This attitude, in spite of the possibility of irresponsible skepticism or anarchism, may evolve into individualism and humanism which would become operative in its ideological and political life.

However, the most notable expression of personal independence can be found in the Japanese people's personal experience of civic democracy. During the past twenty years all kinds of citizens—workers, merchants, housewives—have been participating in the activities of labor unions, parent-teacher associations, groups at their place of work or in their neighborhood, and many other organizations. Almost everyone has an opportunity to participate in some such groups where he can express his own opinions and support his own causes, even though not completely free from traditional social pressures or the influences of mass media. This kind of grass-roots democracy is not yet firmly established, but it has great potentialities.

Modernization

Another area of ideological debate in Asia today is "modernization," whose exact definition has been the subject of endless discussions, by philosophers, political scientists, economists, sociologists, anthropologists, men of letters, and others.

The Marxist method for evaluating the nature of the modernization of Japan has always been based on Marx's five stages of economic development—primitive community, slavery, feudalism, capitalism and socialism—and after the Second World War many intellectuals came to regard it as the most scientific and objective method to evaluate social progress.

Another group, including influential scholars, tried to examine the modernization of Japan from a different perspective. They began with man, his ethos and value concepts, and held that social reform must be directed or accompanied by the renewal of man. Modern ethos is the human basis of modernization.

This approach must be distinguished from abstract idealism or spiritualism. The human ethos functions as a creative value concept and driving force to re-organize and re-create the system and structure of society, including social, political and economic relations, as exemplified in the analysis of Max Weber in his *Protestant Ethics and the Spirit of Capitalism.* Such a position was represented by Professor Hisao Otsuka, a leading Christian economist of Tokyo University. He does not reject Marxian methodology.

But he tried to emphasize the firm position of man—his ethics in the structural reformation of society. Being a Christian, Professor Otsuka himself finds the modern ethos in Protestantism; some others find it in modern humanism. Because of this, some opponents criticize this group as modernists who measure the nature of modernization of Japan by the standard of the West—a measure which comes from without though that is not the motive of this group at all. Their approach is to start with man, his ethos and value concepts.

Another example is Professor Masao Maruyama, one of the most influential scholars, who has carefully examined the root and logic of traditional Japanese thought—particularly political thought —and dug out the potential value concept, the concepts of man or of history which were the internal potential driving forces for the modernization of Japan. His excellent studies of Sorai, the leading Confucian scholar of the Tokugawa period, of Yukichi Fukuzawa, the most influential intellectual of modern Japan, and of many other modern political thinkers are sharp analyses of the ethos and thought pattern of the Japanese. The criteria presupposed in such studies are very similar to the modern humanistic or even Christian concepts of man. Critical studies and analyses of the emperor system have been made by some of us not only as criticism of the political system but also of the deterministic and authoritarian value concept underlying them and which along with some psychological elements are the inner obstacles for healthy modernization.

Another approach of this group also starts with man, but not with the Christian understanding of man or a concept of man similar to the western humanism, but with the stagnant and slavish consciousness of the common people of Asia. Yoshimi Takeuchi, who introduced Lu Hsün's approach to postwar Japan, has persistently taken this stand. "From below and into within, but never from outside and unto upward" is Takeuchi's way. . . . It is a search for the growth and rise of indigenous selfhood from the bosom of the stagnant Asian cultural and spiritual soil. He even cherishes the spirit of resistance against the cultural impact from outside—that is, from the West. In his view this internal motivation is the only potentiality of modernization of Asia for him and for many others who take a similar standpoint. Takeuchi is also interested in nationalism—democratic nationalism—only within this basic approach.

In spite of the differences in their emphases, the common concern of these groups is to distinguish clearly between modernization and westernization—though many admit that the western impact often stimulates the move toward modernization—and to discover the factors for "change" which come from the inner motives of persons, cultures and societies in Asia. In other words, there is a presupposition that man can control or influence his social and physical environment according to his value system. This optimism has positive meaning in Asia where historically religious or political fatalism and determinism have been dominant in the philosophy of life of the people.

A third group is made up of American scholars who, since before 1960 when a conference of American and Japanese scholars was held on the general theme of modernization, have been making studies on the modernization of Japan. Of course, each scholar has his own approach to the subject, but Professor John W. Hall of the University of Michigan, who was the convener of this group, has laid down the following criteria of a modern society: (1) a comparatively high degree of urbanization, (2) widespread literacy, (3) comparatively high per capita income, (4) extensive geographical and social mobility, (5) relatively high degree of commercialization and industrialization within the economy, (6) an extensive and penetrating network of mass communication media, (7) widespread participation and involvement of members of the society in modern social and economic processes, (8) a relatively highly organized bureaucratic form of government with widespread involvement of members of the society, (9) an increasingly rational and secular orientation of the individual to his environment based on the growth of scientific knowledge.[5]

---

[5] See Hall's paper entitled, "Japan Within the Concept of Modernization." Other papers by this group are "Changing Japanese Attitude Toward Modernization" which has just been published (edited by Marius B. Jansen) and "Changing Japanese Social Structure" (Ronald P. Dore, the convener), "Entrepreneurship and Technological Change in Japan" (William W. Lockwood), "Changing Japanese Political Ideas and Institutions" (Robert E.

Some of these American scholars, differing from the average Japanese intellectual's judgment, evaluate the nature and degree of modernization of Japan very highly and some even admit that such a success in modernization was due to the modern Japanese nationalism under the emperor system. Using these criteria, some scholars define modernization as the change from one way of life to another through technological and industrial revolution. On this basis in the past one hundred years, Japan has accomplished remarkable modernization. Many regard Japan as a model for the underdeveloped countries in Asia and Africa. Although Japanese intellectuals regard democracy or democratic liberalism as an essential element in the concept or idea of modernization, these scholars claim that democracy may be a by-product of modernization, but it is not an essential part or source of it. Modernization may imply totalitarianism.

There has been strong reaction on the part of Japanese liberal and Marxist intellectuals to this kind of American evaluation.[6] They criticize the technological and economic interpretation of history, and the evaluation of Japanese society solely on the basis of superficial economic prosperity to the neglect of the inner motives, ethos, and value concepts of the people who give meaning and direction to our dynamically changing society. Even Marxist intellectuals are critical of this modernization theory regarding it as too "materialistic" and technological. There is also criticism of the rather superficial appraisal of the emperor system, imperialistic nationalism, and totalitarianism as producers of material and technological modernization. Thus, value concepts have become of crucial importance for Japanese intellectuals in all efforts to define modernization.

Ward), "Changing Values in Thought, Literature and the Arts of Japan" (Donald H. Shively). These writers are reluctant to admit the universal validity of any analysis based on some fragmentary area of human experience, and they refuse to measure the modernization of Japan by taking western experience as the norm of expectation.

[6] As a matter of fact, there are several outstanding American scholars who are deeply interested in inner values in "change," "progress," or "modernization." However, the above-mentioned approaches and interpretations are introduced more popularly here as the American view.

In spite of differences in expression, definition, or characterization of modernization, there is a common interest in the "change" from a stagnant, hierarchical, autocratic Asia to something new. And the profound interest of Asians—and especially Japanese—is focused, on the one hand, on the value motivations of the Asians themselves and the purpose and goal of change and, on the other, on methods and techniques to bring about structural changes in their societies.

Pacifism

Another dynamic, yet ambiguous idea today is "pacifism." During the Second World War there was little pacifist sentiment in Japan. A few Christians made a strong plea for justice and peace as a national ideal but they were subjected to social or political pressure, or imprisoned. But in postwar Japan secular pacifism became very popular. The New Constitution declared "disarmament" as the national ideal and policy. Most people interpreted "pacifism" as almost identical with "democracy" or humanism. It was a symbolic expression of the renunciation of imperialist militarism and fascism. Another decisive factor in the growth of pacifism was the common desire for "no more Hiroshimas." Almost everybody claimed to be pacifist, and regarded pacifism and democracy as the national policy of postwar Japan. This rosy idealism lasted until the triumph of the communist regime in China in 1949 and the Korean War in 1950. Then a great division appeared between those who wanted to revise the Constitution to justify maintenance of a military force for self-defense, and those who wanted to keep what is called the "peace Constitution" as the very ground of liberal democracy and a barrier against the revival of militarism.

Another division in the pacifist ranks is between communist pacifists and other idealistic pacifists. The former hold that since economic and political conflicts are the cause of war, the social struggle to solve such conflicts is the way to achieve peace. Thus, pacifism is interpreted in ideological terms. Faced with this challenge, idealistic pacifism, arising from people's natural aversion to war, humanist or Christian pacifism, which emphasizes spiritual attitudes such as reconciliation, the elimination of hostility, urged the rejection of war and began to recognize the social and economic causes of war. But idealistic pacifism and the ideological war of "communist pacifism" are basically different. For example, in the beginning of the anti-atomic and hydrogen bomb movement, people of many different ideas and ideologies cooperated in the cause of peace. But division gradually became apparent. One of the vital questions which caused the division was whether the movement should oppose the nuclear experiments of all nations or only of certain ones. Some liberal youth movements and women's organizations and some Christian groups left it. The communist and socialist leaders struggled to gain control of the movement, and it was divided into two or three parts. In the past two years at least three or four conferences were held at the same time, and representatives from China and the U.S.S.R. took different positions.

Even the Christian Peace Organization has split into two groups, partly reflecting the ideological division in the secular pacifist movements, though the apparent cause was disagreement over whether Christian political action should be guided by purely political and social considerations or by a Christian ethical evaluation of the political and social situation. One group sent representatives to China and the other to the World Christian Peace Conference in Prague.

However, in spite of the ideological confusion, "pacifism" has never been so popular in Japan as today. It provides common ground on which supporters of different ideological positions can still meet and exchange ideas in a search for some common understanding or goal. There is a realistic idealism which is trying to develop the idea of pacifism into a national policy in this time of struggle between powers and ideologies in the world. It is an expression of a desire to be independent from both the U.S.A. and the U.S.S.R. and to take a unique role as mediator between the opposing powers on both the political and the ideological plane. It is also an expression of a desire to break out of a narrow nationalism, to participate in the destiny of mankind, and to contribute to the welfare of the world. This sentiment is strong among the people who suffered severely during the war for the glory of the Emperor's nation. They do not express themselves in the same way as intellectuals or scholars or political ideologists, but pacifism might be an expression of their particular desire for modernization.

The Need for Christian Insight

In this conflict of ideas and ideologies in our Asian countries today, Christianity is not functioning simply as one idea or ideology among many. Rather, individual Christians are participating in the conflict, sometimes taking the initiative in the thinking about independence, nationalism, or pacifism. In Japan some are raising critical voices against the revival of old nationalism, analyzing the emperor system, and its concept of man or other dangerous tendencies. Some Christians are taking leading roles in the discussion on modernization and influencing the thinking of the people. Some are involved in the pacifist movements or other social and political groupings and find difficulty in discovering the unique role of Christians in ideological conflict. Sometimes Christians are divided into opposing groups. Though the number of Christians is small (½ per cent of the total population) their contribution in the field of ideas and ideologies is considerable.

Despite individual participation by laymen, the church as a body is not ready to give guidance to its members on how to act realistically and effectively in the conflict of ideas and ideologies. In the churches, study committees have been organized and materials have been collected. But history is moving and changing rapidly and dynamically and the ready-made theories or theological speculation of western or even Japanese theologians is not sufficient. It is essential to mobilize and evaluate these laymen's ideas and experiences and to work out some basic understanding of the nature and meaning of the present conflict. The church has a mission to offer to her members and the world the insights which our Lord alone can give—insights on the true meaning of human and national independence, the search for modernization, the right direction of change, the struggle for ultimate unity and peace, and the true ground for unity in the diversity of ideas and ideologies.

5

URBAN REVOLUTION IN THE UNITED STATES OF AMERICA

by DAVID W. BARRY (U. S. A.)

Nature of the Urban Revolution

AN American sociologist, Kingsley Davis, has graphically shown the world's rapid transformation into an urbanized planet by the following table[1] of actual, estimated and projected percentages over the short span of 250 years:

	Percentage of World's Population	
Year	*Living in Cities of 20,000 Plus*	*Living in Cities of 100,000 Plus*
1800	2.4	1.7
1850	4.3	2.3
1900	9.2	5.5
1950	20.9	13.1
2000	45.0	25.0
2050	90.0	50.0

Urbanization on so vast and rapid a scale constitutes a fundamental change in human history. Until very recently the basic oc-

---

[1] Adapted from KINGSLEY DAVIS: "The Origin and Growth of Urbanization in the World," *The American Journal of Sociology,* March, 1955, p. 435.

cupation of the overwhelming majority was that of wresting from the natural world the fundamental essentials for life: food, clothing, shelter. The cities of the ancient world and of biblical times were concentrations of power based upon the ability of a ruling group to exact tribute from the countryside either by force or by religious authority and occasionally by the more subtle methods of commerce. The largest were not above 200,000 in population, and it took 50 to 90 farmers to support one city dweller. Today fewer than one out of twelve American workers is employed in agriculture, and in this country the common experience of the great majority of people is an urban one. Not only is this true of the United States and of many other industrialized and urbanized nations, but the social policies of large sectors of the world today called "underdeveloped" are directed toward the same goals: larger cities, larger industrial concentrations, fewer agricultural workers. We do not have the answers to the multiple problems of a vastly increased and increasing population, but such answers as we have tend inexorably to be urban ones: urban kinds of employment, of housing, of political life.

It is essential to understand the extent to which the economic values associated with production, distribution and consumption take precedence in this urban society over all other considerations. The economies that built pyramids to the glory of dead rulers or cathedrals to the glory of God are scarcely comprehensible to today's urban mind, which makes its most fundamental decisions in terms of what the effect will be on a producing, marketing and consuming society. Many urban architects deplore the fact that their talents, once used to build permanent monuments to power and prestige, are now required simply to design the most economical use of space for large numbers of people who live and work in a limited land area, resulting in a monotonous repetition of cubicles and a visual sameness of cities all over the world. Karl Marx made many errors in prediction, but he seems to have been right in his assertion that in an industrialized urban society economic considerations would assume primacy over other kinds of values.

This is not necessarily to be deplored, despite the many persons whose sensibilities are offended by the stridently materialistic tone of urban civilization today. The God who made the world and called it good and entered in flesh into its life for its redemption is surely concerned about the material well-being of his children, and this is a consistent note in all Christian history. In almost all previous societies, Christian and non-Christian, the so-called non-material values in life (aesthetic, cultural, even "spiritual") had to depend on social classes that achieved freedom from drudgery through some method of exploitation of others; and the pursuit of such values was impossible for the majority of the population. The urban mass economy aims at achieving abundance for all, and in America it actually achieves an approximation of this goal for from one-half to three-quarters of the population. In other urbanized and urbanizing societies, even the most dictatorial, the goal of mass abundance must be an explicit one, for political revolution is always just around the corner. This is something new in human existence and surely intended by God as one of his good gifts: the technological possibility of a life for all men freed of the pressures of day-to-day grubbing for the sheer necessities of life and rich with the cornucopia of fascinating material inventions that are spilling out of men's creative minds today. It is so new that the increasing masses of mankind in relatively privileged nations, as they emerge into unprecedented material well-being, have little idea of what to do either with their relative abundance or with the increasing leisure that this kind of living makes possible. Where do we go? Toward acquisition and consumption of more and more material things, in accordance with the basic dynamics that make this system go? Or can we begin to turn man's energies away from sheer acquisitiveness to other purposes? Here the churches, which deal in motivation and values, have some serious thinking to do, especially as in their present form they seem to have so close an affinity to the social groups who have had the greatest material benefits from the urbanization of society.

It is still true, however, that the great masses of the world's population and large sectors even of the people of the "successfully" urbanized nations, such as the United States, do not share significantly in the material advantages of those for whom our urban system is working. This brings us to another major challenge. Urbanism rewards the trained, skilled, technologically educated man; but at the same time it penalizes those who do not have these skills. The urban society makes pre-urban man out of date and provides no place for him. This is a radically different situation from the earlier days of rapid industrialization, when factories, railroads and construction could absorb thousands of unlettered farmers from all over the world if they had a strong back and were willing to work, or from the days when pioneer man was transforming wildernesses into farms and plantations. With frightening speed, urban society is turning into a kind of world that has no role for the untrained, unskilled to perform. The productive economy of America is sufficiently advanced to maintain such people by means of the character-destroying, slightly-above-destitution system known as public welfare. Other countries—especially the nations in Asia, Africa and South America—as they struggle toward urbanization, are not yet able to do this; and actual starvation is a constant threat. In either event, urban mass civilization is a destroyer of souls for those who are not equipped to perform the technical, verbal, mathematical, scientific and other advanced functions upon which urban processes depend.

This again may be the kind of challenge in which God is testing our capacity to take his purposes seriously. It is a fundamental Christian belief that God wants the potential of his children developed to the utmost, and this theme has been strong in church colleges and educational missions. Yet in no society, however fervent its protestations of Christian and democratic values, have we ever taken seriously the task of educating the poor or those at the bottom of the social ladder; we have never looked at every child, from every family, to discover his potential to be a doctor, physicist, mechanic, statesman, poet, technician, and then given him the training that his individual capacities, rather than his family's social position, required. Urban society is forcing us to decide either to do this or to allow our world to become permanently divided into those who are within its system of privileges and those who are condemned by lack of opportunity and training to live outside.

This decision is not necessarily going to be made by the kings and princes of this world, or by the "establishment," the policy-making groups and power structures of urban society. In the churches of the West, the groups concerned with the poor and with social change to improve the lot of the poor have long operated on certain assumptions as to how constructive social change occurs. They have assumed that when an informed group of concerned citizens call the attention of the public to the plight of those who are deprived and dispossessed, the response of the community's leadership, supported by the pressures of an essentially humane citizenry, will be a reasonable and honest effort to improve conditions. This approach has won certain limited victories, such as prison reforms and the establishment of social services and protective devices against the worst hazards of poverty, including social security and public welfare. Since, however, the poor have always been perceived as powerless, this approach has always been one of negotiation within the more privileged segments of society about what will be done *for* the poor, rather than negotiation with the dispossessed themselves about their needs.

The Revolution of the "Poor"

The rapid pace of urbanization and the radical nature of social change that it involves have brought some rude challenges to this style of thinking. The "poor" in urban society have begun to make much more drastic and immediate demands upon the power structures than the "friends of the poor" were ever inclined to make on their behalf. In today's urban world, revolution is taking on a new form. Revolutions in earlier days were for the purpose of replacing one ruling class with another. This theme is by no means absent from today's revolutions, especially in continents which are emerging from colonialism, but in the developed urban communities a different form of revolution is appearing. It is the demand of hitherto dispossessed groups that they be included in the benefits of urban life. They do not demand a new kind of system or a revision of social objectives, but insist that historical patterns of exclusion shall be ended.

The new kind of revolution appears in its clearest form in the racial revolution in America. The Negro is not trying to replace one leadership *élite* with another, nor is he revolting against the American system of government, or its economic system, or the value systems underlying what is called the "American way of life." Rather, he is demanding his right to share fully in this scheme of things. In making this demand, he has decided to leave behind him the influential white friends, so often churchmen, who have counseled patience and gradualism, step-by-step change, conciliation and compromise, the making of friends and the development of mutually cordial relationships. Instead he has substituted the threat and reality of social disorder, of civil disobedience and open conflict, modified by a strong but not necessarily predominant theme of nonviolence as a basic technique. He has learned that only by such methods can an otherwise powerless group expose the hypocrisy of a nation that lives by a double standard and force changes in practices that deny elementary principles of justice and morality.

This has been deeply troubling to the American churches, conditioned so long by interpretations of the Christian gospel that equate love only with reconciliation. Not for the first time in history, the churches have had to face the fact that they were identified with an immoral social system, and the fact that systems of special privilege have rarely been dislodged in history without conflict. In a comparable situation in the early days of labor union organization, despite the advanced leadership given by the Federal Council of Churches and by certain churchmen, the churches on the whole deplored the conflict engendered by the organization of the working man to assert his interests, and they maintained their identification with privilege and the *status quo*. According to some analysts, this resulted in the alienation of the laboring man from the church (though others held that he had never identified with it anyhow, so could not be alienated). There are many signs that

American Negroes, particularly their youth, are taking a hard look at the segregated institution of the church with which they have long been identified and are testing it against the realities of their new commitment to achieve full dignity as citizens. The tests are coming largely in the area of how the church deals with conflict, and unless the church's witness can have a real impact in achieving goals of justice and equity, it is likely to be dismissed by many in this struggle as irrelevant. This realization has put many of the more sensitive church leaders on firing lines where they have never been before.

Moral reactions against the peculiar immoralities of the American racial system have thus been caught up and given new content by the revolution of rising expectations that urbanization has brought about. The historic preoccupation of civil rights groups with *de jure* discrimination in basic rights of citizens has been rapidly changing to concern with the *de facto* aspects of discrimination in areas of life such as education and job opportunities which deny the Negro access to the benefits of urbanization. In other countries which are moving toward urbanization the same process will occur and is occurring; the particular social methods of class, ethnic groups, political persuasion, hereditary privilege that have been used to perpetuate the privileges of any given group are being challenged by the vast promises of a life of material abundance for all that an urbanized, technological world holds out. The inarticulate masses whose arduous labor kept others in relative comfort have begun to comprehend that there are now available other ways in which to run a world, and they are becoming more articulate in their demands, especially in cities. There are many obstacles to the achievement of a well-functioning, urbanized, industrialized society, including the need for capital, the pressures of population growth, the training of technicians, systems of transportation and communication. But among all these, the one moral obstacle that we can expect the peoples of the world to reject is the conscious or unconscious assumption that the apparatus of urban society is designed to perpetuate the privileges of an *élite* group, however it may be defined.

The "Mass" of the Urban World

Among many other aspects of urban society that both challenge and perplex those concerned with Christian values is the recurrent problem how to assess the "mass" aspects of the urban world against the stress on the dignity, worth and meaning of the individual life in Christian tradition. Urbanism by its nature implies large numbers of people, too numerous for most social processes to deal with one by one, and in a setting too complex to let social order depend on the vagaries of individual expression (as was possible in America, for example, in the days of family farms). Thus urban answers tend to come by dividing people into large groups with presumably homogeneous needs and tastes and mass-producing the services which their common needs require. Thus we get mass transportation, mass housing projects and suburban developments, mass magazines, mass media of communication, mass production of clothing styles and food, supermarkets and chain stores and all the other new systems of the new urbanism that have begun to erase individuality from American cities and are being repeated in newly developing cities all over the world.

We need some very clear thinking about this characteristic of urban living as it relates to the sense of the individual worth of God's children. It is fairly evident that given the opportunity, most people seem ready to choose the benefits of mass-produced civilization over the lower material standards they have previously known. A mass-produced car is better than no car, even if it is exactly the same as the neighbor's car. New public housing, even if monotonous, is preferred over the most picturesque of unsanitary slums. The village folk singer gets neglected in favor of radio and television, even if programs on the latter are tasteless and full of propaganda. Except for those who have known privilege and its choices, people all over the world seem to respond readily to the products of mass civilization and opt for them rather than for the less-developed, but more individualistic, products to which they have been accustomed.

In more advanced urban economies, mass production for a mass market greatly extends freedom of choice: foods, magazines, communications, housing. In addition, urban concentrations facilitate other specializations that do not develop in a nonurban society: specialty shops, interest groups, religious forms, special libraries, unusual occupations. It can be argued with much validity that as urban culture develops, the opportunities for individual expression and choice become vastly greater than has ever before been possible.

Against this, however, we must see urbanization threats to individuality.

The smaller community may respect a given person neither more nor less than a large urban community, but at least it never forgets that he is there, be he beggar, king or town character. But in the masses of urban humanity, this awareness of the individual gets lost, particularly at the points where broad questions of social policy and structure are determined. The urban masses must be housed, transported, fed, entertained, informed by processes that emphasize, not their individual differences, but their common characteristics. Thus much of urban policy is developed in terms that treat people as statistical abstractions: families that need two bedrooms or three, families within certain income limits, voters for whom a particular phrase will touch off an automatic response—the "Negro," the "housewife," "Labor," "Catholics," "suburbanites."

The term "mass" applies to the products, services and messages that are produced in large identical quantities and offered to the urban public. They are by nature impersonal and provide little opportunity for individual "feedback" from the consumer. We may discuss a pair of shoes with a cobbler, but our only communication to a large shoe manufacturer is through selection of one style as against another, or of a competitor's product. This by itself is so unsatisfactory that merchandisers develop elaborate market research techniques to try to hear the voices of people. In the same way in urban society it becomes increasingly difficult to hear people expressing their real needs and concerns in any area of life: the citizen trying to be heard by City Hall, the parent trying to get the attention of the Board of Education, the unemployed trying to express their anger and frustration.

The clear moral danger of urban civilization is the constant temptation to apply the concepts surrounding the term "mass" to people as well as to products, services and messages. Products can be mass-produced, but people cannot. The message that comes on television is a mass message, repeated identically in millions of homes, but it is received, perceived, reacted to in as many different ways as there are individuals who see and hear it. A thousand apartments in a housing project may be physically identical, but the thousand families who live in them are identical only in whatever crude standards have been used to select them—family size and income level, for example. In style of living, taste, aspiration, integrity of the family, strength of loving relationships, they represent a thousand different human complexes.

When the mass characteristics of urban society do not allow for the expression of individuality, the effects on human personality are not good. Frustration can lead to anger, resentment, alienation, apathy, "anomie," and all the other disturbing symptoms of social processes that are not serving human needs. The struggle for personal integrity can produce artists and reformers, beatniks and delinquents. It can also produce defeated and apathetic persons, alcoholics and addicts. The destruction of personal integrity by mass society can take many forms, including the increasingly familiar and superficially successful urban man who has the appropriate personality for each role he plays—salesman, father, church member, citizen—without relating any role to the other in terms of a consistent pattern of conviction and loyalty. The sense of purpose and meaning in individual life can too easily get lost within the vast impersonality of urban society, where the focus is on the coordination of mass behavior rather than on the coherence and consistency of personal behavior. In such vast urban agglomerations as metropolitan New York, for example, a man can live not only a double life, but five or six different lives—suburbanite father, corporation lawyer, officer of a downtown church, active board member of a social agency, regular patron of a midtown bar, member of a hobby group—with the different roles competing for his time, but almost never intersecting.

The pressure for conformity in urban life is thus not just a matter of a human suspicion of differences, but also a function of the fact that large numbers of people can be handled more easily if they behave alike. These pressures deal largely with externals, and urbanites are characteristically reluctant to get too much involved with the inner workings of their neighbors—motivations, hopes, aspirations, the deeper angers and hostilities. Even in church these are handled gingerly, with the remote objectivity of a public sermon and in the privacy of an occasional session with the pastors, but rarely between layman and layman as members of the body of Christ. Yet this inner life of the individual needs nurture of its uniqueness, for which the apparatus of mass culture is particularly ill-adapted. Bottled up too long, the need for individual expression erupts in many irrational forms in urban life, from meaningless murders to exotic cults.

The church, as custodian of the faith that God not only loves his children individually but has a unique purpose for each one, needs to address itself to the ways in which urban civilization can be a means of fulfillment for each one of the urban millions. It is a tremendous and complex task. The problem is not resolved by nostalgic reversion by the churches to forms that reflect village life of yesterday. Neither is it resolved by uncritical absorption into the life of the church of all the techniques of mass civilization to make the church "up-to-date." It requires the most perceptive and thoughtful examination of what urban life does to mankind, both inside and outside the church, and highly creative responses to the cries of those who are left lost or hurt or lonely in the rushing, uncaring life of the metropolis.

The urban world poses some very real questions as to whether metropolis was made for man or man for metropolis. Change occurs with such speed that we may ask whether the forces behind the processes of change are humane and constructive. The governmental structures that referee, and increasingly initiate and direct, the processes of change are often ill-equipped for the task, designed for yesterday rather than for tomorrow. Human lives and human values get sidetracked by the relentless pressure to get on with the job of urbanization. Problems created by inadequate planning are often not recognized or dealt with until they reach a point of crisis, as with America's "war on poverty" directed belatedly to the needs of the millions for whom the affluent society had not provided a place.

The churches can never afford to be so caught up in the tides of change that they cannot reflect upon the forms that urbanization is taking and judge whether these are the forms which move toward fulfillment of God's plans for mankind and the redemption of a troubled and unfaithful world. It seems fair to say that the churches have by and large simply mirrored the urban world in which God has placed them—the divisions of class and race, the bland acceptance of "progress" and "success," as the secular world defines these terms, the philanthropic conscience offerings to bandage the wounds of those whom the massive urban machine has damaged.

There are many signs of stirring in the churches today, however, which indicate that they intend no longer to be so passive and accepting in the urban world. The church needs to discover what God intended the city to be, and then to hold this standard high before the people and measure our urban civilization against it. The urban process is not a relentless machine; it is the composite of thousands upon thousands of human decisions at many levels. The role of the church is to call urban man to make his decisions in terms of God's will and purpose, that man may achieve the destiny that is his.

6

URBAN REVOLUTION IN LATIN AMERICA

by ORLANDO FALS BORDA (Colombia)

THE counterpoint between country and city—the divergence of values and philosophy of life between peasant and urbanite—lies at the root of one of the principal challenges of culture that affect the role and function of churches today. The weight of tradition is heavy, and religious institutions, rustic by origin, could be expected to experience some maladjustment in the artificial, man-made urban world. The peasant's transmitted behavior tends to recognize man's dependence on God, whereas urban man is inclined to adopt a secular attitude that underscores man's self-sufficiency. The old set of religiously conditioned norms is relegated to the countryside, and among urbanites another normative set makes its appearance: technological rationality. This belief in science to control the natural forces and the environment tends to replace the traditional religious attitude as a dominant factor in society.

The resulting duality in the social structure, that underlines the contrasts between the rural and urban worlds, imposes, therefore, a reassessment of church conceptions and policies. The situation today points toward a strong shift of emphasis in human societies, from an ethos of sacred and passive adaptation to God and nature, to an ethos of the active control of nature. The basic integrative function of religion in societies is passing to other institutions that have responded better to the scientific and technological challenge, such as the state and the economy. These then become the "cement" of society through the diffusion and adoption of new secular values.

Such processes of social change, that appear to be worldwide, are particularly acute in Latin America, where rates of growth are breaking records; in 1950, 75 per cent of the population of that subcontinent was rural, but today it is under 50 per cent. In countries such as Colombia the urban population has increased 126 per cent since 1938; figures that show a similar trend can be produced for Argentina, Brazil, Chile, Peru, Mexico, Venezuela and Panama.

Sociopolitical instability and weakness of traditional institutions were some of the results; the churches, and especially the Roman Catholic Church, that comprises the majority of the population, are "suffering" the growth of the industrial city. This type of urban agglomeration is a rather recent addition. Pre-industrial cities which reflect the patterns of traditional society are still found in Latin America. But the ingredients of transition are already present: there is the peasantry, with an awakened sense of opportunities, and the urban *élite,* which survives on political and economic interests that are based on rural exploitation.

The technological revolution has also reached Latin America with advances of an adaptive nature, formerly attuned to the underlying sacred ethos, but now becoming increasingly secular. The discovery of the importance of self-reliance is looking for ethical support, to legitimize the new sense of intellectual independence, industry and profitmaking. The religious structure of Latin American society, until recent times apparently monolithic, is thus severely hit by the technological revolution that emanates from the industrial city. It is well, therefore, to focus attention, however superficially, on the basic characteristics of the city, as they can be observed in Latin America, as symptomatic of processes that may be occurring all over the world.

The Nature of the Urban Challenge

In the first place, the modern industrial city functions over a network of fluid communication and transportation systems that have revolutionized the concept of community. Traditionally, the biological and ecological idea of community has been paramount in ecclesiastical organization. In fact, church institutions such as the parish have maintained the medieval and colonial kind of community that was brought to America by the Spaniards and Portuguese, with a geographical base and boundaries more or less logically established, and that comprised a number of believers in social interaction. In this case there was justification for localizing the pastoral work and for building temples in which to congregate the flock; the parishioners were on hand and controllable. In the Latin American city, on the other hand, the fluidity of communication and transport underlines the complex nature of other social groups, often stratified and occupational, and with no clear ecological base. Thus, today an urban community is formed by the social interaction of persons and special-interest groups located at quite distant points geographically; propinquity is less important than with traditional rural communities. More important are items such as social activities and interests of people, the means of transportation, the mail, the telephone, the radio and other media required in forming and perpetuating urban social groups.

Louis Wirth took note of this reality, stressing the density, heterogeneity and secondary-group nature of cities. But in Latin America there is also an underlying maze of primary relations in the city, prominent especially in "marginal" groups (slums, workers' sectors) where family relatives often tend to settle at close quarters. True city neighborhoods undoubtedly exist; but unless they have a social history presenting, for example, communality of origins (mostly rural) or class homogeneity, neighborhoods as such are relatively unimportant for city life. This trend, however, is in process of being reversed, as the upper- and middle-class displacement to suburbia (see below) takes its course.

Second, and related to the first characteristic, the Latin-American city functions also on the basis of impersonal media of communication. The personal contact, although existent, does not carry much weight in relation to sheer numbers. One important effect is the tendency to homogenize the population, with the inherent danger of totalitarian control; another is the weakness of informal ways of social control. The use of mass media, still largely untapped in Latin America, presents perspectives and possibilities for new ways of carrying Christ's message. It seems that the old technique of pealing and tolling bells, personal witnessing, corner speeches and band tooting, although effective in certain circumstances, especially among primary groups, would not be so in the modern molds imposed by urban mass civilization.

Third, according to traditional ways of defining man in community, his basic religiosity produced a type of action which was prescriptive. This meant that socio-religious norms would not permit much personal deviation; the group held supreme control over the person, which often expressed itself in strong and extended familial ties. One result was an ethos of passivity or of resignation to God's will or of attributing what happens to mere luck, with a correspondingly low level of aspirations. A pre-capitalistic mentality forbade an agile conception of wealth. Such a community afforded little chance of social mobility, and led to the formation of caste-like structures and ascribed statuses. The consequences in behavior were multiple, as can be seen in studies of rural life in Latin America. On the other hand, through its rationality the new urban-industrial society, of which the modern city is a paradigm, imposes upon the person in community a type of action which is elective, in the sense that he may choose among alternative ways of behavior, looking to whatever is most effective with regard to means and ends. This action is itself institutionalized and expected (social change is institutionalized), thus producing normative flexibility, secondary relations, nuclear, rather than extended, families; and a sense of independence and responsibility in isolation or loneliness. The secular values take the person to high levels of aspiration and his *Weltanschauung* opens, preparing him for a wider participation in society. He acquires a capitalistic mentality and a talent to utilize the channels for vertical mobility that are provided by this new type of society. And, as in the previous case, this conception carries great consequences in behavior: education is valued more highly than land ownership or family procreation (even in Latin America rates of fertility, though still high, are bound to decrease in a few years); traditional leadership gives way to rational or bureaucratic leadership; prestige is gained by engaging in novelty actions and not in traditional undertakings; the nation is discovered as a real social entity; resignation surrenders to rebellion, indolence to action and fatalism to new hopes.

This is a central motor in the challenge of urban civilization, because it is based on attitudes, beliefs and values, that is, on cultural traits found within the very realm of religious intangibles; it is inherent in what has been called "the revolution of rising expectations," the appearance of which in Latin America is dramatic and tumultuous. In a sense, the new characteristics depend in one way or another on the activation of rational-technical norms and values and, curiously, not on the vitalization of religious norms. At first glance it would seem that the former are incompatible with religious norms; some would claim that rational-technical values are entirely materialistic and therefore difficult to syncretize with Christianity. Hence it appears that through science and technology the secular Latin American state is assuming, with a few exceptions, the moral integrative role which religion once had in the past; that bureaucrats and scientists are the new priests; and that the law and the scientific method are becoming the new gospel. Yet Latin American groups do not seem to have found enough satisfaction from these panaceas, judging from widespread urban maladjustment, disorganization and rising psychopathies. In the past there seemed to be a fairly harmonious, communal integration, under the paternal protection of Spanish and Portuguese religious and civil authorities. Now there appears an unstable anomic integration, somewhat contradictory, that depends on personal decision and action rather than on communal control and prescription. But present social arrangements are not satisfactory and people are clamoring for effective outlets.

How the churches are responding to this crucial aspect of the urban challenge is, of course, subject to controversy. It may be that part of the answer lies in sacralizing elective action, individuality and secularity in urban groups, as well as in the machine-world and automation: in siding actively with the people who have rising expectations even though it would require the churches, especially the Roman Catholic Church, to renounce material advantages, prerogatives and powers. (It is well to remember that apparently materialistic technology has its spiritual or nonmaterial side, the discovery of which for religious ends seems essential for religious renovation. It could also be that this self-appraisal should include analysis of possible materialistic aspects of church work.)

In the fourth place, the new ethos of secularity has encouraged in Latin America the formation of large and active groups of people who are at least indifferent toward the religious. Such persons may be influential in political action and policy-making bodies. The modern Latin American *élites* are not as a rule so strongly committed to the sacred as the *élites* of the past. The value structure of city leadership has changed from the days of the ruler-priests or the colonial theocracy of the Iberians, when church and state were integrated. This marriage is still in force in a few Latin American countries, but with questionable results; because then the church tends to become a pawn for political maneuver. The urban challenge in this sense pushes the church aside, to make room for the secular state; but it requires simultaneously that in its marginality the church shall also become specialized in the province of the sacred. Control of behavior is then exercised by a political and economic *élite* whose members have themselves effected the surgical operation of segmenting personal roles, by separating the "normal" or daily, way of life—mainly secular—from the religious (or Sunday) requirements of their status or positions.

Finally, the fact that the modern Latin American city is obviously more complex must affect the ancient role of the church as an integrative institution. Present trends in many countries mark the end of sacred, well-integrated, pre-industrial cities. Urban concentrations are predominantly industrial, economic, political, administrative, recreational or educational in different proportions. The challenge here lies in the fact that religion and the church have been left behind as social institutions, thus making it more difficult to integrate with the other institutions which have moved forward. It should be recalled, nevertheless, that the Christian churches were alert to the economic and social problems posed by the transplanting of western civilization to the new world; their missionary work can be cited as pioneering in such fields as modern education, urban social work, agricultural methods and rational health practices. But their *élan* was lost during the period of civil wars during the nineteenth century, and since then they have been somewhat static in these fields, at least in relation to urgencies in Latin America today.

Aspects of Cultural Lag in Urban Churches

The church has been defined as a historical body of believers who are socially organized. It is a social group which seeks to carry out the norms of religious institutions; these are obtained from revelation, holy texts, traditions and customs, from which the group derives its mystique as a *corpus christianum,* with special charismatic traits. Sociologically, therefore, the churches can be related meaningfully to the rest of human society; they can be regarded, that is to say, as one of the segments of total social structures. In a functioning society, the church is intrinsically connected with the other segments in such a manner that it is affected by them and by the whole.

According to William F. Ogburn, a cultural lag is formed when connected segments of the social structure do not change with the same speed, and it manifests itself through tensions, strains and social disorganization. If these premises are accepted, it can be hypothesized that in Latin America the church, and especially the urban church, is experiencing a cultural lag in relation to economic and technological institutions that impinge on the religious sphere. The *raison d'être* of religious life based on the sacred ethos may be destroyed by secularity and technological rationality.

The parochial conception of church congregations implanted during colonial times in Latin America has already been mentioned. This lag, according to François Houtart, feeds an image of an anchored church that is insufficiently agile for the milieu in which it is supposed to move. Such a characteristic has important implications for the organization and administration of churches, most of which have been conceived on authoritarian and hierarchical patterns. In a sense, control by the church in Latin America has been totalitarian, and this was possible in the ecologically established congregations of which the church was formerly composed. Now such control is outdated. Democracy as a challenge to the churches is also urban in nature. Modern believers often crave for an increased recognition of their self-responsibility. This is another expression of the secular rebellion in Latin America.

Likewise, the style of services and liturgy are often incompatible with urbanization. The manner of singing and praying, even the use of ancient or theologico-technical language in sermons, are survivals of a past in which they may have been congruent and effective; today, they tend to be criticized, especially among intellectuals. The distinctive garb of clergy and nuns illustrates, again, a historical lag, although in a few countries, such as Mexico, it has been made illegal to wear it on the streets. When religious services are broadcast or televised, the cultural lag is plainly visible, for they are not well suited to these media of communication. The urban mail and newspaper circulations are little used by religious leaders to promote concern for the church, because they still cling to old and tested—but now ineffectual—practices of direct personal contact and teaching. The nineteenth-century custom among Protestants to call each other "brothers" (promoted by missionaries in Latin America) served a useful function for urban integration, since it was a family term used to substitute vicariously for the relations left behind. With the passing of time, however, this custom, although still useful in places, has tended to dramatize ghetto-like attitudes in the church. Such attitudes may have been functional then. Now they are inherently ineffectual because they tend to isolate the church, so that it does not participate, as it is expected to do, in the larger society.

A tendency to underrate the layman's role in the churches may be another sign of cultural lag. Clericalism was rampant and perhaps useful in the past; today, it may become a source of discontent and frustration. For example, clergymen often tend to favor beneficence and charitable works which they themselves can directly control, and to mistrust communal action in which the layman takes the lead.

Present evidence shows that community development techniques are important for social welfare and progress. This is another field in which the Latin American church, with its tendency to keep membership within the four walls of the temple while the surrounding community may be in dire need of practical Christian witness, lags behind. Community development work could provide an anchorage for unsettled youths who are leaving the church. Here it is pertinent to recall that the once-effective church institutions, such as "Sunday schools," were formed as a response to the urge for learning experienced by the working class at the dawn of the industrial revolution in England. Today they are an empty shell devoid of their initial social dynamism.

Other examples could be cited to show how inadequately the church is responding to the challenge. One final instance indicates a deficiency in general policy: in several countries, while cities grow and peasants leave their fields, missionaries are continuing to travel mainly to the increasingly depleted rural zones—a policy that contradicts both social reality and demographic trends, but maintains cultural inertia.

Some Other Trends and Symptoms

Religious groups vary in the degree to which they adapt themselves to the urban secular ethos. Orrin E. Klapp finds, for instance, that Protestantism has secularized its ritual more rapidly than Catholicism; his analysis is an interesting attempt at rationalizing the concept of rites, to the point of arguing that even atheists can be ritualistic, and concluding that "ritual is a society-building force which should be used as a *tool* of organization but not become an end in itself." This is a clear statement on past and potential urban religiosity.

It may be that, as elsewhere, the Latin American urbanite needs a remodeled ethical code that would give technology and secularity a framework of dignity and liberty, in order to secure responsible development with full social justice. He seems disposed to accept the basic role of religion in this regard. But, as in similar crises of the past, adjustments are also required within church groups and in the religious norms themselves.

Agility is essential. No one knows quite what to expect in the new urban milieu, and institutional rigidity, like religious inertia, which may be interpreted as an effort to maintain the *status quo,* may be tantamount to suicide. For example, the city may be changing again both in content and in meaning. Since the end of the Second World War a new trend toward deconcentrating the cities has become apparent. The inhabitants who move to suburbia are again forming ecological groups, but on a more complex basis than those of the past, and with a blend of new and old structural elements. It is safe therefore to assume that the neighborhood church may be staging a comeback in suburbia, while the downtown churches are definitely obsolete. Neverthless, the tactics and strategy of the suburban churches should reflect the experience through which the religious institution is passing today.

We need especially to recognize the existence of special-interest groups in the city, which likewise merit special ministries. Of strategic significance in Latin America are the students and the young, the industrial workers, the businessmen and the professionals, the government employees and political leaders, the literati and intellectuals. As we have said, the city functions on the basis of interaction between these complex and disparate groups. They often have no specific nucleus—they are diffuse. But they exist and need an ethical guide. How to minister to them raises many problems. The traditional pattern of ministry is clearly not effective—labor peer groups cannot be equated with the old church brotherhoods and sodalities. An alternative could well be found in autonomous lay movements and the dispersal of church activities according to the real patterns of social organization that are found in industrial cities, and without fear of calling new ideas by their own name. Further sociological research of an applied kind is needed to assist in this important endeavor.

7

URBAN REVOLUTION IN SOUTH AFRICA

by Monica Wilson (South Africa)

Urbanization—a Universal Challenge

Problems of city living recur in all the continents and are uncomfortably familiar. Whether a social scientist or a welfare worker is reporting on Bombay or Leopoldville, Marseilles or Washington, he inevitably speaks in terms of poverty, unemployment and bad housing. The degree and incidence may vary greatly—what is called poverty in Washington might be thought adequate means in Guatemala—but everywhere some portion of the community fails to get jobs or lives in fear of losing them; some portion finds means inadequate to cover basic needs; some lack food, shelter, warmth or any measure of family privacy. Poverty is as old as man and is not peculiar to the city: what is new is the conviction that it can be conquered. This is the challenge of mass civilization. In the villages men reached an accommodation with poverty: in the city where they are perhaps less poor—for they move to the city to seek wealth—they revolt against the old hunger.

Unemployment presses harder in town than in country, where the able-bodied may find some occupation on the land; and it is a greater danger to those who are producing for a market—a demand which may fluctuate—than to those who work to feed and clothe themselves. Therefore organizing our economy, so that all who require them may find jobs and that fluctuations which throw men out of work are controlled, is the second challenge. Poverty and discontent will continue to overwhelm communities that cannot offer productive work to all their members.

In housing, the specific urban problem is crowding. Standards of sanitation and building which are tolerable when there is space around each homestead are intolerable in a city, and the urban family typically lacks privacy, both within the family and from neighbors—something which is commonly enjoyed in isolated tribal societies, even when they are very poor, and by peasants. Crowding is exacerbated by the pace of movement into cities, so marked in many countries since the last war, and frequently also by the absence of intelligent planning by city authorities or government, or by lack of means to implement plans. Then Delhi and Johannesburg, Hong Kong and Buenos Aires are disfigured by shanties and shacks far worse than the rural homes from which the migrants have come. Families camp out in the streets or live in leaky shelters made of sacking and old tins. Unemployment on the one hand and lack of houses on the other imply a failure in organization that does not exist in subsistence economies where every family builds its own hut out of earth, or the products of the bush.

Quest for Community

The problems of living in large concentration are not, however, those of the poor or the philoprogenitive alone. Whatever his income, or the number of his children, the city dweller—and particularly the newcomer to a city—has to adjust himself to new patterns of social relations. The given community of neighbors and kinsmen is often not there for the townsman. In a modern industrial society a man moves where he can best find a job, and this may take him far from kin and from those among whom he grew up. A study of genealogies in an African suburb of Cape Town showed that kinsfolk were scattered not only between town and country but through half a dozen cities, seeking work, whereas traditionally these kinsmen would have lived in one neighborhood. Some writers have seen the chief problem of the tribesman or peasant who moves into the city as loneliness, isolation. Recent studies of migrants in towns of America and Africa suggest, however, that newcomers, moving into a city, are quick to form groups based on the home area—the country, or chiefdom, or district, or village—from which they come. Almost every newcomer in Cape Town, for example, finds some group with whom he can associate as "those from home." Networks of such groups grow up, and they receive newcomers from their home areas. In the African suburbs each such group tries to live together. The members form a mess—or several messes, if they are many—cooking and eating together; they seek employment in the same firms; and they enjoy their leisure together, forming their own choirs, dance clubs and sports teams. These groups of "home boys"—which is what they call themselves in South Africa—recreate country ties within the city, and are of enormous importance in providing the newcomer with a familiar community into which he is received. They are typical of migrants in Africa who circulate back and forth between country and town, and of the first generation of immigrants settling in a foreign country and ignorant of the language. The "Yankee City Reports" admirably describe them as they operated in New England. But "home boy" groups do not continue indefinitely. They do not continue because those who remain in town, or settle in a foreign country, do not ultimately *want* to remain villagers and foreigners. They are irked by the restrictions of the small, intimate community and seek to move out of it, interacting more and more with outsiders with whom they have some common interest. In Langa, an African suburb of Cape Town, the migrant who hankers after some activity in which his "home boys" are not interested is told: "Don't do things on the side: Don't pull your own way: Don't be a goat among sheep." And, as one informant explained: "It is this that makes life in the barracks with 'home boys' intolerable for certain types of men, and they escape . . . as soon as opportunity offers." The man who finds conformity to village patterns, village values, irksome soon becomes independent of his "home boys" and interacts increasingly with townsmen proper, those who are rooted in town. The town-born in Langa have no "home boys." They associate with their schoolmates and fellow workers, fellow churchgoers, or fellow beer brewers, often with a different set of friends for different purposes. The townsman chooses friends in a way the villager cannot. Some may stick to a narrow, close circle, much like that of a villager; many do not.

Many in the city are nostalgic for the virtues of the small group—the security and conformity of the familiar, the given community—and "villages" keep re-forming in cities, particularly among families long settled in one street or neighborhood, but the desire of many for "freedom" or "to get on" keeps drawing individuals out of these "villages" in the city. The price of freedom, of greater choice, is the loss of the sense of security in a small familiar group, and the loss of control exerted in small communities.

The challenge is to facilitate the growth of communities within the larger city which will nevertheless allow the individual to enjoy the advantages of large-scale cooperation. Intelligent town planning can help in some measure by providing for living spaces with schools and churches, playing fields, library, hall and other recreational facilities, as well as shops, where neighbors may grow to know one another, and within which children and old people may move about safely, but from which men and women can go to work, and where they may enjoy the kind of amenities that can be the product only of cooperation in larger groups, such as symphony orchestra, professional theater, a university. The pattern of traffic with some measure of seclusion in the "village," and easy access to the outside, is one of the conditions of growth of such a community; but physical conditions cannot create it; they can only foster its growth. The challenge to reconcile a strong corporate life, affording the satisfactions of the small ingroup, with a reaching out to others, remains.

This challenge may confront a family, a church, a neighborhood, a nation. Often the price of solidarity in the small sect is its exclusiveness; its separation from others. An ethnic church may itself be the core of exclusiveness in a foreign group in a city and the most tight-knit churches may be class bound or color bound, or if indeed parishes including all those of one local area, they may be narrowly parochial in outlook. Perhaps the condition of reaching out is that the individual should associate with different sets of people for different purposes, so that ties which bind men together cut across one another. If a man works and plays and worships only with one small set, he cannot but remain aloof from others; but if he only worships with them the relationship must remain thin. This is the dilemma before the individual and the church. The church, the neighborhood, the nation can no more contain all a man's activities and aspirations than can the family, but both local congregation and family must seek to foster ties between their members through common activities. There is a perennial tension between the strength of the ingroup, achieved through corporate activities, and outgoing to strangers. It can be solved only in the man who remains "one of us"—of his family, his local church, his working group, his city, his nation, but is yet continually reaching out to others. He can remain "one of us" only by continuing to participate in some measure, by continuing to care for his fellows in the small group, but he cannot devote the greater part of his time to his kinsmen or his neighbors as men in isolated societies do.

Another change in kinship patterns is occurring in Southern Africa also. Movement to the city results in the disappearance of wider corporate kinship groups—that is lineages and clans—and they are replaced by associations, that is groups of people who cooperate because they share common interests. The disappearance of the clan and the lineage does not necessarily involve any weakening of the elementary family, nor does it preclude the maintenance of a network of kinship ties, between sisters and brothers and cousins and their children, who are accessible in town. The shift from a society based on lineage and clan to one based on voluntary association has been caused partly by Christian teaching, for the solidarity of lineage and clan as fostered through the cult of the shades, and the church itself—or rather the diverse denominations into which it is split—are the most important associations in terms of numbers and influence in at least some African townships. The church is directly concerned with fostering the elementary family of parents and children: it is not necessarily concerned with lineages and clans, and indeed partly replaces them by creating another loyalty which sometimes conflicts with lineage and clan ties.

But where lineages and clans diminish in importance the security which they provided for orphans, widows and the disabled disappears, and new forms of social insurance must replace it. The aged and the unemployed also present a greater problem than in a primitive or peasant society where everyone can do some sort of work. The adjustment to a new kind of kinship system shaped by a cash economy, industrial employment and city living presents a problem not yet adequately solved in any country, and particularly acute in those countries in which the older generation assume that traditional kinship obligations should be fulfilled and the young, living in new circumstances, find themselves unable to do so.

Effects of Migratory Labor

Cities everywhere have in the past recruited and still do recruit from the country, and the problem of adjustment of the newcomers both from the country and from cities is universal. In some areas, however, difficulties are greatly increased by a continual circulation of men between country and town and back again. Such a circulation has been common enough when peasants or tribesmen moved into cities, often in other countries, to work for limited periods and earn a sum of money with which to marry, or build a house, or start a herd, or tide the family over a bad harvest. But in most countries the great majority of migrants have not continued to circulate for long. Either they settled and married in the city, or returned to their homes to work full time on the land. This process can be traced for the Polish peasants who worked as migrants first in Germany and then in the United States, or the Irish peasants who worked in England and the United States. It has occurred also in Katanga and on the Copperbelt of Zambia.

But in the Republic of South Africa it has been impeded by the policy of *apartheid,* which seeks to exclude Africans from towns except when they are required as laborers for white-controlled industries, and which refuses an African countryman the right to bring his wife and children to live in town with him. Even a townsman may now be refused the right to keep his wife and children in a town where they have already settled. Case after case of such exclusion has been recorded in and around Cape Town. Opportunity for nonwhites is very narrowly restricted by discrimination in education, in employment, in the exercise of political rights, in recreation, in housing and in the enjoyment of social services. Men move to town and become urban workers, but are not accepted as citizens: they are excluded by legislation from the urban schools and universities enjoyed by whites (except under special permit) and, under the most recent regulations even from concerts and plays which in some centers they hitherto enjoyed. They are largely excluded, through job reservation, from skilled employment, and Africans now have no voice in parliament, the final political authority over the whole country. They are excluded by administrative regulations from participating in open competition in sport, both within and without the country, and in housing and social services they are more and more narrowly confined to specified areas, and to differentiated and limited social amenities. Migratory labor has already continued in South Africa for over a hundred years; it is on such a scale that over half the men from country villages are always away from home; and it is envisaged as a permanent system. Indeed, it is a condition of the system of *apartheid,* and it is implied in the proposals for partition now so commonly put forward.

Large-scale and long-term migrant labor has certain very specific social effects: it implies a marked disproportion of the sexes in town and country; it implies that a husband spends the greater part of his working life away from his wife and children; it implies that the acquisition of skill in a particular job is limited, for the migrant, by definition, moves from country to town and back and often returns to different jobs in town. It is hardly surprising that migratory labor is correlated with a high illegitimacy rate, and a higher crime rate than those in the general population. The church is concerned that family life should flourish, and therefore the church must be totally opposed to the perpetuation of any system of migratory labor which involves the separation of husband and wife, parent and child.

Uneven Tempo of Industrial Life

The city has been described as affording the individual greater choice than the village—choice of work, of recreation, of friends. And this freedom to choose now implies, and perhaps inevitably, competition. In most village communities, and in the cities of feudal or caste societies, social position was largely taken as given, fixed by birth. In the new mass civilizations it is not, and they are rooted in the value of competition in production and commerce. Economic competition is the flywheel which drove the industrial revolution; it is built into schools and universities in the system of competitive examinations; and into national economies. Now competition exists in one form or another in all societies, but there are great variations, not only in the permitted forms of expression, but in the degree in which competition is encouraged or restrained. Some hold that the achievements of modern science and the high productivity of the affluent societies of the West would not have been reached without the drive of unbridled competition. But the cost in mental disorders and in conflicts between individuals and groups is obvious. The value of loving-kindness—the *caritas* of the New Testament; of *ubuntu*—humanness—which is so much stressed by many African people; concern for the community—these do not fit with unbridled competition. The contrast in attitudes toward competition is particularly evident in the rapidly changing societies of Africa. The failure of an African peasant to produce much more than his neighbor may be regarded by a westerner as indicating a lack of drive and initiative, whereas a conspicuously large crop, much bigger than that of his neighbors, may be regarded by them as having been achieved by unfair means at their expense. On the other hand, a western professional man may be restrained from competitive advertising by conceptions of professional ethics which may not be felt binding by an African. One of the challenges of the new mass civilizations is to discipline and canalize this competitive drive, that it may not injure the growth of the individual, may not make him incapable of relaxation, or of being content with what he has achieved, or of cherishing his neighbor, and yet be used as a spur to the attainment of those things—knowledge and wealth—which the community as a whole so ardently desires.

Then there is ugliness. When the ugliness of our modern cities is mentioned most people dismiss the subject with one of two arguments. Either they say that "we cannot afford frills, the poor must be fed and housed first," or else "there is no agreement on aesthetics." Some professing Christians may add that beauty is not the concern of the church. None of these answers is convincing, for ugly buildings are often costly: there are many of them in the richest countries, built by the richest industries—filling stations and many of the new supermarkets in the United States are a case in point. There is some measure of agreement among the instructed as to what is ugly; and the church has fostered beauty in building and sculpture, painting and music through nearly two thousand years. The real reason why so many ugly buildings are erected is that few people think that ugliness matters. They are concerned, first, with utility, including speed of construction and speed of access, and, second, with catching the eye of the customer. Difference—eccentricity—is therefore sought after, rather than satisfying proportions. The failure of communities to look ahead and provide a considered plan for corporate living, together with emphasis on the right of each individual to build as he pleases, results in a desert of disorder.

The relation between the psychological and social adjustment of the individual and beauty in his environment is a matter on which we are still very ignorant, but that there is a connection can hardly be doubted. As cities grow so greatly in size and the proportion of people who live in them increases, the need for beauty in urban building becomes increasingly urgent.

Some writers speak of the loss in joy of artistic creation when the craftsman is replaced by the machine-minder, and of the danger of men in a mass civilization being dominated by machines. Such writers lack experience of the drudgery of life without machines, and they overlook the satisfaction which many in this generation experience in running a machine and "keeping it sweet." They overlook also the joy of the draughtsman in creation.

Conclusion

The underlying challenge, which embraces all the others, is that the new mass civilization offers a potentiality for fullness of life. That is why the cities draw country folk into them: they offer opportunities of acquiring wealth, of education, of artistic creation and enjoyment which are lacking in isolation. They offer it not exclusively to a very small class as past civilizations have done, but to the people as a whole. They offer a freedom, a choice, in friends and in values, which is not there in isolated societies. The choice implies a potentiality for good or evil. The new wealth and knowledge and skills may be used to destroy, to injure oneself or others, or for more fullness of life.

8

THE CHANGING FAMILY IN THE WEST

by HELMUT BEGEMANN (Germany)

The Crisis of the Traditional Form of the Family

WORLDWIDE sociological changes, the result of industrialization, have produced a crisis in the family from which it can emerge only in an altered form. In many countries a developing industrial society is destroying the old clan and extended-family structures. The entire *oikos*-system, which has shaped Europe for thousands of years, and supported the system of social classes, is breaking down. People are being forced into gigantic urban housing complexes which change the basic community and social structure in a way that especially affects the family.

The extended-family has become a small limited family. Life in a compact modern apartment forces parents drastically to limit the number of children. At the same time the family is losing its social, educational, economic and legal functions. The home is becoming little more than a place to eat and sleep. Family and business, family and leisure, family and society, family and school, family and church are all developing into different coexistent and frequently conflicting spheres. People are often caught in deep conflicts, especially in areas of rapid social change, because although they still think and react in terms of the old family-community social structures, they must live here and now in the new industrial society. These tensions are bound to be reflected in the family, especially between young and old. The industrial society is steadily expanding all over the world, and societies and cultures which do not open up to its new life-forms have no future. But what is to become of the family?

The family is no longer a stable social unit secure in society. Industrialization has deprived it of its economic basis; culture and tradition no longer necessarily bind the family members together; each member is on his own and independent of the others, individually related to society. Each must rediscover and grasp his changed function in a changed world.

There is much uncertainty in the family about behavior, because the guiding norms are lacking.[1] What holds the family together in a highly industrialized society? How should the members of the family shape their common life? The modern family has become extremely fragile, because it is completely dependent upon the mutual confidence of its members. Moreover this fragile, sensitive, intimate unit is exposed to the powerful influences of economic development, advertisement, television, radio and the press which penetrate every home and threaten traditional family relationships.

The Family and the "Sexual Revolution"

From the beginning of time sexual relations in all cultures have been regulated by certain socially accepted institutions (monogamy, polygamy, prostitution). Today a revolution is taking place in sex relations. Conventions and morals which shaped and sustained the individual's behavior are disappearing, and setting him free.

It is no longer the family but the responsible individual who is the foundation of society. Thus, the tendency toward individualization, toward personal rootlessness, is encouraged. In a mass so-

---

[1] See Report of the Committee for the Department on Cooperation of Men and Women in Church, Family and Society at the WCC Assembly in New Delhi, 1961.

ciety individuals encounter one another superficially at work, and in leisure-time activities. Sexualization of every sphere of life and a flood of suggestive advertising are gradually making sexual license socially acceptable. Sex relations seem no longer to be related primarily to an institution, whether marriage or socially accepted forms of prostitution.[2]

The number of early marriages and of illegitimate children is increasing. One sexual taboo after another is breaking down. Marriage is not sought primarily in order to satisfy sexual needs. Divorce statistics are rising steeply, especially in highly civilized societies.

In the light of these developments, can we still expect that monogamy will continue to regulate sexual relationships? Can sexual relationships be institutionalized? Must they not be given freedom? [3] Sociologists ask whether the traditional structures of marriage and the family are relevant in a modern industrial society, or whether another form must not be developed.

Questioning the Natural Law Argument

According to Natural Law, certain forms of community originate in the nature of man and this "nature" is unchangeable and independent of the social order. But our age is asking whether a "natural"" family order which corresponds to the nature of man really exists, or whether the form of the family has not always developed out of a given society. Has the family ever been an institution developed exclusively from the "nature" of man? The family was and is a social unit and therefore a cultural achievement. Every form of the family and of human community develops not out of the "natural tendencies" of man, but out of human decisions. We need the help of social scientists who study the structure of the family and the relationships between its members in order to discover a family ethic, and the form of the family which God desires

---

[2] See H. SCHELSKY: *Soziologie der Sexualität,* Hamburg, 1955.

[3] The Report edited by Alastair Heron, "Toward a Quaker View of Sex," London, 1963, is based on similar questions.

for our epoch. We shall also have to study the concept of the family as it has developed in the Christian tradition, and to test whether it is still relevant today.

The Concept of the Family in Christian Tradition—The Biblical View

Though the Bible did not develop a special doctrine of the family, we can trace certain basic lines.

The patriarchal family is accepted as a matter of course in the Bible (*oikos* = house). The house-father ruled his wife, children, slaves and the whole *oikos*. He had complete authority not only in the economic but also in the religious realm. In the early history of the Israelites the tribe (namely, the clan with its patriarch, or its tribal father) was the inclusive society in which the individual grew up. The tribal organization gradually disintegrated as individuals gained possession of large areas of land; and cities were formed under Saul and David, which disappeared completely after the exile had torn the tribes apart. The father-house, the smallest social unit, then became independent and became very significant in the rebuilding of the Jewish people,[4] as the essential cell of the national life and worship.

The background of the social laws for the New Testament *oikos* is found, first, in the patriarchal structure of both Jewish social and religious life (as described in the Old Testament), and second, in the equally patriarchal system of Hellenistic society. The New Testament writers do not question the social system of their age, because social reform was not their purpose. Jesus was not a social reformer, but the proclaimer of the kingdom of God. Nevertheless, his disciples realized that through their membership in the eschatological family of God they stood in a new relationship to the *oikos*-family.

a. Jesus Christ's call to discipleship freed men from the bond-

---

[4] L. ROST: "Die Vorstufen von Kirche und Synagoge im Alten Testament" in *Beiträge zur Wissenschaft vom Alten und Neuen Testament,* 4th series, No. 24, Stuttgart, 1938.

age of the *oikos*-family and made them members of God's family (Mark 3 : 31–35; Matthew 10 : 21, 34–37; Luke 9 : 59 ff.; Luke 12 : 51–53; 14, 26; I Corinthians 7 : 25 ff.). Did Jesus reject the earthly family? Did he place himself above the order of the *oikos?* The message of the New Testament is that Jesus made absolute claims on people, that his authority is greater than that of the *oikos,* that his word carries more weight than tradition and custom and that he is the undisputed Lord.

b. It is recorded in the New Testament that Jesus respected the relationships between man and wife, parent and child, and that he regarded the home as an appropriate place in which to have fellowship with others. He did not remove people from their domestic relationships, but sent them back into them. He charged many whom he had healed to return home (Mark 2 : 11; 8 : 26; Matthew 9 : 6; Luke 5 : 24) to testify to what Christ had done for them (Mark 5 : 19; Luke 8 : 39; see also: Mark 2 : 15; Matthew 9 : 10; Luke 5 : 29; 15 : 17; John 2 : 1 ff.; Luke 19 : 1–10). In the epistles we read that the *oikos* was the place where the early Christian congregations gathered (I Corinthians 1 : 16; 16 : 15; Romans 16 : 3; Philemon 2; Colossians 4 : 15; Acts 11 : 14; 16 : 15; 40; 16 : 31–34; 18 : 8; John 4 : 53).

c. A unique relationship developed between the *oikos* and the church which is reflected in the admonitory sections of the New Testament. In Christ there is no difference between man and woman, slave and free, Jew and Greek: all have received the same grace and are charged with the same responsibility. In the *oikos,* however, differences remain. How can this tension be overcome? Christ enters the reality of the *oikos* and fills its structures and relationships with his love. The order for the *oikos* rests no longer within itself; it has its validity and strength in Christ. He lays new obligations upon the members of the *oikos.* All find their head in Christ and derive their unity not from their house-father, but from him.

d. Theologically speaking, the assigning of positions in the *oikos* to man, wife and children is founded in the divine creation (I Corinthians 11 : 1 ff.). However, this order of creation is nowhere found in its "original" form, but only in the historical form it has assumed in various social systems. The order of creation and the social order penetrate each other and are inseparable. God remains true to his creation and seeks to fulfill the true order of the *oikos* through Christ's love. The *oikos* is not the essential element of community within a family and a people, but rather the sustaining power of God's faithfulness as revealed in Christ, which has found expression in the order of the *oikos*.

e. Christ, as lord and servant, embraces the *oikos*-society, with all its members—husband and wife, children and slaves—and unites it in love. The balance shifts from the patriarchal order to personal categories such as love, devotion, sacrifice, responsibility and confidence. In Christ, the *oikos* members see themselves in a new light. Each should respect and love the others in Christ. The Christian congregation is called to draw the social relationships into its congregational life, to order and to heal them. Christ affirms and sanctifies the family as God's creation, but he sanctions no definite order or concept of the family.

f. The Bible speaks even more clearly of marriage than of the family. There are indications that a monogamous concept of marriage was already beginning to develop in the Old Testament society. The monogamous concept of marriage originates in the covenant of love which Yahveh made with his people and which has its correlation in the marriage of man and wife. According to the New Testament the relationship of Christ to the congregation is to be reflected in Christian marriage (Ephesians 5). Jesus understood marriage as a gift of God and testified to its indissolubility (Matthew 19 : 6).

Thus the understanding of marriage and the family which developed in the Old and New Testament differed from that held in the existing society. The basic New Testament concept of the relationship of the Christian congregation and the earthly *oikos* indicates the direction in which we must seek a valid pattern for the family today.

The New Testament approach did not prevail in the church which eventually adopted the natural law dogma of the Graeco-

Roman economy and gave it a theological interpretation. In the seventeenth and eighteenth centuries the Christian teaching about the home was developed, in terms of the relationship found in the patriarchal *oikos* as a divine order. In this view the home (the clan-family) is a community for living, for working and for worship. The house-father has complete authority. The home is the basis or "primary cell" of the state.

Natural law teaching (especially as developed in Roman Catholic thought) derived the constitution and communal form of the home hierarchically from human nature: the man is the head, the woman the heart of the family.[5] The main purpose of marriage, according to natural law, is to reproduce and bring up children. The individual family, as the basic cell of the state and society, broadens to the universal family of man.

H. W. Riehl, a German family sociologist of the nineteenth century, described the patriarchal family as an "eternal structure." [6] The natural law explanation of the family still predominates in Roman Catholic theology, although the industrial and social revolution has severely challenged it.

Valid Functions and Structures of the Family

A search for the valid functions and structures of the family must start from the "worldly" and "spiritual" dominion of God which established the family and is constantly active in it.

We can say that God in his worldly dominion desires a family structure which will form people who are capable of serving their society; but it is doubtful, however, whether we can deduce specific family functions and structures from this. There is a danger that such a rationalization may assume an ideological character. We can go further only if we inquire into the relationship of God's

---

[5] See the Encyclical of Pope Pius XI, *Casti connubbi.*

[6] H. W. RIEHL: "Die Familie" in *Die Naturgeschichte des Volkes als Grundlage einer deutschen Sozialpolitik,* Vol. 3, Stuttgart and Berlin, 1925, 13th edition.

spiritual dominion to his worldly dominion. God's desire for order in the world is not an aim in itself; God preserves the world for Christ's sake. Christ is the hidden basis of natural law and religious law, and of all social structures which make human life possible. Even the secular *lex* of the family has a spiritual significance; ultimately it is identical with the *lex caritatis*. The norms for earthly community relationships lie in the rule of God as revealed and eschatologically realized in Christ. Thus it is important both to differentiate between worldly institutions, human society and the spiritual reality of Christian brotherhood and to question whether any given form of the family best serves Christ's rule.

We must expect that sociology and the other secular disciplines will conclude that the family as a community of parents and children is not sufficiently flexible or adaptable to meet the demands of modern society; and must give way to other forms. However, Christians who base their teaching and life on Holy Scripture, must declare categorically that God, for man's own sake, does not want to give up the family, that the eternal fellowship of God in which human nature is fulfilled bears the charactor of a family (*familia Dei*).

In any theological interpretation of community, we start from the brotherhood of all in Christ (Galatians 3 : 28). We are children of God (Galatians 3 : 26), (Ephesians 3 : 14 f.) through our faith in Christ. This eschatological community of Christ's brethren has thus three elements which are the basis of all communities: fatherhood (as creative power), brotherhood (as self-sacrificing love), and sonship (as confident obedience). God's reality embraces in itself these three elements. In other words, God is the primal community. When he created man in his own image (Genesis 1 : 27), he allowed his creature to participate in his own communal nature and made man a responsible counterpart to himself.

These dogmatic statements still do not answer the question: what form of family does God want? Must not the answer be: if God has called men and women to share responsibility for society, then he must want that form of family which best equips people to meet the demands and duties of the society of their time, and which helps people to become persons. The secular sciences can participate in the search for new patterns of the family but they encourage the family to become a law unto itself. Today the family lives in tension between its secular form and the coming Lordship of Christ. Because the family (as a limited fellowship) looks toward the future kingdom of Christ, its institutional form is open to change. The family is related to the eschatological brotherhood in Christ, which is the aim and the consummation of all fellowship. In this way God is creatively at work within institutions such as the family, using them to bring his eschatological reality into the world. The eschatological hope, coming from faith in Jesus Christ, liberates forces in men and women which are the very basis of family life.

When we look back on the history of the *oikos,* we see how the eschatological reality of the fellowship in Christ, influenced the *oikos* and vice versa. Although the patriarchal system has obstinately maintained itself in the church's teaching, the Christian concept of love and loyalty, responsibility and obedience, freedom and obligation, has had a decisive influence on marriage and the family. The idea of monogamy, the practice of eating around the same table, the practice of conversation and the esteem for confidence and love within the family have their origin in the Christian message.

The eschatological fellowship of God's kingdom provides indispensable norms for the concept of the family in Protestant social ethics. Three of these norms are listed here:

1. *The principle of the family.* In creating man for fellowship with him God also wants man to fulfill himself in fellowship. In his mercy he has bestowed on man marriage and the family—the provisional community. Christian social ethics must therefore approve the family in principle and must not consent to the breakup of the family for political, economic or ideological reasons. However, this says nothing about the form which the family should take.

2. *Monogamy.* Faith in Christ brings the realization that full fellowship is attained only through undivided love and devotion. Christ lived in a fellowship of this kind with his own people. Marriage should reflect that same fellowship. Through monogamy marriage becomes what God intended it to be. It leads the two partners into complete fellowship, body and soul, in which they each experience the full happiness of fulfilling their different natures. This does not mean, however, that Christian ethics could insist on legal monogamy. Monogamous marriage can be maintained only where men and women have experienced God's love in Christ. Where men and women respond to Jesus' call to discipleship, their marriage assumes a "corresponding" form. The church has not to preach monogamy: it has to preach Christ.

3. *Family-community as partnership.* The guiding norm for the family-community is the eschatological reality of the Church of Jesus. Within the church the fellowship in Christ should manifest both unity and diversity. On the one hand, Christ is one: one Body, one Person (Romans 12 : 5; I Corinthians 12 : 12; Galatians 3 : 28); on the other hand, there are many members. Christ combines both things: being-a-person and living-in-community. If this eschatological church is the norm for fellowship within the family, it also reveals the form which the family should take. When the members of a family come under the power of Christ, they are called to partnership. Partnership is the expression of an ethos, a claim, which is made when people become members of the Body of Christ. In this sense it means living-for-one-another, losing our egocentrism through fellowship and living in fellowship. If this egocentrism really does die, then a man and a woman receive their real function: they become a father and a mother. All members of the family, parents and children, find themselves through this fellowship. It does not destroy personality but matures it and relates it to others.

If these three norms are indispensable in a Christian approach to marriage and the family, what are their implications for the social functions of the family today?

The Family's Function in Modern Society

Despite the crisis which threatens the family today its stability amid social revolution has been repeatedly demonstrated. This fact has been emphasized by sociologists both in Europe and in America. It was particularly evident in postwar Germany.[7] In modern industrial society the family is maintaining its stability. Sociological studies show that its importance, both for the individual and for society, is increasing.[8] The loss by the family of one function after another has recalled it to its primary function.[9] Wherever modern civilization establishes itself, the family detaches itself from its social environment and is thus able to re-establish its own sphere. Personal relationships, human contacts and active cooperation among family members become increasingly important and both the weakness and the strength of the modern family are revealed.

1. *The family creates personality.* In defining the task of the family today, we must bear in mind the social-psychological fact that "man is not born human." [10] The loving Thou which a child encounters in the family, and to which he learns to respond, forms his spiritual life and enables him to mature. He becomes capable of speaking, answering, loving, adapting himself, of having consideration for others, of subordinating his ego in society, of obeying, of helping in the family.

Authority (*auctoritas*) in the modern family which is organized as a partnership has become a responsibility in which the entire family shares. The *patria potestas* has become the *familiaris potestas*. As such, the family is a creative power, capable of shaping man's social-cultural personality as no other institution can. R.

---

[7] H. SCHELSKY: *Wandlungen der deutschen Familie in der Gegenwart,* Stuttgart, 1955, 3rd edition.

[8] See R. KÖNIG: *Materialien zur Soziologie der Familie,* Berne, 1946; *"Sozialpsychologie der gegenwärtigen Familie"* in *Universitas,* 1957, Vol. 12, pp. 124 ff.

[9] R. MCIVER: *The Elements of Social Science,* London, 1944, 7th ed., p. 162.

[10] R. E. PARK and E. W. BURGESS: *Introduction to the Science of Sociology,* Chicago, 1921, p. 79.

König speaks of this "second birth," a building of the "social-cultural personality" as the central and primary function of the family.[11]

The family provides an opportunity for decisive encounter with God. Because the elements of the family correspond to God's creative nature, the family can encourage and practice faith in Jesus Christ more effectively than any other institution. Faith which is expressed in love should not "metaphysically" transcend the natural family ties or bonds, but should intensify and deepen them, and thus form and strengthen the whole personality. Therefore, for the sake of God and of man, we must not acquiesce in social trends which lead to the breakup of the family.

2. *The family preserves personal values.* The family should give a growing child his freedom neither too soon nor too late. As a child becomes acquainted with the world he begins to oscillate between the family and the kindergarten, and school, and, later, leisure time, political activities and a job. The modern producer-and-consumer-society, which is abstract and anonymous, estranges man from himself and deprives him of his personality. Yet the society can survive only if there are men and women who are free and responsible in their dealings and decisions. The social processes destroy the very humanity of man which they desperately need. The indispensable function of the family today is to build and preserve man's personal values. Men need the community of the family (even if it is geographically dispersed, trust, love and care can be expressed in the family through invisible personal bonds) if they are not to lose the living elements of their personality, which are increasingly pushed aside by artificial organizations, the hegemony of machines and mechanisms, automation and technology.

The Christian family is open in two directions: to the worshiping congregation and to society. It is pre-eminently in the family that the problems of church and society confront each other and behavior-patterns are worked through in daily life. Through the

---

[11] R. König: "Sozialpsychologie der gegenwärtigen Familie" in *Universitas,* 1957, No. 12, pp. 124 ff.

congregation the family participates in the eschatological glorification of God and acknowledges its provisional character in the light of the coming kingdom. It receives the eschatological gifts of love, goodness, forgiveness, hope and patience which renew the family community and thus serve the world. Through society the family is drawn into the economic world where it is thus constantly threatened by forces that are foreign to it. The family and the world of work, the intimate community and rational organizations have become sharply opposed, but each in fact need the other.

The coming of a society of leisure, as hours of work are reduced and automation progresses, is likely to make important demands upon the family. We shall need a rich, intensive, deeply harmonious family-life if we are to use our leisure to good purpose. Where, if not in the family, should people spend their leisure time creatively? Where else should they learn that life is something more than consumption and work, that it is essentially conversation, fellowship, concern, play, growth and maturing? Christians who have been freed by Christ from the curse of law, who are called to be children of God and brothers of Christ, should be able to make crystal clear the purpose and meaning of the family in an industrialized leisured society.

3. *The family transforms sexual relations into socially responsible forms.* Sexual behavior is undergoing far-reaching changes. There are no standards to regulate sexual relations which have degenerated into an egocentric, temporary and almost instinctive experience, with antisocial effects. We should not, however, describe it as perversion since the social realm which anchors sexuality and transforms it, simply does not exist. We can counteract this sexual crisis only by restoring the family which as a social institution has the ability to transform sexuality into sociality. The God-given purpose of sex is to create community. God has placed men in families through sexuality, so they may help and care for one another. The social forces which direct, vitalize and stabilize sexuality work through the community of parents, children, brothers and sisters. The family creates a sexually neutralized zone in which the child learns to direct his sexual instincts and his egocentric physical

pleasure-sensations toward a Thou of the opposite sex, and thus to build a partner-relationship. He lives in the family at an institutionalized distance from his own sexuality, and thus becomes free and able to encounter a Thou. Unless the family forms the child socially, perversions like homosexuality, inability to make contact and antisocial sexuality may develop. In the marriage relationship, the vow of fidelity is one of social as distinguished from sexual fidelity.[12] A couple may remain sexually faithful without necessarily being bound in personal oneness and community of life. But if the sexual encounter does not presuppose the will to total community of life in which one serves the other, everything will be destroyed.[13] The sexual relationship as an expression of mutual love within marriage confirms and deepens the oneness of man and wife in every area of their life.

The Traditional Christian Concept of the Family

A revision of the church's traditional concept of the family is necessary at several points.

1. *Is the family the basis of society?* The Bible provides no grounds for the view that the family is the basis of society. However, the theology of natural law as developed by the Roman Catholic Church (Thomas Aquinas) confirmed Aristotle's thesis that the family is the primary cell of the community. This thesis can be challenged today on two counts:

a. The church is not the sum of the families within it. The natural family is not a building-stone of the large community of the supernatural family, the *familia dei.* On the contrary, the church, the Christian congregation, encompasses and anchors the family. Unless the family is upheld by the confidence and love of

---

[12] "Social" in the sense of complete personal loyalty to one's partner and responsibility for him or her, not in the sense of recognition of a particular social expression of marriage and family.

[13] "Towards a Quaker View of Sex" clearly overlooks the fact that sexuality is the concern of sociality, and ignores the basic connection between sexuality and marriage or the family as a social institution. (See footnote 3.) In some places the Report therefore draws conclusions with which I cannot agree.

the believing community which witnesses to the Lordship of Christ, it can scarcely remain stable. The family does not live from itself but from the love and in the forgiveness of God which is given to us in Jesus Christ.

b. The concept of the family as the primary cell of the community has been destroyed. Family and community no longer form an organic unity. The family is a unique group, and other social groups and organizations of modern society are built upon their own laws and not upon the family.

Society in the "personal age" [14] is founded on and maintained by responsible individual personalities, and nothing can replace the family as the former and protector of personality. However, although the family is a certain form of community, it is not the basis of community, for there is community in other social groups. Theologically speaking, God as the primal community is the basis and origin of community.

2. *Is the patriarchal system specifically Christian?* The biblical statements about marriage and the family clearly reflect the patriarchal social system. But the sociological components of theological statements are not part of the gospel. All systems become relative in and through Christ's coming kingdom. Thus the Christian church may acknowledge a given system of society (polygamy, matriarchy), while waiting to see what new social structures may appear as a result of the preaching of the gospel. The patriarchal system is not specifically Christian because there are no Christian systems, only Christian obedience, and Christian conduct within the systems.

3. *Is marriage indissoluble?* Marriage has become extremely fragile in modern society, and makes greater demands on the individual than ever before. Its stability depends on the creation of a partnership and of personal community. Unless these criteria are met, marriage does not fulfill its purpose, it destroys fellowship instead of creating it, and destroys personality instead of strengthening it. According to the Christian concept of marriage, it is in-

---

[14] D. VON OPPEN: *Das personale Zeitalter,* Stuttgart, 1960.

tended to be permanent and indissoluble, but this indissolubility is not a metaphysical essence which functions through the marriage partners. If it were, the innermost core of marriage would be law; but in its nearness to creaturely reality marriage is a gift and a help. The church must accept responsibly the possibility of divorce as a last resort for the sake of man, because man is not made for marriage, but marriage and the family are made for man.

4. *Is sexuality merely the power of procreation?* Throughout the ages church tradition has condemned sex as sinful. Marriage was supposed to direct sexual instincts, which were regarded as evil in themselves, along ordered paths. The real purpose of sex was supposed to be procreation. This narrow view must be revised, for it ignores the community-building force of sexuality. God designed sex for social reasons and not exclusively for marriage. Through it he brings people into relationship with one another though he has restricted its practice to marriage. The primary purpose of marriage is not to regulate sexual relationships: marriage creates a social community which includes man's whole life and which makes sexual love into a social force.

In the light of modern sexual behavior, the preaching of traditional sexual morality becomes irrelevant. The most effective approach or strategy today, in conditions of greatly increasing sexual freedom with its antisocial tendencies, is to develop the meaning of the family-community as an expression of an intensive communal life, in which people of both sexes are bound in partnership.[15]

---

15 See H. BEGEMANN: *Strukturwandel der Familie,* Hamburg, 1960.

9

"RACIAL" MAN IN THE MODERN WORLD

by DAISUKE KITAGAWA (U. S. A.)

Ethnos as a Vital Dimension of Human Existence

THROUGHOUT the history of mankind the individual has always found himself a member of an ethnocultural group. He has seldom questioned the basis of the *ethnos* into which he was born, and to which he was proud to belong. It provided him with "the homeland of his soul," the vantage point from which he saw his universe, the perspective in which he saw other people, and the basis for his sense of importance and self-respect.

In the more primitive eras, *ethnos* was basically a kinship group: the extended family, clan, tribe and the like. In the course of history such groups were consolidated to form a nation in the modern sense of the term. The growth of the nation led to the emergence of a common ethos, mores and culture among all its subgroups. Those who did not share the same culture were strangers (*xenoi* over against *ethnoi*). Here is the crux of ethnocentrism and xenophobia.

In dealing with the moral and psychic problems of man as an individual, we overlook at our peril the dynamics of group membership as a dimension of human existence. What we call race problems cannot be fully understood without an adequate knowledge of how they are rooted in this very issue. Man as a natural being is born free from prejudice, but as a cultural being he is conditioned by the prejudices of his group.

Though the race problems of our day cannot be understood apart from the ingroup and outgroup feelings which membership in *ethnos* inevitably evokes in man, it is only in relatively recent times that race per se has come to be regarded as *the* basis of *ethnos.* The Christian church has helped to create the race problem throughout the world by acquiescing in the linking of western white culture with racial superiority.

The Race Problem in Historical Perspective

The intellectual, social and technical revolutions which succeeded one another as a result of the Renaissance transformed the West into a dynamic, self-expanding society. Though it was divided into several nations, these were all Christian in religion (with Jews as a minority) and Caucasian (or "white") in race. Thus the western missionaries represented a dynamic civilization and were often supported, in presenting the gospel, by its technical superiority. The close association of the early Roman Catholic missions with Iberian maritime imperialism, which resulted in every conquered territory being claimed for the Pope as well as for the crown, and the church being planted there even before a single convert had been won, whatever the theological or missionary justification, in practice identified the missionary movement with territorial aggrandizement.

The Protestant missionary movement was, almost from the outset, linked with colonial imperialism. The Protestant missionaries tended to be puritanical or pietistic in outlook and preoccupied with saving souls rather than with territorial aggrandizement. (But the underlying *motif* was the conquest of paganism by Christianity, and Christianity was presented as *the* religion, incomparably superior to the religions of the native people.) The aim of Christian mission was spiritual conquest; to teach, to give, to help the inferior and to enlighten and to civilize the primitive. When Ziegenbalg wrote glowingly of Hindu philosophy, his supporters at home reprimanded him: they had sent him to convert the pagans, not to be impressed by paganism. An outstanding American missionary of the nineteenth century, Rufus Anderson, propounded his theology of missions on the assumptions that pagans had only "vacuity of mind and plenitude of errors." Many similar examples of such religio-cultural imperialism could be cited.

The inadvertent coupling of the western missionary movement with the economic, industrial, cultural and political expansion of modern Europe into all parts of the world helped to produce a feeling of superiority in the West. The collective experience of western people, religiously Christian and racially Caucasian, with people outside of Europe over four centuries, led them to conclude that non-Caucasians who were also pagans were without question inferior to them. The various, pseudo-scientific theories of European racial superiority evolved about a hundred years ago represented attempts to rationalize this feeling. It also inevitably found expression in the ethnocentrism which, as we have seen, is inherent in human existence. Paradoxically, ethnocentrism becomes a dynamic force in a society in which all forms of *ethnos* based on a people's natural background become increasingly irrelevant. This is precisely the kind of society that industrial civilization has produced, first in the West, and then throughout the world as a result of the colonial imperialist expansion. Latin America, Asia and Africa were first made an extension of the West, but they soon became involved in its industrial economy, and a reciprocal dependence developed within the framework of an emerging global society which is becoming increasingly urban, industrial and technological. In it, mobility of population tends to be accentuated; man's worth depends upon his technical skill, industrial creativity and economic marketability, rather than on his ethnic background or membership. In such a multiracial society, people either become sufficiently emancipated to do without their group affiliation, or they feel uprooted and unstable and are therefore unable to relate themselves to anybody. It is at this juncture that the hitherto vaguely felt sense of racial superiority expresses itself as race prejudice on the part of many people who, because of their racial background, formerly occupied positions of privilege. Thus, the social forces which make racial ethnocentrism totally untenable are also driving people to find an escape from emotional insecurity in some kind of outmoded *ethnos*. This is the meaning of race prejudice as it is found in modern men, especially those of the dominant racial group.[1]

The Problem: A Racially Stratified Society

Racial differences inevitably produce class differences polarizing society when other social forces are working toward its unification. The industrial economy puts a premium on man's technical knowledge and skill, and on his productivity, and encourages mobility of population creating everywhere an increasingly open and dynamic society, in which man's racial background becomes irrelevant. However, the attitude of the dominant white group as it seeks to defend the threatened *status quo,* arouses resentment among the subordinate groups, and the two can no longer coexist in peace. They may face each other with hostility, or they may ignore each other in cynicism and suspicion.

There is, moreover, evidence from many parts of the world (the Southern U. S. A., the Copper Belt of Zambia, the Republic of South Africa) that polarization also takes place within each of the opposing racial groups. The white community is polarized around the two extremes of those who want reconciliation with the colored people and those who seek at all costs to maintain their privileged position, with the majority of people uncommitted between the two. Similar polarization occurs within the community of the colored people.

The result is a general breakdown of communication, between the two communities, and between different groups within each. Members of the white community no longer hear the genuine voice of the colored people, and the voice of those within the white community who dare to maintain contact with colored peo-

---

[1] For the basic insight into the problem discussed in this section, I am indebted to KENNETH LITTLE: *Race and Society,* in the UNESCO Series on *The Race Question in Modern Science*.

ple falls on deaf ears. Mutual trust disappears and a state of general demoralization ensues.

The collective hostility and resentment of the colored people toward the white community, as it seeks to defend its privileges, and their collective suspicion, mistrust and cynicism toward acts of kindness by white people are also directed against the Christian church, since it has been identified, rightly or wrongly, with the white race. Herein lies the church's predicament in the present race conflict. Because of its involvement in the race divisions of our time, the world, with its majority of colored people, does not believe the church when it expounds the principle of equality laid down in the gospel. How can the church be God's instrument in redeeming the very history of which the church is both a responsible maker and a helpless victim? Today, the church stands in the presence of God and of his created world, inescapably bound up with past history. It knows what the gospel says on race relations, but when it attempts to articulate it and implement it, it is faced by these contradictions. A racially divided society and a racially divided church—the two are completely interwoven—support each other. And yet the church has a conscience, the gospel, and indeed the church is meant to be the conscience of the world. To reintegrate a racially stratified society is beyond the possibilities of men who have been born into it, nurtured by it and have become part of it.[2] Take, for example, the matter of communication. How can one part of a society, which either cannot hear or deliberately refuses to hear what the other part is saying, be an instrument to re-establish communication? We need a community of men and women who, under the impact of the gospel, have been reunited, who have transcended their racial differences to form a reintegrated community, and who may be able to act as an integrating force within the still divided world. Such a community may be found within the organized church, but not necessarily. It will not always be made up exclusively of Christians. It can be brought

---

[2] Integration does not mean dissolution of racial groups or the assimilation of minorities into the majority groups. In an open society racial communities have a right to maintain their group identities.

into being only through the intervention of God's Holy Spirit whose action is not restricted to the organized church or to those who call themselves Christians. The church must be humble and open-minded to discern when a breakthrough of the Holy Spirit takes place and must dare to obey.

The Problem: The Racially Prejudiced Person

It is important to distinguish between prejudice in general and racial prejudice in particular. No one is born with racial prejudice, but no one is free from the risk of becoming prejudiced. The creaturely finiteness of man makes this inevitable. Man has a limited vantage point and his knowledge is bound to be fragmentary, partial and biased. But as he lives in the community of men where each is looking at the same thing from his own vantage point, the interaction of many different views saves him from being completely *frozen* in his own biased outlook. The basic ill of the racially stratified society is that it hinders this natural corrective; man becomes prejudiced; and bias, unchallenged, becomes a part of his "second nature" warping his personality.

Of the several basic issues involved in the problem of a racially prejudiced person, bred by the racially segregated society, three are crucial:

a. *Stereotyping*. A racially prejudiced person puts all men into rigid categories purely on the basis of racial background: he refuses to see in them human persons each with his own individual talents, traits, characteristics, skills and other abilities. To a racially prejudiced white person, a Negro man is a Negro. Whether he is a citizen of the U. S. A., or of one of the African nations, a university graduate or illiterate and unskilled, makes no difference; his being a Negro is sufficient to exclude him from all human relationships which require mutual respect and equality. A Negro person (man or woman) may be more than welcome as a domestic servant, but never as a social equal. A missionary may be sent to work among Negro people, at home or overseas, but never with the expectation that they will one day claim their places in the sun on an equal basis with white people. Affection may be showered upon a Negro woman as a maid, with no respect for her inalienable honor and dignity as a person. Much philanthropic work may be carried out for the benefit of Negro people as long as they stay "in their place."

Moreover, the fact that racially prejudiced people are acting in accordance with the mores of their own society makes it all the more difficult to convince them that their treatment of people of other races is wrong. In the deep South of the U. S. A. and in the Republic of South Africa, this problem reaches its logical extremity.

b. *Closed-mindedness.* Prejudiced persons become intractably closed-minded. Confined within their own circle, they do not come into contact with people of other races, and have little chance to have their eyes opened. Man as a person can be known by others only in so far as he reveals himself, and no such self-revelation can take place apart from interpersonal engagement, or dialogue. The basic problem of the racially prejudiced person is that in the presence of people who are of a different race he "freezes up" and destroys their opportunity to disclose themselves to him.

To a prejudiced person encounter with people of different racial background is terribly threatening. But the dynamics of modern industrial society no longer permit the rigid separation of racial groups, and the racially prejudiced person is therefore in a desperate position. The segregated society which has made him what he is and which is his refuge is crumbling. And yet, he cannot bring himself to enter into dialogue with people of races different from his own. Short of conversion, or rebirth, he cannot be freed from the race prejudice which has made him what he is.

c. *"Fool's paradise"—collective hallucination?* Objectively prejudice is nothing more than a crutch on which the prejudiced person depends, but subjectively it is far more: it is that which defines for him his universe. It does so by excluding people of other races, or by confining the range of human, that is, interpersonal, relationships to the circle of his own race. Like the proverbial ostrich, the prejudiced person seeks escape from reality. He creates within his mind a cozy little community made up of himself and his kind in which he feels secure and comfortable, and he yearns to stay in it, come what may. Nothing is more self-deceptive than this burning desire to perpetuate racial segregation. The basic problem in dealing with the racially prejudiced person lies in his constitutional incapacity to see how false is his imagined world because it is so absolutely real to him.

The problem must be seen in the collective dimension as well. One person suffering from hallucinations is difficult enough. When thousands do so, the difficulty is multiplied and intensified.

Approach to the Prejudiced Person: A Reconsideration

The problem of racial prejudice cannot be adequately dealt with by exhortation or even by scientific analyses. The problem is not only how to correct and remove a certain kind of misinformation about different racial groups. The outlook on man of prejudiced people is warped in spite of all the scientific findings in the area of biology, cultural anthropology and even moral theology; and this outlook defies rational argument. Therefore moralistic preaching on the evil of race prejudice falls on deaf ears. It is time we learned that something entirely different is required. Two related actions may be suggested.

The prejudiced person is a product and continues to be an integral part of a racially divided society and so every effort should be made to change the social pattern itself, without waiting for every individual to be freed from his race prejudice. Both legislation and social action are needed. At the same time, every effort must be made to help prejudiced people to look at themselves from a wider perspective, to gain insight into themselves. Here, modern psychotherapy will prove more helpful than anything else, in dealing with both individuals and groups as a collective entity.

The Stance of the Oppressed

Negro-white tensions entered a new chapter in the U. S. A. with the bus boycott led by Martin Luther King, Jr., at Montgomery,

Alabama 1955–1956. By then "the Negro masses were more than just resentful and angry; they were also informed." [3] James Baldwin had written: "At the rate things are going, all Africa will be free before we can get a lousy cup of coffee." [4] The Negro Americans had reached the conclusion that they could not simply rely on the white people to shelve the problem of racial discrimination. Not that all Negroes hated or mistrusted all whites, but even the moderate Negroes knew that unless the Negroes themselves demonstrated strength and determination the white Americans would not and indeed could not act forcefully.[5]

Under the pressure of world history, Negro Americans have become unabashedly and avowedly militant. "After so many years of submission," it has been said, "the Negro suddenly discovered that he had a collective purpose and a collective courage and, what was more, the collective power to make the white man take notice of, and even yield to, his wants," and "to the vast majority [80 per cent] they [the demonstrations] were an exhilarating exercise in racial pride and accomplishment." [6]

The Negroes of the U. S. A. have become convinced unequivocally that justice is on their side: in terms of the Constitution of the U. S. A., the Judeo-Christian religion and ethics, and plain human decency. They have sensed that it was time to bring the longstanding conflict in their relationships with the white citizenry into the open. Confronted by the highly organized power-structure of the white-dominated U. S. society, the only course open to Negro Americans was to organize themselves. Spontaneous mass movements led by skilled leadership have developed strategies and tactics. Thus the Montgomery bus boycott led to the formation of the Southern Christian Leadership Conference; the most spontaneous

---

[3] LOUIS E. LOMAX: *The Negro Revolt,* Signet Book, T2273, p. 87.

[4] Quoted by LOMAX: *op. cit.,* p. 88.

[5] D. KITAGAWA: *Race Relations and Christian Mission,* p. 21, New York: Friendship Press, 1964. See also, WILLIAM BRINK and LOUIS HARRIS: *The Negro Revolution in America,* Chap. 8, "What Negroes Think of Whites," New York, Simon and Schuster, 1964, pp. 125–137.

[6] BRINK and HARRIS: *op. cit.,* p. 66. An excessive instance of this is the Black Muslim movement. See ERIC LINCOLN: *The Black Muslim in America,* Boston, Beacon Press, 1961.

movement of all, the sit-in demonstration of college students (beginning at Greensboro, North Carolina, February, 1959) led to the formation of the Student Non-Violent Co-ordination Committee and revived the Congress of Racial Equality. These organizations have driven both the National Association for the Advancement of Colored People and the National Urban League to become increasingly oriented toward direct action.

None of these organizations is exclusively Negro; but in all of them the initiative and the leadership rest with the Negro Americans. By 1963 the enlightened white leadership came to realize how inadequate their own efforts had been, however genuine their goodwill and concern for the Negro American, and they willingly yielded the initiative to Negro leadership. This also explains the significance of the extraordinary action taken by the National Council of Churches (U. S. A.) when they organized the Commission on Religion and Race, whose avowed principle of operation is to cooperate with the above-mentioned civil rights organizations.

Racial Tensions as Power Struggle

It is essential to recognize that the racial tensions in the U. S. A. have reached the point at which a solution is impossible without a power struggle between the dominant white community and the subordinate Negro community. A similar situation prevails in Southern Africa (including the Republic of South Africa, Rhodesia, Mozambique and Angola) though in the U. S. A. the law is unequivocally on the side of the Negro community, while in Southern Africa the contrary is true. For this reason Negro civil rights leaders in the U. S. A. can afford to adhere, and are unqualifiedly committed, to the principle of nonviolence, however much they may advocate and practice direct action and public demonstration, often at great personal risk. The focal point of their action is either to convince racially prejudiced white men of the folly of defying the law or to test the willingness of the local authority to abide by and implement it. In short, the law provides the leverage for the civil rights movement to be daring without resorting to violence, however much the movement itself is organized to gain power.

In Southern Africa any attempt by nonwhite Africans to organize themselves is prohibited by law, so that if they want to become powerful enough to make the dominant European community listen to them, they have no option but to organize themselves for illegal action and resort to violence of one kind or another. In the U. S. A., all organized demonstrations and direct actions aim at forcing the white group to sit round the conference table to negotiate on greater rights for the dispossessed.

In Southern Africa any demonstration or direct action initiated by the Africans leads to government suppression by force, and the Africans are therefore driven in desperation to resort to violence. In the U. S. A. the final court of appeal is the citizen's conscience, and the collective conscience of the nation; organized demonstration by the Negro community helps to compel the white community to listen to the voice of its own conscience. In Southern Africa, on the other hand, the Africans cannot count on the European community's conscience, collectively or individually with a few notable exceptions.

But whatever the basic difference in the situations in the two countries, the Christian church is inescapably involved in both. It cannot escape, either within its own institutional structure, or in the national society of which it is called to be the conscience. The church thus finds itself in a precarious position. It has little to say, either to the Negro community in the U. S. A. or to the African community in Southern Africa. The church in the U. S. A. is fortunate in that the recognized Negro leaders are almost without exception committed to the principle of nonviolence. The church in Southern Africa is in an almost impossible situation because the government in power through its highly organized injustices committed in the name of Christianity, is alienating the African community.

For diametrically opposing reasons, it would for the time being be more prudent in both countries for the church to concentrate its efforts primarily upon the "conversion" of the dominant group: in the U. S. A. following the lead of the Negro community in penitence and humility, and in Southern Africa working with greater determination to change the outlook of the government in power. Before it can do anything constructive in the area of race relations, the church is called to be penitent and to be humbled.

What Then Can the Church Do?

The church's pronouncements on racial matters have excelled in idealism and in general moral exhortation, but have given little guidance on how the principle believed to be right should be put into practice in a given situation. Sending missionaries to Africa, but giving no thought to racial segregation in one's own church or neighborhood illustrates the inconsistency to which a moralistic attitude can lead. The church's approach to the race problem has tended to make the Christian complacent, satisfied with personal friendships with people of a different race, and with display of a liberal attitude freed from race prejudice.

Second, the glib conception of the identification of Christianity with the "white" and the "European" has made the church incapable of a sympathetic relationship with the colored people, the oppressed and the socially ostracized. At best, a paternalistic attitude toward the minority group, and, at worst, indifference or apathy, have emerged. No one in a privileged position can begin to appreciate the scope and depth of the plight and frustration of the dispossessed or even be capable of hearing what they are saying.

The church as an institution, along with the people of the West, is suffering from what might be termed "a majority psychology"; although it is a numerical minority and only one of many social institutions within a pluralistic society, it still seems to believe that by its own unilateral action, it can solve the race problem of our day. Before it can make any positive contribution, the church needs to be freed from this kind of conceit and to become more humble, acknowledging its own shortcomings and limitations.

Generally speaking, the church can do three things:

a. It should make every effort to become a community in which people of various races are united by their common commitment to Christ and his gospel and together try to deepen their insights into the true nature of the problem. In this process, the church may become an agent to restore interracial communication.

b. It should participate in all organized efforts, political and legislative, to restructure society in such a way as to make it easier for people of various races to meet one another as fellow human beings and as citizens of the same society.

c. The church should emphasize a therapeutic ministry among those who are frightened, who feel threatened, and who, unable to face the future, are driven to look backward to the past. Such a ministry demands a renewed theological perception of what God has been doing in modern history. Racially prejudiced persons cannot be tricked into accepting people of different races by psychological manipulation. A therapeutic ministry is prophetic, manifested through preaching, teaching and bible study, especially in small study groups.

PART III

CHRISTIAN BASES OF MAN IN COMMUNITY

IO

THE ERA OF THE PERSONAL

by DIETRICH VON OPPEN (Germany)

Origin in the Gospel

THE outlines of a human society are traced in the Sermon on the Mount (Matthew 5–7) with special attention to the following: the protection of life—"You shall not kill, and whoever kills shall be liable to the judgment" (5 : 21); the keeping of one's word—"You shall not swear falsely, but shall perform unto the Lord what you have sworn" (5 : 33); just punishment—"An eye for an eye, and a tooth for a tooth" (5 : 38); concord among members of the same community—"You shall love your neighbor" (5 : 43 and 5 : 46–47); and with it the exclusion of the stranger—". . . and hate your enemy" (5 : 43); purity of motive in public worship—"Beware of practicing your piety before men in order to be seen by them" (6 : 1); the acceptance of standards applicable to all—"For with the judgment you pronounce you will be judged" (7 : 2); the right attitude to property and work—"Do not lay up for yourselves treasure on earth" (6 : 19); "Do not be anxious about your life" (6 : 25–31). However, these foundations of human society are called into question by a repeated, "But I say unto you . . . ," which involved, first, an exciting, revolutionary and not easily understandable step into undiscovered territory; and, second, the immediate extension of the discussion of social ethics beyond the limits of Jewish legalism to the point of universal importance.

The Sermon on the Mount thus challenges point by point the features of institutional life, and presents a coherent picture of a new form of human responsibility. This new approach emerges most clearly at the heart of the Sermon on the Mount (6 : 1–18) where the old attitude is confronted with the new, in the commandments about giving, praying and fasting. The revolution has four aspects:

1. The old institutional order loses its absolute character in one simple, but all-changing step, motivated by an encounter with the living and personal God.

2. For him who takes the step a new reality appears behind the established order. He is able to transcend order based on power which is characteristic of public life. He is no longer either controlled or supported by institutions. He becomes an individual.

3. A new source of strength and new relationships replace the established order. Man is confronted with God (in praying), with his neighbor (in giving) and with himself (in fasting); and is led to respond to this challenge.

4. Social action, when placed in this new perspective, changes its character completely, or more precisely, takes on its real character. . . . Only when nothing is received in return does the gift become really a gift.

The guidance and supervision of man—the responsibility for his right action—now comes from a new direction. What was an institutional responsibility becomes a personal one because it derives from a new relationship with the person of God, the person of the neighbor and with his own self. The Sermon on the Mount does not address man first as a member of a social or political order, of a transitory "kingdom," but as a citizen of the kingdom of God which is greater than any human kingdom.

What is the meaning of this transition from an institutional order to the personal responsibility of the individual before God?

The transition is a process of secularization, of personalization, of mobilization; it is a movement toward the achievement of true manhood: "You must be perfect, as your heavenly Father is perfect."

Actually the Sermon on the Mount does not suggest a "transition" from the institutional to the personal form of life; but rather an "historical juxtaposition" of the two patterns, a taking of the new into the old, a fulfillment of the law. There is, however, a clear definition of priority: "But seek first his kingdom, and his righteousness; and all these things shall be yours as well" (6 : 33). These things refer to security which is the theme of institutional life. The "personal attitude" is the more important, because it lays the foundation for the institutions; it is the rock upon which the house is to be built (7 : 24–27). The personal attitude relativizes the institutional life. Hence the hostility of the institution toward the individual who acts on free personal responsibility and accepts the institution only conditionally.

The Secular Character of the Organization

A new type of institution has become the main governing form of order in our era. It may be called the "organization." It has many variations, but it can be reduced to certain basic types: the enterprise, the private association or club, and the state. In order to understand our era the difference between the phenomenon of the "organization" and the older sacral and traditional order must be clearly grasped. In a certain sense it can be said to have its spiritual origins in the gospel, and from that derives its great strength.

1. The basic qualities of the organization are openness and flexibility. It is amenable to change as tasks, methods of work and situations change.

2. The organization does not live so much in the past as in the future. Future interests, future achievements, and the like decide its forms and dimensions. It depends for its very life on thinking ahead and not looking back.

3. The modern organization is secularized. Adherence to it is

no longer confirmed by oath or pledge, but by a written contract. Nothing in it is sacred and inviolable; methods of work, limitations of competence, and other factors may change.

4. The organization has only limited and conditional power because its purpose and competence are limited.

5. The organization is structured to provide room for the freedom of the persons related to it. The member of a club, or of an enterprise, is more than this; essential parts of his life remain outside its control. This freedom of the individual in the organization liberates him for personal responsibility; moreover, only the "free" person can give the organization the form required by circumstances. The organization differs strikingly from the older sacral order precisely in the direction indicated by the gospel itself. This may well mean that the gospel provided the motivation for the changes.

Club, Enterprise and State as Basic Types of the Organization

The great diversity of organizations may be reduced to three basic types: private association (club), enterprise and state.

The *private association* or club is, in its basic structure, both institution and organization. Its institutional characteristics, such as its exclusiveness *vis à vis* those who do not belong to it, its constitution, its achievements and so forth, are decisively limited by the freedom of the individual and his rights within the association. He can join or resign, he can vote, his individual interest takes precedence over the common interest, so that the emphasis in the life of the association actually rests on the individual. However, this basic structure has been fully realized only in contemporary society.

The modern economic *enterprise* which developed with the separation of the worker from the household community bears all the characteristics of an organization. It calls increasingly for personal responsibility. The constant expansion of technology makes for professional differentiation and qualification; specialized training is required and work is becoming more and more individualized.

Mechanization means that only the complicated work remains for human beings. Personal qualities, such as experience, knowledge, precision, responsibility and dedication are required at all levels of the enterprise.

Just as the relationship to work has changed, so has the relationship to colleagues. Increasingly the worker belongs to the "working group." The highly technical work of today is marked by its "coglike" structure of cooperation, in which the "individual" is not an isolated individual but is in a specific and new way related to others, detached, yet closely attached through work.

At the same time, the function of the "boss" has changed. The "crisis of the hierarchy" consists, on the one hand, in the growing responsibility of the workers, and on the other, in the growing importance of the cross connections in the firm, that is, cooperation between the departments without going through the boss. The boss transmits instructions and supervises, but instead of his issuing commands and demanding obedience, one responsible person converses with another.

The relationship of the modern *state* to its citizens has also changed from institutional to personal. In this respect it bears all the characteristics of an organization. The state has itself furthered the new principle by establishing government offices, by legislation guaranteeing the inviolability of the private life of the citizen, and so on. The basis of the citizen's attachment to the state is no longer his obligation to a ruler, but primarily his right to personal freedom. The emphasis lies on an attachment which is the reverse of the attachment to authority: the latter was an existential obligation of the subject to the ruler; everything today encourages responsibility in the form of an engagement in a relationship of confidence. The citizen is able to undertake this responsibility of self-engagement because of his basic rights as a citizen.

The institutional powers left over from the old dominating form of the state, such as the ethos of civil servants, patriotism, military regimentation, are important but, being powers of the past, they no longer constitute a major basis.

The Pluralism of Society and Its Integration

The pluralism of our society threatens not only its unity but also the welfare of the people in it who are affected by "organizational" conflicts. The question of the integration of the pluralistic society therefore arises.

For Hegel this integration is the task and mandate of the state. Yet it is this increasing responsibilty for the whole of society which has caused the state to grow gigantically and which has thrust upon it an organizational and pluralistic structure. Although the modern state has legally, socially and economically a steering, and thus integrating function, the possibilities of comprehensive integration by the state are in fact reduced. Today the state itself must be integrated.

Opposed to Hegel's conception is the liberal faith in the independent and automatic integration of interested liberalized bodies. In actual fact, interests today are so diverse and contradictory in themselves that they have both an explosive and a harmonizing effect. And it has been demonstrated that this liberal type of integration is inadequate to steer the development of society. Actually, the appeal to the authoritarian and to the liberal state both go back to an outmoded concept of a "total system of order."

However, the pluralism of society opens a new challenge to personal responsibility hitherto dismissed because all action based on pluralism seemed relative, selfish and divisive. Responsibility in a pluralistic society implies openness, flexibility, the finding of answers to constantly new situations, possibilities, difficulties and conflicts. It suggests an imaginative readiness to build bridges in all directions.

It is the person who will achieve the integration of modern society since he bears the main responsibility in modern organizations. Because the organization threatens the lives of persons, the individual must bring about the integration of the different powers in his own interest and for others. He must confront the opposing elements at the point where he becomes involved in them; he must take his position and do the responsible thing; he must assert himself or give way or find an adequate compromise—while always understanding and appreciating the need of maintaining mutual relationships.

What Is Personal Life in the Era of Organization?

The organization lives by the two centers of responsible human stewardship: the institution and the person. It is without doubt an institution. At the same time, however, because of its structure the organization requires a special kind of personal responsibility and stewardship. Organizations today stand or fall according to the extent and quality of personal responsibility which pervade them. The institutional framework can never be discarded; its functional reliability depends ultimately on the personal responsibility in the group. But in our society the institutional structure is such that left to itself, it becomes numb and lifeless. It presupposes a free personality, and its life depends on this presupposition.

The crucial fact about modern personality is that it is demanded by the social structures. They do not establish it, they do not determine it, and they do not give it its particular stamp, but they require it. This is something fundamentally new and peculiar to the organizational pattern and in contrast with the old and religiously sanctioned orders and traditions which have produced their own type of personality.

The calling of personal responsibility implies "objectivity," "partnership" and responsibility for one's own life. Objectivity is our relationship to the subject. It involves flexibility and awareness of the unlimited possibilities and the pluralistic patterns of human relations. The constant possibility of change requires flexibility of judgment, a willingness to re-examine pre-judgments; a readiness to expose narrow and one-sided viewpoints and to accept a necessary broadening of outlook. It also involves acceptance of the variety and the contradictions of the material world. These attitudes depend on intrepidity and the will to surmount the situation without which objectivity is meaningless.

The relationship to other people calls for partnership. Here, too, there is a structural principle of dialogue; an attitude is required which is in itself contradictory and which includes three elements: individualization, dependence and equality.

There is no doubt that the modern person is a very lonely "individual" in a mass society. . . . He is always unique among all the other people. He is always someone we can reach, guide and represent only marginally; he has to be respected as a separate and impenetrable entity. All this keeps people in a state of unusual alienation from each other.

At the same time there is this "unusual dependence" in which we find ourselves. Precisely because our "situation" individualizes, it also binds us together. We Germans, we Europeans, we coworkers in a production process—we are all held together in concrete collectivizing situations. This dependence presupposes that we have confidence in each other. The complexity of the objectives, the specialization of the functions, the circle of relationships make confidence the absolute presupposition of our life in every sphere.

Self-responsibility which is required for the relationship of a person to himself also contains the elements of detachment, self-criticism and impartial action. The modern world requires us to keep a self-critical detachment from ourselves, our thoughts and actions. The actual center of responsibility lies in ourselves and no longer in the institution.

However, this detachment from ourselves must be within the unity of a community; otherwise we are confused and lose our self-assurance and capacity to act. It provides a type of free impartiality alongside the self-criticism and overcomes the tensions and contradictions of objectivity and partnership. The attitudes of objectivity, partnership and self-responsibility are marks of a profound "coming of age" which tolerates no regimentation, which has to be independent *vis à vis* the material world, others and oneself.

Objectivity, partnership and self-confidence are at the same time the buttresses of dialogue. Our world is not suited to unilateral decision. All forms of association demand communication relating all spheres of life and work. This dialogue is a basic element of modern society. Conversation is the expression of being a personality, and the personality is required by the modern world for the sake of its existence.

The Endangering of Personal Society

The movement from the established order into organizations, and the parallel transfer of responsibility from the institutional to the personal, has created a new danger in the world: the brittleness of the modern concept of existence. This brittleness is due to the fact that the attitudes which the new situation requires of us have not yet been fully realized and have not become habitual. Moreover, since attitudes are discovered in relation to structure, they cannot be known in advance and this makes for insecurity. In fact to call the historical (*geschichtlichen*) man to personal responsibility is to ask too much. The transfer of responsibility from the institution to the person thus increases the danger for the world.

The specific danger of the organizational world is totalitarianism in all its forms, best seen in the omnipotence of the machinery of the state. The totalitarian state is an organization through and through; in other words, it seeks to carry the tendency of the modern state toward flexible expediency to the ultimate, but endeavors at the same time to revive the absolute authority which was discarded in the process of objectivity (*Versachlichung*). Totalitarianism is the lack of personality in the sphere where it should be given scope; it has exploited the consequences arising from the failure of personal responsibility. It is obvious, however, that in the long run there is no return to a pre-personal era. The direction of the course of history cannot be reversed.

History as the Way of the Person

The gospel by its call has made the sacral orders of life unimportant and has led the human being to the new status of a "person." But nevertheless, the "historical" (*geschichtliche*) man has a part in the institutions; he has a kind of double history, which in its completely developed forms shows that responsibility has shifted from the institution to the person. At the same time individual status, on whose granting the existence of our modern world depends, overtaxes the "historical" human being; this was recognized in the gospel.

The origin of the strength of the person lies in Jesus Christ, who not only taught how to be a person, but who lived as one and who, according to his words, will continue so to live. He formulates very clearly the three elements of personality in the commandment: "Thou shalt love the Lord thy God with all thy heart, and with all thy soul, and with all thy mind, . . . and thy neighbor as thyself" (Matthew 22 : 37–39).

The person of Christ represents a transforming entry into the world. The historical orders of the world look to this person as to someone "presently expected." The fact that the world's demand for the "person" becomes more and more pressing, points to Jesus as the one who will come, who was and will be.

We do not here refer to categories of "natural theology," which would adapt Christian belief to scientific thinking, or to secular constructions of history; but to unchangeable and irrevocable directions of world history. We can and must look at history as a whole from the perspective of Christ's appearance, his influence and the anticipation of his return. It is in this referral of world history to the person of Christ that we return to the gospel and to the concept of a history directed to a goal.

The changes which the world has experienced through the coming of Christ made it "qualitatively different" from what it was before. This does not mean, however that it is now a Christianized world in the sense that it has been improved, but rather that it is full of the disturbance, the restlessness, the confusion, which Christ himself said that he would bring—must bring—for the realization of the final aim.

The qualitative difference lies also in the nature and cause of the confusion: the specifically new fact is the emphasis on the person. This is what we find so agonizing and devilish, so perverse and lethal. As the gospel so soberly predicted: personal responsibility is too hard for the natural man to bear. The way of personal responsibility leads through deeper and deeper crises. But the same gospel also says that this will finally be the way of fulfillment. But this is known only by faith.

The Christian Congregation

In the course of the disintegration of the medieval "order" and the formation of pluralistic world of organizations, the church itself adopted the criterion of organization. It became more independent, its forms changed and lost their sacral strength.

The church continues to change its forms because it has to fulfill its task—the proclamation of the gospel to the world (see Matthew 28 : 19 ff.)—in changing circumstances. Three illustrations of this new situation can be given:

1. Today the church no longer comprehends the total life of man. Like all organizations, the church is limited in its apprehension of man in society. The church shares in the pluralism of society where many organizations compete for influence on the human being, but where the personal responsibility of the individual has always to be taken into account. Regimentation is no longer accepted by anyone.

2. The church has lagged behind its own influence. Consequently its main purpose cannot be to "win back" a world that has "turned away" from the church. Since in our day the thesis of the "turning away" is considered to be "unchristian" we often fail to recognize its Christian origin and its hidden Christian center. For it is not that the modern world has turned away from the church, but that the church has not been able to keep abreast of its own influence. It is not the duty of the world to follow the church; it is the duty of the church to follow the world, especially on a way which it has itself prepared. Since the desacralized, pluralistic, organizational forms of the world, based upon personal responsibility, have developed from Christian roots, the church can and must be desacralized, pluralistic and organizational in its

own forms and must encourage personal responsibility. The more it does this, the better are the conditions for the proclamation of the gospel, for the implementation of the church's aim as an organization.

3. Moreover, new aspects have emerged in the orientation of the Christian mission toward the non-Christian nations. The process of industrialization has also penetrated and introduced organizational forms of life to non-Christian nations, and with them the challenge to personal responsibility in mastering the modern world. In their tradition, the Christian nations have at their disposal categories of understanding and a "Christian heritage" which can be mobilized to meet the challenge. But how do non-Christian nations master the new situation?

At this point we can see two factors which are decisively interrelated: on the one hand, there are nations which, through industrialization and organization, are increasingly turned to personal responsibility, which is in its origin Christian; on the other, there is the church, which teaches these nations and all others the value of the individual: this has always been its task and if it neglects it, it betrays its true nature. Thus in the course of history plans for a bridge (the church) have been designed and material has been found with which it is possible to build this bridge.

The church is an organization and yet, in its true nature, it is something else and something more. The power by which it lives is not introduced from outside—as in an organization, but dwells in the church itself. Jesus Christ, who demonstrated to the world this concept of being an individual person in all its purity, is a constantly present power in the believing congregation; and it is in this way that being a person is realized in the church, in the congregations: here, as nowhere else, a distinctive relation to reality is established and lived. Christian faith has abandoned the idea of absolute secular values; it has introduced the individuality of the human being and the equality of men before God, and has enabled man to adopt an objective and controlled attitude toward himself. There is no way back from this today, and the existence of the world depends on these spiritual powers. Therefore it is imperative for the congregation, because of its "life in Christ," to keep alive the knowledge of the eternal origin and validity of its standards. The congregation—by its nature and its manner of life—stands not on the fringe of modern society, but right at its center. It is not defending an island which has to be saved: it is the foundation on which the modern world is built.

Knowing that it is impossible to escape from its trespasses—an experience which was formerly that of only a few responsible persons but which has now come upon us all—the congregation keeps its view fixed on the deeper reality of the world, which those who strive for secular perfection fail to perceive. Once we have recognized, however, the impossibility of escaping from our trespasses, three ways are open to us: (1) either we accept it with cynicism and loosen our restraints; or (2) we continue to work, even without deep spiritual understanding, though this is a dubious procedure which becomes less possible with every decade that separates us from the orders of the past; or (3) we accept the experience within the fellowship of the congregation. Here alone is the power that can overcome the lethal whirlpools of trespasses and revenge: the forgiveness of our trespasses. When God forgives us and we forgive one another, the most profound personal event takes place in the congregation, making it possible, over and over again, to begin anew when the whirlpool has overwhelmed us. The world today is everywhere gripped and tossed about by the force of such whirlpools. No organizational means can ever decisively overcome them alone.

II

BIBLICAL UNDERSTANDING OF COMMUNITY

by JULIO R. SABANES (Argentina)

AT certain epochs in its history the church has stood at the crossroads, and some doctrine has provided a clue to an interpretation of the Christian message, a kind of master key to open the way to a new understanding of Christian theology and mission. During the Reformation era, this role was played by the doctrine of justification by faith or of the priesthood of all believers. Dare we say that today the Christian doctrine of community has become the main focus of theological thought, and that it is of decisive relevance for the Christian approach to society?

Many Christians would answer this question in the affirmative. God wills community, and he summons man to communion with him and with his fellowmen. When God takes the initiative of redemption and intervenes in human history, he does so in order to restore the broken communion and the disrupted community. He wants to draw us out of our isolation and egocentrism and to bring us into a community of love. In his study of the Epistle to the Ephesians (commenting on Ephesians 2 : 14), Professor Markus Barth says that the metaphor of the broken wall points to the true meaning of the work of Christ who has broken down every division between men.[1] And he adds: To say Christ means to say com-

---

[1] MARKUS BARTH: *The Broken Wall,* Judson Press, Chicago, 1959, p. 43.

munity, coexistence, a new life, peace.[2] And Dietrich Bonhoeffer has written: "There is in fact only one religion from which the concept of community is essentially inseparable, and that is the Christian religion." [3]

The Biblical Meaning of Community

In the New Testament *koinon-* and its derivatives appear repeatedly: *Koinonos* (partner or companion), with the same meaning reinforced by the prefix *syn;* the verb *koinonéo* (to be a friend or a companion, or to share with others) and its cognate *synkoinonéo;* and *koinonia,* sharing in community, the abstract formation of *koinonéo.* Synonyms, like *metecho* (verb) or *metochoa* and *synmetochos,* appear as adjectives or participles. This remarkable group of words is used to convey several related meanings:

a. Sometimes, words of the *koinon-* group are used in relation to two or more persons who share in the same reality. For example, all Christians have a *koinonia* in Christ and his benefits. They share in God's grace—" . . for you are all partakers (*synkoinonous*) with me of grace" (Philippians 1 : 7); in the gospel—"I do it all for the sake of the gospel, that I may share (*synkoinonos*) in its blessings" (I Corinthians 9 : 23); the promise—". . . the Gentiles are . . . partakers (*synmétoka*) of the promise in Christ Jesus through the gospel" (Ephesians 3 : 6); the glory to be revealed—". . . as a partaker (*koinonos*) in the glory that is to be revealed" (I Peter 5 : 1); the Holy Spirit—"so if there is . . . any participation (*koinonia*) in the Spirit" (Philippians 2 : 1); and the divine nature of Christ—". . . you may . . . become partakers (*koinonoi*) of the divine nature" (II Peter 4 : 1), ". . . you were called into the fellowship (*koinonian*) of his Son, Jesus Christ our Lord" (I Corinthians 1 : 9), ". . . for we share (*métochoi*) in Christ" (Hebrews 3 : 14).

---

2 *Ibid.*, p. 44.

3 DIETRICH BONHOEFFER: *Sanctorum Communio,* Collins, London, 1963, p. 92.

b. They also signify our sharing with Christ, and this is generally denoted by "syn" used as a prefix to other verbs. In Philippians 3 : 10 Paul says: ". . . that I may know him and the power of his resurrection, and may share (*koinonian*) his sufferings." This sharing with Christ is conveyed by several verbs: (*su-then*) "to live with" (Romans 6 : 8; I Corinthians 7 : 3); (*sympaskein*) "to suffer with" (Romans 8 : 17); (*syntauroszaii*) "to be crucified with" (Romans 6 : 6; Galatians 2 : 19); (*synapozanein*) "to die with" (II Corinthians 7 : 3), and (*syndoxazein*) "to be glorified with" (Romans 8 : 17).[4] In many passages, these verbs are in pairs, one pointing to the abasement and humiliation of the incarnation and the other to the exaltation of the resurrection and ascension ". . . and you were buried with him (*syntaféntes*) in baptism, in which you were also raised with him (*syneghérzete*) through faith in the working of God" (Colossians 2 : 12).

For Paul, the present sharing in Christ's suffering is the promise of future glory, and communion with Christ is for all the congregation of Christians. We share in Christ's life, sufferings, passion and glory because he has shared with us our human nature: "Since therefore the children share (*kekoinoneken*) in flesh and blood, he himself likewise partook (*metésken*) of the same nature . . ." (Hebrews 2 : 14). This fellowship with the Father and the Son is truly an extraordinary and marvelous possibility. ". . . our fellowship (*koinonia*) is with the Father and with his Son Jesus Christ" (I John 1 : 3).

c. The *koinonia* manifests its reality by creating a genuine community among Christians. This fellowship has a value in itself: "If we walk in light . . . we have fellowship (*koinonian*) with one another . . ." (I John 1 : 7). It was a living reality from the very beginning of the church: "They devoted themselves to the apostles' teaching and fellowship" (Acts 2 : 42).[5] This fellowship was the new power that even the enemies of Christianity came to admire.

---

[4] A full consideration of this is found in G. Kittel, ed.: *Theologisches Woerterbuch zum Neuen Testament,* von Kohlhammer, Stuttgart, 1957, Vol. III, *ad locum.*

[5] Some commentators seem to suggest, on the basis of the dative in the original text, that a better translation would be "and to the fellowship."

According to Paul, *koinonia* becomes most real in the Lord's Supper. "The cup of blessing which we bless, is it not a participation (or communion) in the blood of Christ? The bread which we break, is it not a participation in the body of Christ? Because there is one bread, we who are many are one body, for we all partake of the one bread" (I Corinthians 10 : 16–17). Paul introduces these questions to a discussion of Christian participation in meals where the meat has been sacrificed on the altar of pagan deities. In ancient time it was believed that those who shared in sacrificial meals became associates or partners of the gods. This is implied in verse 18: "Consider the practice of Israel; are not those who eat the sacrifices partners in the altar?" Paul declares that through the Lord's Supper Christians become partners with the heavenly Christ. The Eucharist brings to reality our *koinonia* with Christ and with one another. But, Paul also implies that one can also have *koinonia* with obscure and demonic powers. "I do not want you to be partners with demons'" (v. 20). There can be *koinonia* in sin, in idolatry, in moral corruption. "Do not . . . participate (*koinonei*) in another man's sins" (I Timothy 5 : 22); ". . . what fellowship (*koinonia*) has light with darkness?" (II Corinthians 6 : 14); "take no part (*synkoinoneite*) in the unfruitful works of darkness" (Ephesians 5 : 11). Just as there is an antichrist, so there can also be an antikoinonia.

Koinonia and its derivatives are also used in relation to the sharing of material goods and to the collection of gifts for impoverished brethren. This readiness of the early Christians to share their possessions was not confined to the apostolic community at Jerusalem; for example, the congregation in Antioch sent relief to the Christians in Judea (Acts 11 : 30). The tendency in current biblical scholarship to attribute this practice to the early Christians' hope of an imminent end of the world is acceptable up to a point, but it does not account for the extraordinary fact that for the first time in human history, groups of people from different religious backgrounds, races, nations and tongues were ready to share their goods with others whom, in some cases, they did not know personally. Expectation of a near end has not always led people to give away their wealth: it has sometimes led to withdrawal into the desert or to an attitude of "let us drink, and be merry." Overwhelming brotherly love made the difference.[6]

In this connection, certain passages in the Pauline epistles have deservedly received much attention, particularly Romans 5 and 8, I Corinthians 13 and 15, Galatians 5. But II Corinthians 8 and 9 also deserve consideration. Here Paul is appealing to his Corinthian brethren on behalf of the collection for the poverty-stricken mother church in Judea, and he does this with theological insight, human understanding and an ability to interpret the spiritual and religious meaning of the handling of material possessions. He calls this collection by a variety of names, among them *"tén koinonian tés diakonias,"* meaning literally, "the communion of service" or "of ministry" (II Corinthians 8 : 4). The same intention is found in Romans 15 : 27 (". . . if the Gentiles have come to share (*ekoinénesan*) in their spiritual blessings, you ought also to be of service to them in material blessings") and in Romans 12 : 13 ("Contribute (*koinonountes*) to the needs of the saints").

Thus, in the New Testament we find *koinonia* playing a major role in the whole range of Christian doctrine, from the communion between the Father and the Son in the Godhead to the Christian basis for stewardship of material possessions. It becomes the focus of a new relationship. A new sense of communion and fellowship between man and God, and a new sense of community between man and his neighbor are the result of the change brought into all relationships by God's redemptive work in Jesus Christ. The love of God shed upon men's hearts through the sacrificial self-giving of Christ creates a bond of fellowship and solidarity among them and transforms strangers and sojourners into fellow citizens of the kingdom of God.

Toward a Theological Understanding of Community

The biblical concept of *koinonia* is at the core of the Christian understanding of community. If *koinonia* is "a common and mu-

---

[6] L. S. THORNTON: *The Common Life in the Body of Christ,* Dacre Press, London, 1941, pp. 7-8.

tual interest and participation in a common object," the character of the community gathered on this basis is determined by the nature of that common object. The Christian community is the body whose head is Christ; Christ himself is the "I" of that community, being present himself in the church. The believers share in this presence of Christ in his church and, in "all the benefits of his passion," or rather in "all the benefits of his incarnation and redemptive work."

Christians partake also in "the fellowship of the Holy Spirit" (II Corinthians 13 : 14). For Paul and other New Testament writers, the expressions "Spirit of God," "Spirit of Christ" and "Holy Spirit" are interchangeable. The Holy Spirit is no other than the Spirit of Christ working in the inner life of the believer and bestowing his gifts upon the church. *"Opera ad extra Trinitatis sunt indivisa":* where one of the three persons of the Trinity is at work, this work can be ascribed to the other two or to the entire Godhead. The Christian community has much in common with other communities, but it stands over against them in being the community of the Holy Spirit. The Holy Spirit is not bound by the limits and possibilities of this particular association, but the community is made up of those who confess that Jesus Christ is Lord, and "no one can say that Jesus is Lord except by the Holy Spirit" (I Corinthians 12 : 3).

This biblical idea of community throws light on many Christian doctrines and on the whole Christian ethical approach. We know that Christian ethics has been guilty repeatedly of individualistic and legalistic interpretations. The concept of community can save us from framing Christian ethics in individual terms alone. Even the greatest mystery of Christian theology, the Trinity, can be illumined by an interpretation of the relation between the Persons in terms of community and of the intimate communion of the Father with the Son and of both *with* and *in* the Holy Spirit. Our *koinonia* is then not only an ethical value, but is grounded and rooted in the nature of God himself.[7] This contributes to a new

[7] JOHN MCINTYRE: *The Theology of Community,* in *The Coracle,* the Journal of the Iona Community, Dec., 1953, No. 24, p. 5.

understanding of our relation with our neighbor, in whose knowledge and service we also know and serve God: "As you did it to one of the least of these my brethren, you did it to me" (Matthew 25 : 40).

The Christian community which is rooted in *koinonia* transcends the sociological community, and therefore its meaning cannot be thoroughly exhausted by any sociological or psychological investigation. Who are the members of this community? How is it distinguished from other religious communities? How does it stand in relation to the whole of humanity? Dietrich Bonhoeffer wrote that there are two basic misunderstandings of the nature of the church. One—a historical and secular misunderstanding—occurs when it is regarded as one religious community among others, and the other—a "religious error"—when it is identified with the kingdom of God. The first misunderstanding springs from overlooking God's action in the calling and gathering of the community and the second from failing to take seriously the historicity of man and the limitations of his earthly works. The reality of the church as the community of the Holy Spirit, willed by God and established by Jesus Christ, can be grasped only from the inside, by those for whom communion with God has been made real. "The new mankind is focused together in one point, in Jesus Christ; and as the love of God through Christ's vicarious action restores communion between God and man, so the human community too once again becomes a living reality in love." [8]

Therefore, when we define the church, we are not describing an institution or a human structure, because the church is the *koinonia* of the Holy Spirit, and this *koinonia* is an indispensable element in the redemptive event. The "history of salvation" did not come to an end with the resurrection and the ascension: it continues in the creation and constant renewal of the *koinonia* by the Holy Spirit.

---

[8] Dietrich Bonhoeffer: *op. cit.*, p. 114.

12

A THEOLOGY OF CHRISTIAN COMMUNITY?

by JAMES M. GUSTAFSON (U. S. A.)

ONE of the more overworked clichés about modern technological society and the churches' participation in it runs something like this: In modern society there is a profound alienation of man from the structures of work, politics and other aspects of life. The large, powerful public world seems to be managed by a few persons in the seats of power or, in the view of analysts, appears to be running not only itself, but the persons who are supposed to manage it. The church has no way of influencing these centers of real power in the world, for in an age of secularization its moral authority is no longer recognized, and it lacks the modes of exercise of social power to become a significant pressure group to countermand the tendencies that appear to be against its understanding of what life is meant to be. Alongside this powerful ordered public world is the private world of person-to-person relationships, of family life and of individual existence. It is in this sphere that some of the protests against the alienation from the structured world take place—the rebellions of youth or the efforts to achieve some compensating meaningful life by concentrating on family activities. The church, we are told, has become functional with reference only to this private sphere. And even here its role has become supportive, therapeutic, pastoral and even idolatrous, for it functions to give religious sanctions to a culturally defined pattern of life that is itself not sufficiently subjected to theological and moral criticism.

The effect of much persuasive writing in this vein, by Marxists and existentialists, by theologians and some Christian sociologists, by world-renowned philosophers and street-corner culture critics, has been to create a mood of hostility toward the church even on the part of many who continue to call themselves Christians. The churches are seen to be part of the problem of alienation, for they have been attending to institutional demands for self-preservation, to cheap piety and to concern only for the private sphere, none of which rectifies in the least the moral impotence of institutional Christianity. They represent religion, and this, on testimony from antibourgeois theologians, is bad. The *avant-garde* Christians then call us to a radical secularity that, we are to assume, overcomes the embarrassment of church life which seems to be merely pious and private in its morality, and institutional in its demands. Secularity also presumably overcomes the distance between Christian faith and the centers of power where things that really matter for the life of man are taking place.

Certain assumptions that inform this perspective need to be brought under serious question. They are both sociological-historical and theological in character. We may ask whether the division between the private and the public, the personal and the structural is not too sharply drawn, and whether significant relations do not exist between them. We may also ask, from a social-psychological perspective, where the person-forming communities are going to be in a program of action that looks with disdain upon the church and other "private" spheres. What is to shape the mind and the spirit of the person who is told to be completely identified with the "world"? What is to provide a center of his own personal existence which informs his involvement in the secular order when religion, as a historical movement influencing persons and cultures, is apparently not to be cultivated? What kind of sociological assumptions lie behind the view that Christians can be socially more effective by involvement in secular institutions, since it is through these that history is being shaped, while at the same time the institutions and the religious culture that shape the Christians are judged to be increasingly useless? Where, also, is the positive place of custom and of cultural values, of *ethos,* in this critical material? In the antibourgeois stance, have critics failed to distinguish between false and suppressive moral customs and order, on the one hand, and the positive significance of cultural morality, on the other?

There appear to be theological assumptions lurking in this kind of social analysis as well. They are many, and they do not form a single consistent school. Insofar as the social analysis moves to the cultivation of an existentialist mood, one wonders if God is not seen primarily in terms of the accepter of persons, the lord who wills meaningful moments of self-realization in personal terms, rather than the sovereign ruler of depersonalized institutions as well. The mission of the church becomes focused too exclusively on the personal and interpersonal. Insofar as the social analysis leads to the glorification of the secular world, where Christ's lordship is presumably being worked out, one wonders whether that world, like the church, is not also deeply corrupted by unfaith and rebellion against God. One wonders sometimes whether we cannot rely upon Christ's presence and lordship in the church, and indeed through religion, as much as we can rely upon his lordship being exercised through social crisis and social change. There is a stress on secularity without adequate delineation of how Christians judge the secular. Insofar as the social analysis separates the realm of the personal from the impersonal, but assumes that God's dominion is pressing in upon both, one wonders whether there is not the legacy of a Lutheran theology and a Brunner theology that sees God doing work with persons through the gospel with his right hand and with institutions through the law with his left hand, in such a way that these are spatially or chronologically separated. The realms of redemption and of preservation become sharply divided, with a different ethic for each.

Debate over adequate social analysis and over theological assumptions has some significant effects on the actual life of the Christian community within the wider community. Our institutional forms and activities are guided in part by the sociological perceptions and theological interpretations. The establishment of "coffee houses" as places of ministry adjacent to college campuses in the United States, for example, is informed often by crypto-sociological assumptions about what the actual situation of society is—one in which students are alienated and thus must be ministered to in terms of that alienation. It is also informed by crypto-theologies, believing that God's grace is known in the intimacies of coffee, poetry and jazz, and is not known in the course of study or in the world of "establishment." The founding of centers for discussion of vocational and political problems may assume not only that the churches as they are now organized cannot effectively speak to the world, but also that conversation about the world without embarrassing reference to theological conviction and to religious interest is the way in which God (if there is a God) works in the modern world. I do not intend to be overly critical of the new forms of witness and mission, since for both sociological and theological reasons I affirm their place in the life of the church. As many have noted, the traditional routinized activities of institutional churches in all parts of the world also certainly rest upon sociological perceptions and theological interpretations that have to be brought under question.

It is my intention in the main body of this essay to suggest an interpretation of community, based upon sociological and theological perspectives, which I hope is more adequate to sources of truth and of insight than some perspectives that are currently in vogue or are historically influential in the life of the Christian community.

The Functions of Community in the Light of God's Purposes

What purposes of God are being realized in the existence of men in community? We should have in mind all three aspects of human community: cultural ethos, interpersonal relationship and institutions. My answer to this question hinges on a number of verbs: God creates, sustains, restrains and makes possible better qualities of life through the existence of men in all three aspects of community.[1]

Common life in various segments of humanity is a means by which God's *creative purposes* bear fruit for men. What is new emerges out of the common life of the old. Human creative achievement takes place within the patterns of life in which persons are related to each other, whether one is thinking of biological procreation, development of new forms of social organization, novel patterns of art and music or scientific and technological developments. Creative work is related to the past in dependence upon it, as well as in rebellion against it. Creative persons are sustained by communities as well as by defending themselves against them. The continuities need to be stressed in an age that is preoccupied with finding discontinuities and with celebrating the novel. Underlying these achievements of men is the potentiality and purpose of newness, or creativity, which is part of God's gracious gift to men in the giving of life. Two examples will make clear how God's creative purposes are achieved through human community.

Newness in human understanding of the physical world is one of the forms of creativity that dazzle the mind. The fresh interpretations we are given, not only of the minutest possible sources of life and energy in the physical world, but also of the relations of the constellations of "universes" to each other, enable men not only to understand the natural world of which they are a part, but also to participate in it with greater intelligence and to master aspects of it for human purposes. Creativity in the world of natural science, however, is not a matter of one person in isolation contemplating introspectively or calculating on the basis of his individual observations. It is a communal enterprise. There is a community of scientists, evoking criticisms and responses from each other, building upon each other's observations and theories, in communication with each other through their own abstract sym-

[1] This section has clear echoes of the thought of my late colleague and teacher, H. Richard Niebuhr, which I readily and gratefully acknowledge, although he would not necessarily have approved of precisely what I have done here.

bols and words. Creativity in perception and understanding, surely in the divine providence a possibility and purpose given by God, is born of intense life in a human community.

Even where the individual appears to "break through" with radical novelty, he is participating in an ongoing community. The rejection or transformation of a traditional pattern in one of the arts, for example, does not come into being as a creative act out of nothing. It takes place as a creative virtuoso responds to the inadequacies of a tradition for the purpose of expressing what he perceives in the world, or what he feels about himself and his world. Novel forms are not *de novo* forms; they are creative responses to patterns that have been given. The discontinuities can be great, as for example in the development of the twelve-tone scale in music, but nevertheless a community is present—one over against which the new is defined; and quickly a new community is born, developing the fresh pattern. Newness, creativity, comes into being through the existence of common life.

Common life is a means by which God sustains human existence in the world. There is an ordering of existence, changing in its particular forms, to be sure, that provides for the continuity of life. Human life is sustained by the continuities of custom and belief, of values and ideas, as well as by the creative perceptions which alter the traditions of men. The ethical importance of custom and of ethos is an area neglected by many Christian interpreters of society today, probably because a defense of it seems in the West to be a defense of a bourgeois outlook, and many Protestant theologians wish above all to be differentiated from that. Life is sustained by the meaning that one person has for another in friendship and marriage, in pastoral relationship and teaching. It is sustained by the ordering of economic and political power through civil law and through institutions of commerce, police power, trade unions and family. Even when men revolt against a given institution or custom that has sustained them in the past, they seek not the absence of community, but a new community organized by a different institutional form, or by a different set of customary standards. The sustaining power of the tribe is cast aside in the aspiration that the nation will take its place as the formative community. The rigid extrinsic code morality of nineteenth-century tradition is rejected in the hope that a more meaningful morality, intrinsic to man's deepest needs or to his Christian life, will come into being. Sustaining patterns of life deserve a dignity in a Christian interpretation of community that is sometimes overlooked, particularly in a time of revolutions and when individuals find custom and tradition to be so oppressive that authentic human existence is often defined in terms of radical freedom from them.[2]

A part of the sustaining function of community is the restraints that it places on individuals and on other communities. The organized interests of one nation act to restrain the aggressive interests of another. The fighters for justice for those who are oppressed are limited in the means by which their struggle can be executed by the existence of a community that concerns itself for the preservation of civil order. The willful inclinations of the antisocial individual are restrained by the existence of mores and customs, as well as by the civil law and the powers of police enforcement. The personal community of family is not only a pattern in which its members sustain each other physically, mentally and spiritually, but also one in which limits are set upon the activities of each other by the obligations of its members toward one another and toward the family as a whole.

Through communities the ordering (sustaining and restraining) work of God for the sake of men takes place. New patterns of this work come into being, and older patterns pass away. One of the

[2] A question is implicit here that deserves long and serious study. One gets the impression that much of the Christian social leadership and experimentation is now directed toward those who are alienated from the past and from present communities, and some of it makes for an attitude not just of criticism of "establishment," but of sheer rebellion against establishment as a prime virtue. I do not wish to suggest that particular attention to the depressed and the "outsiders" is not important, but some of it is being given to the neglect of meaningful interpretation of the significance of pattern and order for human beings, and of the ways in which old orders can be reformed to fulfill better the necessary functions of human social life. We seem to be much clearer about the oppressions of custom and institutions that sustain us than we are about their positive functions in the sustaining of human life, and thus about how these patterns themselves can be altered better to fulfill their essential moral purposes.

mistakes of those who define "orders" of creation and preservation is that they often find a kind of revealed positive sociology in the fact that men exist within family and state, as if there were a clear pattern for these institutions ordained by God. This, as has often been seen, can lead to a false identification of an existing historical pattern with the divine order, and thus to an uncritical, conservative acceptance of a *status quo*. We have now properly learned to speak of ordering rather than orders, in the light of the errors of the past. Or to use a different set of words, community can be interpreted functionally, as accomplishing purposes needed for human life. Its particular form or order is to be judged by its effectiveness in fulfilling its morally purposive functions. God sustains and restrains life through the functions of state and family and other institutions, as well as the historical occasions for them occur; through the development of mass public education, through the work of universities and their institutes, through political parties, through labor unions and through international organizations.

Through community, God also makes better qualities of life possible for men. Indeed, while sin is not redeemed by community, God's redemptive love can take particular historical force and form through the relations that persons have with and for each other. Even civil law, as an establishment of new patterns of justice and order in human society, functions to bring new possibilities or qualities of life into being in particular societies. The order of law and the order of society can be the means by which God's love makes possible better existence both for social groups and for individuals.

Community, then, through God's creative use of it, has a high order of theological dignity in a Christian interpretation; it is not merely something oppressive, hostile to authentic life, embodying sin and prejudice. The social mission of the church, in turn, needs to be related to each of these aspects of human community, with each of the aspects of God's purposes in view.

It would be very one-sided, however, to acknowledge that the corrupt, the demonic, the sinful did not also exist in human community. At least since the time of A. Ritschl and W. Rauschenbusch we have come to understand the existence of "kingdom [or perhaps better, realm] of sin." To cite the positive significance of custom and tradition for human commuity in the economy of God does not imply that custom cannot be perverse and run counter to God's purposes for man. The embedding of racial prejudice within social custom is one case in point. Tradition can also be oppressive, functioning as an idol that prohibits men from responding to the call of God in the openness of the present. To cite the sustaining and even redeeming importance of interpersonal relations, of being for the other person, is not to imply that such relations cannot be demonic and destructive, cannot be the means by which perverse domination of one person over the other takes place, or the means by which inhuman servility of one person under the other is justified. To suggest the positive ethical importance of institutions and civil arrangements in the human community is not to deny the existence of unjust laws, or the magnifying of the effects of human selfishness through the use of economic and social power over workers, or over a nation. Indeed, corruption, perversion, distortion of purpose exist within each of these aspects of human community; human relations are a realm both of sin and of God's creative, ordering and redeeming presence. They are constantly under the judgment of the presence of God; they are constantly in need of prophetic criticism and reformation; indeed, they also await the full redemption that is to come. But we err if we see only their perversity, or if we fail to give them a high level of dignity in our understanding of God's work for men.

Community and Moral Action

These same patterns of God's care for man that are apparent in human community are also the patterns of mutual service, responsibility and obligation within which men are called to moral action. Christians together in the church are particularly called to interpret their existence in community as the location in time and space of their responsibility to God for human society and for other persons. To participate in a cultural ethos, in a moral tradition, is to have responsibility for that ethos and tradition. To be personally related to another is joyfully to serve the other and to be obligated for his well-being. To function as a person within an institution is to see the power of the institution as the means for the upbuilding of humanity and to acknowledge the responsibility of the institution for the preservation of justice, liberty and order in the world. The patterns of common life are patterns of service, responsibility and obligation in a Christian interpretation of community, to God and to men. They are patterns in and through which moral activity takes place.

In response to God's goodness man freely and joyfully serves not only individual neighbors, but the common life that binds men together. This is most easily seen in the realm of interpersonal relations. The other is one whom I love, one whose good I can seek, one whose presence I can sustain, one whose despair I can help to overcome, one in whose presence I have delight and joy. Existence in family life makes the details of this clear. In his love, God has given the others to me: wife or husband, and children. In their love for me, the others sustain my life and bring to it joy and delight. In response to the love of God and the love of others, freely given, faithfully given service is an expression of moral action. But service is not confined to the interpersonal.

Participation in a location of responsibility in an institution is also a call to service. Consciousness of the care of God for the human community through government and university, through voluntary associations and political parties, evokes a response of grateful service to others through these institutions. They are the spheres in which freedom, love and concern are expressed. Their own internal structures can be shaped in part by expressions of freely given love and care. They can be shaped in part to be consonant with purposes that express the Christians' response to God's goodness.

Life in community is also life in common responsibility.[3] It is the acceptance of accountability for the shaping of the values and cus-

[3] For a succinct account of the nature of responsibility, see H. R. NIEBUHR: *The Responsible Self,* New York, Harper & Row, 1963.

toms that inform much of the unconscious responses and actions of the members of the human community. Community is held together by custom and tradition; good and evil are embedded in custom and tradition; custom and tradition shape the character of persons and institutions so that loyalties and convictions drawn from them inform the responses and actions of persons, even when they are not aware of them. Persons with a minimum experience of cultural pluralism within a nation or across national boundaries are conscious of the fact that attitudes, emotive expressions of moral convictions, words and sections often express cultural values different from their own. Part of the pattern of responsibility in community is responsibility for these often inarticulated values, customs and traditions.

The Christian community has the responsibility to articulate and criticize this glue of custom that holds societies together. If tradition and custom regard Negroes or certain castes as inferior and dictate prejudiced attitudes and actions toward such groups, it is the responsibility of the Christian community to engage in the alteration of these forces. If tradition and custom sustain respect for personal liberty and inviolability of conscience against powers that seek to invade and manipulate men, the Christian community has a responsibility to maintain and strengthen these forces. Such forces have in many instances no definite location: there is not always an institution that is dedicated to the cultivation of the evil or the good that is present in an ethos. Yet through instruction, prophetic writing, the nurturing of the minds and spirits of children and other means, the Christian community can exercise influence in shaping the forces that in turn invisibly shape the attitudes, responses and actions of men.

Interpersonal relations are relations of responsibility. They exist not merely as occasions of joyfully given service, and certainly not merely as occasions for self-realization. Faithfulness of one for the other is an aspect of the interpersonal. To be for the person is to be faithful to the other person, to accept responsibility for the well-being of the other. Through interpersonal relations, God cares for the well-being both of the self and of the other. As active persons in these relations, Christians interpret them as occasions of responsibility to God for the care of others. As the promises of the marriage service so vividly suggest, to be related as husband and wife is to be related not only in freely given affection, but to be responsible for each other. Indeed, responsibility for each other is a structure of love, not merely the occasion for love. It is a pattern of service and responsibility. Parents are located in a pattern of responsibility to God for the well-being of their children. Friendship, if it is not confused with mere acquaintance (as it often is in the United States), is not just the enjoyment of each other, taking delight in the presence of each other; it is also the acceptance of responsibility for the needs of each other. To be for the other person is to be responsible for the other person.

The formal and informal patterns of relationships established within institutions and between them are clearly patterns of responsibility. As active agents in institutions, Christians particularly interpret them as centers of power and influence the conduct of which has moral consequences in the society, and therefore institutions are to be understood in terms of moral responsibility. This responsibility is not a thing, a substance, as it were, that institutions could have. It is rather to be articulated in detailed terms for particular institutions; for the political party, the management of a small business and so forth. Christian interpretation asks certain questions of institutions: For what is this institution responsible? How do its purposes cohere with an informed understanding of the manner and ends of life that Christians believe to be consonant with what God is seeking to say and to do? How can persons in institutions act to give direction to their activities so that the well-being of humanity is sustained and improved by the policies and activities of institutions? In the divine economy, institutions and their relations to each other are patterns of social life in and through which moral responsibility—to God, for the human community—are exercised.

Obligation—a stronger word than responsibility—also enters in. Life in community is life in a structure of moral obligations, of claims upon persons and of claims upon groups. To participate in the community of custom and tradition is to be obligated to God for its rectitude and its nurture, for its continuity insofar as its effects reflect an understanding of what God wills to do for men, and for its alteration insofar as it is a corruption of what God seeks to do and to say. To be sure, the Christian community is in a sense emancipated from cultural ethos; it certainly does not find its final righteousness and justification in its responsibility for the customs and traditions of the society of which it forms a part. Its loyalty to God gives it a position over against custom and tradition, its faith gives it a freedom from bondage to social custom and tradition. But this freedom ought not to imply that the Christian community has no obligation to God for the sustenance and cultivation of those customs and traditions which can be a means of God's governing and edifying work in the world. I have sought to make a case for the positive function of culture in the divine economy; if such a case is made, the Christian community is obligated to God, who rules and upbuilds through culture for the moral quality of that culture.

Mutual obligation is an aspect of interpersonal relations as well. Personal relations, if they are significant, exist over long periods of time and across the boundaries of spatial separation. To be for the other person is to delight in his presence; it is also to be responsible for him, to be obligated to him. In many forms of personal relationship there is a formal rite which not only confirms that two persons will be faithful to each other, but that they are obligated to each other. The marriage service is again an excellent example of this fact. There, a covenant is made between two persons, before God and a congregation of his people, which details some of the obligations that exist, by virtue not only of the freely given love of one for the other, but of the fact that this love is a faithful and responsible love. As such, it is fitting that there be an articulated, determined detailing of the structure of obligations that both express love and nourish love. Obligation in personal relations is not antithetical to love; it is a form of responsible and faithful love. Marriage is not the only interpersonal relationship in which this is the case.[4]

"Steadfastness" or faithfulness as an aspect of interpersonal relations, with the implied duties and obligations toward each other, is a part of the Old Testament interpretation both of covenant and of love. It is not a nineteenth-century or post-Kantian imposition of extrinsic rules or duties upon persons. It is part of the Christian conviction, born of God's revelation of himself, that informs the church's understanding of relations between persons. In the time of a "new morality" that comes into being under Christian auspices, a morality that smacks of a kind of shallow concern with self-realization, it is perhaps even more important to see the significance of the structure of personal relations as a structure of mutual obligations of persons to each other and for the consequences of their common life.[5]

In the institutional spheres of life, the aspect of obligation is more clearly seen. Institutions have rules and laws which articulate the obligations that persons have toward each other, and the duties that they have toward the institution. But a Christian interpretation is not a mere support of obedience to institutional laws and

---

[4] An American is constrained to comment at this point upon the difference between the casual interpersonal relations of his society and the formalized relations of the continent. Friendship and acquaintance have come to mean virtually the same thing for many Americans: there is no sense of being responsible for the other person by virtue of friendship, and no sense of obligation that gives the other a serious claim upon one. There are no little rites that signify a transition in the character of the relationship. By contrast, the mutual consent to move from the polite to familiar form of "you" in more traditional societies symbolizes not only that two persons are at home in each other's company, but that they virtually pledge themselves to a kind of faithfulness to each other which may entail responsibilities and obligations. The interpretation I am giving to interpersonal relationships obviously would place a high value upon such articulations of a "covenant" even if made only in the mutual consent to address each other in the more familiar forms of speech.

[5] One looks in vain for any serious discussion of obligations in the books that often are covered by the appellation "new morality," such as J. A. T. ROBINSON's chapter, "The New Morality" in *Honest to God,* and PAUL LEHMANN's *Ethics in a Christian Context,* New York, Harper & Row, 1963. One suspects this is so because obligation suggests law, and law seems to be antithetical to an ethics of grace in which the "divine indicative" has such clear centrality of attention.

rules; it is rather an understanding that institutions and those acting in and through them are obligated to God for the conduct of affairs, and thus obligated to the persons and society of which they are a part for the actions and effects of the state, the economy and so forth. Institutions are locations in which man's obligations to God and to other men have a concreteness, a virtually material quality, which expresses man's moral discernment and care. The Christian community is obligated first to God and then to and for the institutions in and through which duties toward God and the neighbors can be carried out.

Implications for the Mission of Church to Society

Some suggestions about the implications of this interpretation for the work of the church seem to be in order. It is not for me to spell them out in terms of practical programs, but only to indicate stresses and correctives that appear to be required in the present situation.

First, and most obvious, is the need to keep all three aspects of community in view. Those activities of the churches and other agencies that view the Christian concern to be primarily personal obviously tend to neglect the institutional patterns of society. The concern for the personal often leads to a disengagement from the realm of the technical and the impersonal. Indeed, there are theological options that encourage this disengagement by judging the realms of technology, bureaucracy and other forms of organized social and economic power to be virtually demonic, and at least to be detrimental to the ends that the Christian message seems to have in view. It becomes difficult to move from the existential and the personal to the technological and institutional if one's interpretation of modern communities, in theological and sociological terms, places the weight of importance and dignity on the realm of subjectively meaningful existence. The kind of mutual involvement that develops between persons through the impersonal patterns of large-scale social organizations provides, in the light of my interpretation, both for significant, meaningful life, and for moral activity in giving some direction to the course of human events. God's purposes, as discerned in the Scripture and in tradition, relate to the historical course of events, and *ipso facto* to technology, bureaucracy and other aspects of industrial societies that are of crucial importance in our time.

Second, these activities on the part of churches and other agencies that are institution- and "world"-orientated must not lose sight of the importance of the "private" and the personal as spheres that sustain persons in their institutions, and more particularly as places in which there is a formation of outlook and of values that in turn deeply affects the kind of judgments and actions that persons make in their "offices" or institutional responsibilities. The private sphere is not only a place of escape from the pressures of the institutional sphere; it is not only the location of a pastoral and therapeutic concern that can never be ruled out of the purposes of the Christian gospel. It is a place in which are formed the attitudes, reflective moral commitments and motives that persons carry into the institutional and technical world. Choices, moral judgments and actions reflect in part the commitments, loyalties, values and motivations that are nurtured and reshaped in the sphere of interpersonal existence. If an understanding of community as a process of action within orderly patterns has validity, attention has to be paid to the spheres within which moral habits, character, decisions, indeed, virtues and their opposites are shaped.

Third, the interpretation given in this essay calls for a far more extensive place for the virtues than popularly exists in Protestant ethics today. Basic selfhood is shaped in the "private" and interpersonal spheres, in the family, the congregation and other centers where the attitudes and values of persons are formed, criticized and in part re-formed. Protestant theology has for too long tended to assume that the language of the "virtues" necessarily implied an uncritical approval of bourgeois attitudes, or suggested that to take the task of shaping the conscience, or of shaping virtues seriously is to live by self-righteousness and law rather than by grace. Indeed, in societies which are undergoing rapid change, with traditional external standards in flux, it is all the more important that the basic loyalties and convictions of persons shall have a measure of stability and clarity, so that their participation in the world may receive direction and purpose.

Fourth, participation in institutions on the part of the members of the Christian community ought to be governed in part by their life of faith, and by purposes, objectives, means of action that reflect the Christian gospel and are informed by the ethical reflection of the community. Life in the church is life revivified by fresh apprehension of God as the sovereign ruler of the world, by renewed dedication to his purposes that is engendered by worshiping him, by informed conscientiousness about the responsibilities and actions in the world that are coherent with the church's understanding of what God seeks to have this world to be. It is in the common life of the church that both intentions and dispositions on the internal, subjective side, and purpose and patterns of life on the external, objective side are to be engendered, fashioned, critically scrutinized and articulated. There is no doubt that the churches as we know them have been remiss in fulfilling this moral function, but we have no other historical social unit within which these functions, in allegiance to Jesus Christ, are performed.

Fifth, culture, or ethos must not be left out of the purview of Christian interpretation and action in society. It is notoriously difficult to influence, since its values and styles are developed by so many different agencies. Protestant churches, and others as well, when they have addressed the problems of culture, have often made sweeping critical attacks about "materialism" rather than finding ways in which to influence the goals and purposes that persons seem to absorb from their milieu. The place that is given to culture in the interpretation offered in this essay calls for a continuous dialogue between the Christian community and other groups, all of which are involved in the shaping of culture. There are signs that this is occurring in the critiques of movies, television, advertising, novels, business ethos and other distillations of culture that have been published under the auspices of Christian churches. Rejection of culture is largely gone as a stance of the Christian community. But apart from persistent critique of it, accompanying our constant involvement in it, we are seriously faced with the temptation to become a new generation of culture Christians, and in our critique of it we often fail in two respects: the faith becomes too readily identified only with the movements of protest against mass culture, and it begins to look as if the Christians had their stakes exclusively in the causes of angry young men; and in our anti-bourgeois sentiments, some of which are in harmony with the claims of the gospel, we are prone to isolate the critical concerns for culture from the daily involvements in it of unexciting, humdrum mothers, children, clerks, executives, laborers and professional people. Too often Christian critiques of culture are critiques of the Christian cultural *élite* who, by virtue of their own advanced tastes and training, have separated themselves from the masses whose daily involvement in ordinary affairs God uses and on whom the *élites* depend.

Finally, we need to find a way in which to reintroduce the idea of obligations and responsibilities without falling into the traps of legalism and heteronomy. These are the traps that ethics is most conscious of today, sometimes at the expense of the right sense of duties and obligations. Indeed, it becomes easy to slip from an antilegalism into an ethic of self-realization in which immediate fulfillment of desires, rather than deepest human needs, is the goal of life. Grace and love drive us from within to become involved in the needs of the neighbor and in the suffering of the world, but under God's sovereign rule we are obligated to take on the burdens of the world as his responsible deputies, even when inner disposition is weak. Life is to find fulfillment in the relations between persons of each sex, but the fulfillment is also one of the duties and obligations that we have toward each other by virtue of these relationships in the divine economy. Faith and love bring us a new sense of freedom, but a pattern of responsibilities and obligations exists to keep that freedom directed toward those things which are helpful and which build up. Neither we nor the world is as "mature" as we are often told, and in the absence of such maturity the necessity of rule and authority under God in determining conduct and activity is indispensable. God's concern for the ordering of human society so that freedom and fulfillment can abound is as much a part of his purposes as is his emancipating men from the bondage of false orders and outdated rules. The interpretation given in this essay calls for more detailed understanding of the church's activity in society in terms of the ordering of institutions and of the duties and obligations of persons at each place of Christian life in the world.

PART IV

MAN AND COMMUNITY IN SCIENCE AND CULTURE

13

CULTURAL MAN

by MARGARET MEAD (U. S. A.)

The Task of Anthropology

ANTHROPOLOGY brings to our knowledge of human beings the results of several specific kinds of research. This knowledge, in turn, broadens and deepens our understanding of man as one among all the living creatures inhabiting this planet in this solar system. Some anthropological research reaches back millions of years in time to place man in the context of evolving living creatures and to trace the evolution of man's various organs and the development of his capacity to perceive, to organize, to question and to begin to understand the universe in which he lives. By a comparative study of the many forms of culture which have existed in the past—studied reconstruction of fossil and archeological remains of language and other aspects of culture and surviving living forms—and by direct field observation of behavior and analysis of currently used symbolic forms, anthropology explores the range of man's capacity to build cultural systems. As a result of the comparative and historical studies which have been conducted during the last century and a half two earlier theories about human history have been called into question. Although our present knowledge leaves no doubt that social forms have gone through large-scale evolutionary changes, in which simple food gathering and hunting have been succeeded by agriculture and animal husbandry and that these in turn have developed into man's present industrial and technical control of nature today, the nineteeth-century assumption that all other forms of culture—man's artistic, intellectual, social and religious life—were tied to this evolution of technical culture, is no longer tenable. Detailed work has revealed a tremendous variety of cultural behavior, with complexity of symbolic forms often associated with simplicity of technical or social organization. It has also called in question the latter assumption, made so often by social commentators who claim to base their statements on anthropological and sociological evidence, that the process of urbanization results in some kind of deterioration in human behavior. Against this assumption they would place the material that shows that small isolated human communities may also represent profound deterioration in human relationships—the peoples of the Baliem valley,[1] the Mudugumor of the Yuat River, in New Guinea,[2] the isolated peoples of the mountains in many Euro-American communities—and that the deterioration which results from urbanization is a function of transition and of ensuing social disorganization, and not of the process of civilization itself. Though not exalting the present state of our own culture to a position of absolute improvement over all preceding cultures, modern anthropological evolutionary theory recognizes the correlates of technical advances in man's increasing capacity for communication, for organization into larger and larger communities of individuals all defined as members of one group and for greater understanding, and the resulting enlargement of possibilities of effective ordering of human social behavior. As a correlate of this extension of our knowledge of the particular steps by which man has developed to his present physical, cultural and social condition, anthropology is also concerned with possible future change. We know that man's body and physical capacities have responded to long-time changes

---

[1] PETER MATTHIESSEN: *Under the Mountain Wall: A Chronicle of Two Seasons in the Stone Age,* New York, Viking, 1962.

Dead Birds, a film produced by Robert Gardner. Film Center of the Peabody Museum, Harvard University, Cambridge, Mass.

[2] MARGARET MEAD: *Sex and Temperament in Three Primitive Societies,* Apollo a-67, New York, Wm. Morrow, 1963.

in the conditions of life, as men acquired and elaborated on the ability to grow, store and prepare food; the ability to provide shelter and clothing as protections against inclement weather; the ability to work with and transform the earth's natural resources, creating implements and machines and new sources of energy and even new kinds of raw materials; the ability to record and transmit —at a distance and to future generations—much that men have experienced; and the ability to organize themselves into even larger and more complex communities, especially as they acquired new and increasingly rapid forms of communication and transportation.

It is, therefore, also the task of anthropology to consider the possible future development of man under new conditions: great density of population, the burden of the knowledge of how to bring about a catastrophe to which not only warring groups but all mankind and perhaps all living creatures might be destroyed, the possibilities inherent in the new technologies. In the distant past inventions like the wheel, the sail, the plough and the loom increased men's simple mastery over their external environment. In today's technology, machines have been substituted not only for the most complex manual tasks, but even for every complex activity of discrimination, memory and decision—tasks which once were performed by the human brain without external aids, just as men once tilled the soil with nothing but digging sticks in their hands.

A Wider Perspective on Mankind

This, then, is the first contribution that anthropological thought can make to Christian thinking: an increasingly detailed and concrete specification of the steps by which man has attained his present physical, cultural and social state; a growing recognition of that state as itself a changing one; and, because of man's newly acquired ability to understand his own past and present, a growing awareness that man's state is increasingly coming under his own control, be it for good or for evil.

Traditionally, as men relied on the concrete terms in which the Scriptures were cast by their writers, men whose inspiration was informed and shaped by their location in time and space, the sense of man as a changing creature, living in a world which man himself was altering, was little emphasized. Biblical parallels to urbanization might be sought in the fall of Sodom and Gomorrah, and the ploughshare and the pruning hook were likely to be treated as if they had been placed in man's hands at the gate of the Garden. For men whose widest knowledge of the world extended to parts of Asia and Europe—for whom most of Africa and all of the Americas and Australia were beyond the widest stretch of the imagination—the constricted nature of the ancient world was accepted as a kind of prototype of civilization. Men might temporarily progress. They might build great cities, wage great wars and carry out great enterprises. But then a great civilization would collapse and fall back again, apparently without intrinsic change, into broken and lesser versions of the past, as the tower of Babel, which men in their temerity attempted to build, collapsed into ruin.

Anthropological research also introduces questions about the possibilities and the limitations inherent in man's physical being, as expressive of the paths he has trodden, and a wider consideration of human perception and the kinds of human social organization—and, therefore, of human communities—which have existed, do exist and may exist in the future on this planet.

Perhaps the simplest way of stating this is to emphasize that our view of man today must include men who lived half a million years ago, men who had only the crudest and simplest of tools and the most rudimentary forms of social organization and, equally, men living today who represent technical stages not unlike theirs, who still can be found living in remote parts of the earth, whose traditions are as old as ours but far simpler than the traditional way of life of the Hebrew people at the beginning of their recorded history. Underwriting the Christian extrapolation to all men of man made in the image of God and man within whom Christ can be perceived, there is now the detailed accumulation of research materials on fossil man, ancient man and primitive man—materials which make possible a general outline of human history as the history of a species. And this species, like other species, can be described as one; that is, as a living group in which even the most remotely separated individuals in space can, if they are brought together, mate and have offspring. But in addition to these characteristics which men share with other related species and with some species very far removed in the evolutionary scale—for example, care by both parents, the importance of vision and uprightness are shared with birds—men have depended on a human ability to develop into persons within the setting provided by the group, yet responsive to the individuality of each.[3] Underwriting the biblical admonition to love one's neighbor is our knowledge of the many thousands of ways in which small groups of men have struggled toward wider conceptions of neighborliness. Underwriting the Christian insistence on the unending nature of man's struggle on earth to reconcile his natural impulses with Christian ideals of conduct, there is the long record of the struggles of human societies, sometimes succeeding and sometimes failing, to develop a social order within which men could follow Christian admonitions. Comparative studies also reveal the perennial struggle in every society so to rear children and support adult individuals that the ideal of the good life, however differently defined, may triumph over man's conflictual tendencies toward good and evil.

Modern anthropology also places in a new context the problems which arise from a belief in inevitable progress and those which arise from a belief in man's essentially unending battle between his original nature and his aspirations. During the nineteenth century and into the first years of the twentieth, the difficulties encountered in reading the fossil records on the one hand, and the continuing ethnocentrism of Euro-Americans on the other, had as one result the tendency to treat evolution, the progressive transformation of biological forms through time, and social progress as in some sense interchangeable concepts, leaving little room for the eternal nature of the struggle as seen by the Christian. But modern anthropology, following the lead of modern biology, broke away from the simple notion that all biological evolution is in and of itself progressive;

---

3 A. Irving Hallowell: *Culture and Experience,* Philadelphia, University of Pennsylvania Press, 1955.

and the accumulating record of early cultures freed our thought from the ethnocentrism which underlies the assumption that all civilization originated in Asia. The elaboration of the many ways in which biological specialization, on the one hand, and cultural forms of learned behavior, on the other, can become blind alleys—or can be lost—increases our understanding of the ephemeral and fragile character of man's present and past. It also clarifies man's future temporal-spatial relationships both to the rest of the biological world and to the societies he builds, within which he must live. Thus, modern cultural anthropology and modern biological theory have summarily resolved the conflict between Christian ideas of the person and nineteenth-century conceptions of man which developed out of that century's very partial understanding of man, in his temporal and spatial extent, millions of years back in time, spread over the entire globe and living at very different technical and social levels.[4]

Modern anthropological theory provides a scientific background for the acceptance of man as part of the living world of God's creatures, for our creatureliness and for continuity within the whole creation. It provides a scientific basis for man's view of himself, in spite of all the differences among various localized races and physical stocks, as one species and for the relevance of a spiritual message to all men, regardless of their historical or spatial relationship to the Hebraic, Greco-Roman and Euro-American traditions. And it supports the recognition that the entire sociocultural framework of human life—including the forms of the family, the organization of the community and the technique of survival, travel and com-

---

[4] It is relevant to note that today, when the idea of inevitable progress is introduced, as it has been by Sir JULIAN HUXLEY in his title essay in *The Humanist Frame* (New York, Harper, 1962), it now enters in a religious—although not in an articulately Christian—context, and it becomes a matter of faith instead of a matter of science. Congruently, Père TEILHARD DE CHARDIN, when he affirms the singleness of human existence as limited to this planet, although it may take eons to evolve and to reach a final conclusion, states his position, in *The Phenomenon of Man* (New York, Harper & Brothers, 1959), as a matter of scientific faith, admitting that the postulation of other forms of life in this and in other galaxies is scientifically equally plausible.

munication—are historically dependent on specific cultural conditions. So man may, through the civilizations that he builds, advance or regress or even threaten the existence of his own species.

Within this wider perspective on mankind, many of the barriers to the ecumenical movement crumble away. Great civilizations which arose outside the specific tradition within which the Judeo-Christian sequence came into being need not be equated with barbarism. The relative readiness of members of different races and different societies to assume the full burden of ministry need not be attributed to race or to some conception of "higher" or "lower" levels of civilization which itself suggests the natural superiority or inferiority of some groups of men to others. Change of all kinds can be recognized and accepted as inherent in the historical process through which men have become what they are and without which human society would not flower but would stagnate. Some particular period in the past need no longer be artificially deified into a period of virtue, stability and harmony with God's will. The written word can be seen as *one* historically developed form of recorded inspiration. And no one vehicle of communication—through script or oral communication, dramatic ritual, radio, television or communications satellite—need be treated as somehow more divinely inspired or blessed than any other. There need be no opposition between simple and "natural" ways of life—tilling the soil, planting the vineyard or shepherding the flock—and the fabrication of goods by machines, between walking and traveling by train or car or jet plane, between laboriously preparing a concordance of the Scriptures by hand and using a computer. Repudiation of the machine can be seen as the local response of men at a particular time and place when machines were first and with great difficulty being incorporated into the sociocultural life of the community. It can be regarded as one response to sociocultural dislocation, not as being due to any inherent opposition between the religiously blessed life and secular or satanic versions of life.

In earlier anthropological work, the delineation of concrete behaviors which were thought of as good and as evil by the members of particular cultures served as one means of stressing the contrast between different societies and cultures. This stress on concretely different views of good and evil often seemed to those who approached the problems of Christian ethics to promote a sterile relativism and to remove any scientific basis in the study of man for the recognition of universals. This interpretation of anthropological findings failed to take fully into account the interconnectedness of culture—a failure in which some anthropologists also shared. The statement that in a certain society, elders were permitted to choose their own death rather than endanger the survival of their grandchildren, and that their children were bound to assist them in this purpose, or the statement that in a particular society, marriage was enjoined with one kind of first cousin or, in special cases, was enjoined with a sibling, seemed, to some, to indicate the absence of any scientific basis for universal ethical restraints on murder or incest—or even the absence of any scientific basis for legal restraints.

The present position in anthropolgy emphasizes the universality of an ethical sense as part of man's inherent human capacities; and anthropologists agree with the biologists who have identified the role played in human evolution by the capacity to accept from trusted elders a standard of behavior.[5] Thus the natural order, scientifically explored, provides, as at present understood, no basis for the sterile relativism which so recently was seen (and residually is seen) as a scientifically based position in opposition to that taken in Christian ethics.

Exploration of the forms that man's imagination takes—even in the simplest primitive societies, untouched by contact with culture-transcending religion, suggests that there may be a biological basis in man, and in man alone, for the capacity to relate to the universe —which has been called the sense of wonder or the cosmological or cosmic sense.[6] This would involve recognition that biological

---

[5] C. H. Waddington: *The Ethical Animal,* New York, Atheneum, 1961.

[6] Margaret Mead: "Cultural Determinants of Behaviour," *Behaviour and Evolution:* Anne Roe and George G. Simpson, eds. New Haven, Yale University Press, 1958, pp. 480–503. Edith Cobb, "The Ecology of Imagination in Childhood," *Daedalus* (Summer, 1959), pp. 537–548.

evolution includes not only the extension, elaboration and specialization of biological capacities found in prehominid species, but that there may be specifically human, biological needs which are an intrinsic part of man's search for God. The need to make the perceived universe meaningful and coherent, to each individual person, to apprehend and in some measure re-create the universe may be likened to a need as biological as the need for oxygen, for water, for food and for rest—a need that is not denied in any human being without consequences.

The Transcendency of Christian Culture

Comparative anthropological studies of cultures in different parts of the world, at different levels of technological development, complex as well as primitive, have led to the recognition that no item of culture is carried in the genes. Each individual is dependent on learning to become a full human being—a person who speaks a language, shares with his fellows a view of other human beings, has acquired techniques for sustaining life and relates himself and all men to the universe. Once this is recognized, it is clear that no aspect of any culture is irrelevant to the Christian ideal of man in community with his fellowmen. Each facet is crucial—the relation between men and tools and machines, the development of political organizations within which men, with however much difficulty, live at peace with one another, the development of forms of communication which make it possible for those of like mind to share their vision of God in a world of accelerating change. And, to the extent that men are called upon to live in accordance with the Pauline definition, "we are members one of another" (Ephesians 4 : 25), no ground plan of the church militant can afford to ignore these findings.

Like all men, the man who dedicates himself to the Christian way of life has been reared in a particular society. Like all men, he has, in the course of his upbringing, become a human being, capable of understanding what he hears and sees and of conducting his life with others. But to the extent that the culture in which he has been reared is in some way lacking—is able to integrate only a few individuals within a common membership; is weak in the authority necessary for the maintenance of peace and order; is deficient in the production of food and goods and lacking in devices for sharing them equitably among its members; is clumsy in handling the growing child's perception of the world; or is deficient in the expression of the brotherhood of man—to this extent is his ability to lead a Christian life impaired. However diverse the requirements may be—from the ability to accept guidance in matters of ethical choice, the capacity to treat sex relations as a responsibility, the ability to read, the ability to learn foreign languages (often an unrecognized demand that churches make upon new converts), the ability to accept stewardship, to the ability to appreciate the finest points of the Christian ethical concept of a personal relationship to God—the requirements themselves, the individual's view of them and his ability to fulfill them depend on the culture within which he has been reared or which he has accepted as a learning individual, accepting full membership.

The history of Christianity has been a history of continual reinterpretation of the Old and New Testaments in terms of particular cultures and periods. Over and over again, the revelations of the Scriptures have been clothed and reshaped by the language and the imagery, the minutiae of the local social scene, the local forms of family, community and national social organization. The fate of Christian understanding has been a very different one, depending on the cultural context in which it is embedded. Very different aspects of belief have been emphasized and elaborated in cultures with strong patriarchal or monarchical institutions and in cultures with bilateral systems of family organization or more egalitarian, democratic institutions.

In the past, this diversity of forms has been used, quite appropriately, to stress the universality of the Christian message. It demonstrated that a message from a God of all men, speaking to all men, could cross every barrier of culture or society, could cross any language barrier and defy any frontier and could be embodied in the poetry and the artistic forms of any group of men. Cultures were diverse, but Christian culture could become universal. The preaching of the gospel in Japanese and Bantu, in Hawaiian and Gaelic, in Italian and Swahili, was in itself a tribute to its universality.

Historically, however, this emphasis on the transcendency of Christian culture has been compromised in several ways. It has been implicitly assumed, for example, that the language and imagery of Hebrew, Greek and Latin (and, later, English, German and French) are somehow closer to God's purpose than the languages and imagery of peoples who are not the descendants, direct or indirect, of the writers of the Old and New Testaments. From this it followed that members of other cultures could understand the Christian message only if their own basic imagery were altered. The demand for change has taken many forms—sometimes explicitly expressed and sometimes only implicit in some set of rules or expectations. So it is sometimes demanded that converts learn the languages of the seminaries and the languages in which commentaries have been written. Or it may be insisted that trousers for men and skirts for women are somehow more "Christian" than skirts for men and trousers for women, or that sex distinction in dress is essential to the Christian life or that a given number of meals a day—as well as food to sustain life—is intrinsic to God's purposes.

The anthropological approach introduces here a double consideration. As human behavior is always viewed in context, no detail of language or dress or political organization can be seen as intrinsic to a religion which explicitly states that its mission is to all men. Thus, anthropological analysis would support the effort to strip Christianity of culturally limiting elements in the language of worship, the form and the materials of the church building and the character of the church polity.

But the same approach leads anthropology also to recognize that Christianity is a historical movement, localized in time and space, historically cast in a certain mold, embodied in the imagery and the vision of a particular group of prophets and saints and brought to its present state as a culture through centuries in which its primary relationships have been with the cultures of Europe and the Near East, not the cultures of Asia or southern Africa, Australia or the Americas. A message of the depth and complexity of the Christian message can be communicated from one human being to another and from one generation to another only through the medium of a particular language, a particular set of social forms, a particular set of images. Therefore, in recognizing both that these are historically given and that the Christian message is applicable to all men, whatever language they speak, whatever historical tradition they may share, whatever their level of technical advancement may be, it is important also to recognize that a process of cultural transformation occurs as the message is received and transmitted in different cultures. Then the humanity conferred by the local culture becomes the foundation for a wider understanding of total Christian culture, as it has been enriched and elaborated, pruned and shaped by men of different cultures, all of whom share its great culture-transcending tradition.

An anthropological understanding of culture provides not only an appreciation of how members of each generation in a particular society are enculturated in their local language, community and nation, but also of the systematic interrelationships and interdependencies within larger cultural units—of which Christianity, among the other world religions, is one. Thus, the futile struggle to create a kind of historical situation in which all non-Christian cultures are equated, regardless of their level of civilization, is replaced by a recognition of Christianity as a culture that transcends local cultures, comparable in this respect to Buddhism or Islam or modern Communism—each of which also has developed a culture-transcending system which crosses the bounds of local cultures and can be learned by men of many different cultural backgrounds. The special nature of Christian truth and Christian revelation is not involved or compromised by such a recognition. Rather, Christianity is seen as a system which in some matters overlaps with other great religions and ideologies, but which is unique in its total configuration and which presents mutually exclusive choices to those who profess to be Christians instead of members of some other worldwide system.

The anthropological approach to the study of man has led to an understanding of man as becoming human within the culture in which he is reared and to the recognition that the purely human values of any one culture should not be elevated above those of any other. But it would also support the proposition that the Christian church itself represents a culture into which individuals may be born or which they may enter (or leave), the versions of which may have a more or less systematic relationship to one another at any historical period.

From this viewpoint, strain within the church occurs as the Christian community feels and responds to change within other parts of a constituent culture-change which may be expressed through technology, scientific knowledge, political organization or new conceptions of man's relationship to man. As the Christian church is almost never coextensive with the whole of the culture of any society within which it exists, there is inevitably a tension between changes in values in those parts of the culture which have a different focus—for example, technical or scientific innovation, taxation, trade unionism—and the desire for the conservation of values in the Christian tradition. Particularly in the modern world, as an accelerating consciousness of social change has led to a sharpening of ethical issues, this tension has increased and the positions taken by the various Christian churches have become less well articulated.

Seen from an anthropological viewpoint, the ecumenical movement can be interpreted as a way of dealing with those historical inconsistencies and discrepancies, as the attempt is made to arrive at a new community of understanding among churches with very different conceptions of their responsibilities in regard to the quality of the relationships of widely separated peoples, the mounting pressure of world population, the crucial necessity of developing new methods of conflict resolution and the care, protection and education of those who stand in need in the worldwide community.

In the early days of the Christian church, language—Latin in western Europe and Greek in eastern Europe—served as an integrating mechanism, drawing together a whole part of the Christian world. Today, the common effort to relate Christian theology and Christian ethics to the findings of science, the growth of technology, the changing size and form of political units and emerging ideas of social responsibility also can become a unifying mechanism. With such a focusing of attention at the higher level of the culture-transcendent Christian community, the kinds of problems which have been worked out in some Christian communities but not in others—concern about evolution, or machines, or supranational organizations or the welfare state—will be seen not as barriers, but as removable stumbling blocks. Furthermore, as we have come to understand the importance of social structure in permitting or preventing or promoting more inclusive and sensitive human relationships, it has been recognized that changes in the organization of relationships—such as changes in forms of association, in residential patterns, in the worker's relationship to his job, in the communication of contrasting forms of behavior associated with national, ethnic or class differences—can go far toward reconciling groups once in conflict. The comparative study of different cultural forms gives us access to a variety of forms of reconciliation and also a knowledge of destructive possibilities against which we must be watchful as we realize that any type of behavior which is found institutionalized in any human culture must be regarded as sufficiently human as to be capable of becoming actualized in any other culture.

Within the wider context it will be apparent that many controversies about the Christian role in determining the type of community which the larger society should choose and maintain are reconcilable. Differences among men which are essentially the products of social history—differences based on ancestry, rank, caste, class or race—will be recognized as irrelevant to the Christian view of man. (For the Christian member of a western society, looking at caste in Hindu society, this is an obvious conclusion.) Similarly, any exclusiveness of community which draws on such historical differences will be recognized as contrary to the Christian conception of man's relationship to man. There is no basis, other than the historical one represented in local cultures, for separation at worship, exclusion from the ministry or prohibitions on marriage or on any forms of social, political and economic equality because of membership in one physical stock rather than another.

Anthropological research can give no support to the belief that any particular form of division of labor, any one set of rules for fixing social status by age or sex or race, any inalienable attachment to the land is an embodiment of God's laws. Clearly, all such practices have changed through time and vary in different cultures; and in their different forms all have been looked upon as according with Christian principles. Ideas about the use of money, usury or interest, just payment and credit—all of which have, from time to time, become interwoven with the prohibitions and admonitions of Christian communities—are equally the products of social history, subject to change and open to examination, within a given context, for the extent to which they enable men, within that context, to come closer to God.

The refusal to make use of the possibilities of the modern world—the refusal to use technology, to fit a church with a loudspeaker, to permit an eye-graft that will preserve sight or a blood transfusion that may preserve life, the refusal to travel by plane or to use new materials for ritual garments—all these things, mere stumbling blocks as they may be, reduce the capacity of the Christian church to be a time-binding and a culture-transcending institution.

No single institution, as such, is more Christian than another. For those who are concerned with the problem of the Christian community and the congruence of institutions within Christian culture, it is necessary to raise the discussion to a higher level. We may then appropriately ask: At a given time and in a given place, within the sense of ethics and the economics of possibility, which kinds of institutions, organized in relationship to each other—international, national, local, concerned with work, with men's formal and informal relations and with the life of the family—best provide for the life of men together, through which men may become more human and better able to relate themselves to God?

New Areas of Integration

The technical-functional view of man is, in the eyes of some theologians, opposed to the personal-cultural view of man. However, it can be better understood as a response to new organizations in an emerging world society, with larger populations, larger units of organization, greater interchangeability of roles, higher rates of lateral and vertical mobility and far more inclusive systems of communication.

The close-knit relationship between parent and child, teacher and child and child in the church, which, even in the recent past, provided for an almost complete integration of what was taught, learned and experienced, has been altered by relationships with far greater diversity and spread. Marriages take place between individuals who differ profoundly in culture and belief. Schools are taught by teachers whose backgrounds and life are exceedingly diverse. The child's relationship to the church is only one of the multiple relationships to sources of authority and leadership.

In most parts of today's changing world there is a search for new kinds of integration of different aspects of life. In some of the most socially mobile parts of the world, as in the United States of America, it is the church which can provide new areas of integration as all members of the family may be part of the church's extended social milieu. At the same time, the newly recognized obligation of the church to play an active role in breaking down class, race and ethnic barriers gives special weight to the demand on the church to be receptive and inclusive, not to sacrifice this mission to the wider world in the interests of a narrower and superficially more spiritually comforting like-mindedness. And these two functions of the modern church—to provide a center of like-mindedness and to welcome and comfort the stranger within the community gates—are everywhere called into play as people move from primitive life to peasant life, from peasant life to urban life, from one region of a country to another and from nation to nation, sometimes willingly, as immigrants, and sometimes under pressure, as refugees.

Certain of the necessary adjustments will be made more easily if, instead of concentrating narrowly on the present, a deeper and broader time perspective is invoked. That is, we can enlarge our sense of what is possible to the extent that we look at questions of inclusiveness and exclusiveness (the breadth of communion which should be sought; the depth of the hold which the religious community, within the wider community, should have on the child) within the widest framework, placing the growth of Christianity within the perspective of the growth of all religions.

It is necessary to realize that throughout man's history there have been periods and occasions, even in very primitive communities, when sudden and intense inspirational emphases have resulted in attempts to form totalistic communities. In a community of this kind every detail of life is made subject to a particular religious rule. Over time some of these attempts have shrunk, fragmented and died; others have diffused and have been reabsorbed into the wider stream of life; and still others have become the foundation for what may be called a church which exists within and as part of a wide community.

Occurring particularly during periods of change and transition, the totalistic approach to the religious life—whether it takes the form of individual retreat into isolation, as in the case of the hermit, or that of the ascetic community, or that of the economically self-contained cult—is, in these circumstances, an almost predictable expression of renewed inspiration and of the struggle to achieve a more integrated approach to the universe. There is, of course, a difference in scale between the small cults that spring up by the thousand among primitive people in parts of the world which have been more recently penetrated, the religious orders that have been formed during periods of social disorganization or even chaos, the quietist cults that developed during the Reformation, the utopian communities that came into being in response to the ideas of the Enlightenment and the types of political integration that we have designated as "totalitarian." But in certain respects they are all similar in kind. Any facet of life can temporarily be regarded as having an overriding value which should take precedence over every other consideration in life and in terms of which the whole of life should be organized.

But significantly, in the long history of man, those religious and political philosophies have survived which have been capable of providing inspiration and leadership in a thousand diverse contexts—which have been meaningful to rich and poor, the possessors and the dispossessed and disinherited, the landowner and the landless, the healthy and the sick, the intelligent and the simple-minded, the intellectual and the craftsman.

It is understandable that in the world today there should be, within the Christian church, movements toward each of these two kinds of inclusiveness. It is understandable that there should be a movement toward withdrawal from the world into a totalistic way of life in which each detail of food and drink, each detail of work and worship, each detail of companionship and solitude, each thought that is allowed to pass through the brain is minutely regulated in terms of some special vision of a close, exclusive and all-exacting relationship to God. It is equally understandable that there should be a complementary struggle to widen the tenets of Christianity, guarding against the possibility that Christianity might become the religion of one race, one part of the world, one political or economic system, and strengthening the assurance that as the scientific and technological sectors of culture increase the number and kinds of contacts between all societies, the church will be able to speak to them all.

The recognition that total withdrawal of the faithful, on the one hand, and far-reaching spiritual participation in the intellectual heritage of the modern world, on the other, are both responses to the consciousness of change in the world and to the fact that each has a long history—sometimes productive, sometimes deadening—as a response to change, can do much to prevent an unnecessary cleavage. For, however different, these are related responses to change. There is no basis for arguing, for example, that those who advocate withdrawal into the religious life or into a total religious community must necessarily be the advocates of conservatism and obscurantism and that only those who stand for full Christian participation in the world today should be regarded as modern, contemporary-minded, future-orientated and intellectually and scientifically sophisticated.

It should be recognized, in fact, that this particular division between conservation and innovation, taken as a whole, represents only one of the many lines of tension between religious concentration and religious diffusion. Many other combinations are possible. Totalistic sects may well embrace modern technology. Religious orders may work concentratedly on modern biological research. Those who have put distance between themselves and mundane cares may do far the best work in restoring the physically handicapped through the most modern prosthetics.

The World Council of Churches can draw upon the widest possible range of Christian forms; among its members there are new cults, old orders, wise old churches and energetic revivified older religious communities. One of the functions of the Council may well be to prevent the occurrence of single lines of cleavage on the issue of the mission of the Christian church to the world and to reidentify the contributions which can be made by those who withdraw to work or to play with the contributions which are made by those whose work lies in the world, as these different groups may become in a wider sense the conscience of the Christian world.

In the Midst of Time

The contribution of anthropology lies principally in providing a longer time perspective and a wider context for the consideration of the problem of the Christian as person in community. By placing man in his long evolutionary history, anthropological research can help to correct the limited and limiting image of man as the user of simple agricultural tools who, when the machine loom and the steam engine were invented, was betrayed into worldliness and removed from the labor decreed by God; as the simple reader of the Bible whose piety has been corrupted by radio and television; as properly the inhabitant of the small, hierarchical community in which each person had a hereditary place, whose sense of right order has been corrupted and lost as a result of migration and urbanization; as the simple stargazer who saw God's perfection in the starry firmament and who was driven to doubt and disbelief by the new vision of the universe made possible by the telescope; as the believer who, identifying sumptuary laws and dietary practices and the eschewal of small pleasures with the will of God, is corrupted by a wider perspective on human morals. Anthropology can help us to recognize, instead, that all these have been—and are—temporary expressions of a deeper human ethic which, to be meaningful, must strive toward the universal.

This sense of perspective illumines and revises the images of historic man so that it is possible to appreciate man's tremendous struggle, in his dawning humanity, to make the world a place in which new generations of men and their children could live more safely and more fully, more wisely and more meaningfully. This in turn makes it possible to recognize that today's world, with its enormous, intercommunicating population, its burgeoning technology and its newly aroused consciousness and conscience, is not the evil and corrupt end of a historical epoch, but, rather, represents one stage on a long, long journey—a far longer journey than the majority of Christians have imagined.[7]

Each stage—each step—on this journey not only is marked by technical mastery over some aspect of the environment which man has accomplished by effort (the real meaning of "work"; for animals do not alter their environment, they merely live within it); it is also characterized by the widening of human horizons which accompanies technical change. Within this perspective, agriculture (a very late human invention) ceases to be the prototype of life on emergence from the Garden. Instead, we see a human creature, frail and almost defenseless against other creatures, equipped only with the capacity to know good and evil and the capacity to shape his environment—to invent tools and weapons, shelter and clothing, institutions and laws—as his special resources in the struggle for survival. By including the thousands of years before

[7] HUGH C. WHITE, JR., ed.: *Christians in a Technological Era,* New York, Seabury Press, 1964.

the invention of gardening (the simplest sowing and harvesting and keeping of seeds for another season) and herding (the simplest gathering in of animals and guarding their young), the whole of our perspective on more recent history alters. It becomes easier to plan the rise of town and urban settlements, when food which was planted and stored was sufficient to feed large numbers of people, and the beginnings of trade and communication, as men ventured across the land and down the rivers and even out of sight of land on the seas. And so it becomes easier also to visualize our life today as part of man's long history, presenting new complexities, but complexities that are no less open to comprehension and mastery than those that followed on earlier innovations.

In this larger context it is apparent that it is as human to invent and use a computer as it was to invent and use an abacus, and as human to invent and use an electric clock as it was to invent and follow the moving shadow of a sun clock. This opening up of the past allows us also to look forward to a future as far removed from the present as we today are removed from the time when men had as their only tool a chipped stone axe.

But this accomplishment—this ability to place ourselves in the midst of time—is dependent also on a willingness to revise our view of man, made in the image of God, to include an understanding of man as a temporally emerging, growing and changing being. It includes the incorporation into our perception of the Christ in all men, a recognition that it is through the very diversity of human culture that the universal in our humanness may be found. And this accomplishment becomes fully meaningful only as we recognize that man, struggling over and over again with the loss of innocence and today possessed of powers almost as dread as those refused by Christ in the wilderness, needs a greater and more vital spiritual vision, not a lesser one, than when men planted vineyards and gathered the grapes in a pastoral community two thousand years ago.

14

QUEST FOR THE "SUPERMAN"—MODERN MAN AND BIOLOGY

by RICHARD KAUFMANN (Germany)

From Conflict to Dialogue

NO other scientific discipline contains so many possibilities of conflict with Christian concepts as does modern biology. This is no accident. The classic sciences kept their distance from man and from psychosomatic phenomena. Astronomy, mechanics, mathematics, physics and the older forms of chemistry concentrated mainly on inorganic phenomena, that is, phenomena which are less complex; they seldom cross the frontier into the sphere of philosophy or theology.

In order to comprehend this fact, we must take another look at the other sciences. Neither the law of gravity nor the laws governing the atom are historical. There have always been atoms; and gravity has always existed. Although scientists today are cautiously speaking about a process of "the aging of matter" (which assumes that to a certain extent matter is also "alive"), they can nevertheless leave out of account the question of the divine origin of matter while they concentrate on their observations. In biology, on the other hand, everything was immediately situated within a historic-scientific sphere; and a new finality appeared, related to man. It started by recognizing natural "history" as a chain of developments in time, from the prehistoric animals to the molluscs, from reptiles to birds; but sooner or later it was bound to clash with the spiritual disciplines.

Where did life come from? When did it start? How did it start? That was one limitation. The other was the unavoidable question: where does man belong? Was he created by the hand of God who breathed into his nostrils (as Christian tradition would have it)? Or is he an animal like the others; even as a Christian man is he merely the end-product of an evolution which has taken millions of years? The last answer is the true one, said science. But the idea of man's being a descendent, brother or cousin of monkeys, lemurs and birds shocked the churches to the depths. Today, however, evolution is widely accepted in Christian circles. Teilhard de Chardin, for example, wrote in 1950, "Mankind appeared basically in the same way as all the other species" and he speaks as a matter of course of *"le group zoologique humain."* Nevertheless, this concept was resisted throughout the nineteenth century.

This problem, however, is still with us today, although in a different form. The intellectual position today is fixed; the scientist is objective, unprejudiced, free from presuppositions, thoroughly capable of defending himself. He occupies a position which is equal in status to that of the church, if not higher. The church and its faith are regarded as outdated; science, on the contrary, represents what is absolutely new—knowledge. In the meantime, a whole series of new questions have been added to the original one, whether man has evolved from the hominids (a group of mammals akin to monkeys). For instance: did originally a single couple (Adam and Eve) separate off from the animal kingdom and start a process of humanification (this theory is known scientifically as monogenesis)? Or did a whole group of hominids separate off in this way (polygenesis)? Today science rejects the theory of monogenesis, which would have retained something of the biblical tradition. A letter written by Cardinal Tisserant in 1964 to the Swiss biologist Johannes Hürzeler assures him that Rome has no intention for the time being of dogmatizing about this question of monogenesis or polygenesis. The Vatican Council leaves science an entirely free hand.

It is evident that the relationship between theology and biology has become more objective during the last eighty years, and this seems to be true of all confessions. Not only has the church abandoned its former attitude of superiority (and sometimes of irony) in order to try to enter into a dialogue with science; some biologists today seem to be more open to theological arguments. When asked at what time in history man had appeared, Hürzeler declared it was the task of another discipline to define the critical moment when consciousness broke through in the process of evolution. This belonged to the sphere of religious debate; he would confine himself to the material realm.

Today the idea is gaining ground that those limits—even if they cannot be exactly defined—must be fixed to some extent. This idea is not entirely new. Already in 1880 Thomas Huxley spoke quite clearly about the scope of natural science and summed up his views in a phrase which even today has lost none of its force:

> I have often wished that the expression *"applied science"* had never been invented. For it is an attempt to persuade us to believe that there is a kind of science which is applicable, or of practical use, which can be studied quite independently of another kind of science which has no practical use and is called *"pure science."* But what is generally called "applied science" is in reality only the application of pure science to a certain group of problems. . . .

This phrase is still extremely apt today. In the meantime biology has become one of the most important of the natural sciences and has set up an impressive apparatus which is universal, speaks an international language and obtains more and more Nobel Prizes and other awards. It has also created a number of smaller subdivisions, the meaning of which is no longer clear to the layman. To the older forms of biology and the study of behavior have been added biochemistry, biogenetics, virology, human genetics (and more recently embryology) and even the fields of molecular biology, population-genetics and quantum biology. A highly specialized team of scientists is engaged consistently and purposefully in research on life. Every year the results of some 50,000 experiments are recorded, all of which have not only to be planned and carried out, but also understood, evaluated and classified, and coordinated with knowledge previously acquired. Knowledge does not grow arithmetically, by adding one fact to another; it grows geometrically. Our knowledge is multiplied from decade to decade. The progress in knowledge during the last twenty years has been breathtaking; but what we shall come to know during the next twenty years is quite unimaginable. Together with their complex activity, biologists now claim a new position in society (such as has already been granted to nuclear physicists). They are also beginning to change man's traditional *Weltbild.* It is an attempt to build a bridge between what were formerly thought of as two coexistent worlds, the *organic* and *inorganic.* If this attempt were one day to succeed, then creation—the origin of life on earth—would be taken out of the realm of divine mystery and brought down to the level of an ordinary, everyday event. In that case (since all scientific research is based on the criterion that it must be possible to repeat the same experiment under the same conditions in all the laboratories in the world) "life" would be a process the control of which would henceforth be in the hands of man.

This idea may be shattering to the naïve Christian. The legitimate task of science, however, which since Galileo has been to explain the inexplicable and to measure the immeasurable, cannot be questioned. Science has a *"right to research."* If that is denied, science is no longer science. Another question, however, which is fully justified, is whether the scientists who have the intellectual knowledge to enable them to stimulate the production of life will also have the necessary ethical qualities to cope with the consequences. These doubts are strengthend by the fact that Thomas Huxley, the father of modern biology, emphatically insisted that there is no difference between applied science and pure science. This statement is of course true in both ways: if applied science is only a branch of pure science, then the findings of pure scientific research will certainly be "applicable," that is, they will be applied.

An example from another branch of science shows how, within the relatively short period of seven years, the "pure" discovery made by Hahn, Meitner and Strassmann that it is possible to split the atom was directly "applied" to the production of the atom bombs dropped on Hiroshima and Nagasaki.

However, the last word has by no means been spoken on this point. It is not yet certain whether biologists, despite their highly concentrated efforts (generously supported by the taxpayer) will ever succeed in achieving the final step and creating life. But during the next twenty years they will probably succeed in doing something else, the consequences of which (although less important ideologically) may cause even more confusion in their practical application.

Dynamism of the Cell Structure

Recognition of the fact that men, animals and plants are the outcome of an evolution which has taken millions of years has naturally focused attention on the key-process in selection which is the determining factor in evolution: heredity. Exactly a century ago the Augustinian Abbot Gregor Mendel explained his "Mendelian laws" in a lecture at Brünn, showing mathematically what happens when two parents with slight deviations in their genotypes produce children. This was the first attempt to bring order into the microcosmic realm of heredity. What the actual processes were, however, no one at that time knew. The conditions for this kind of research were still so bad that Mendel's important discoveries were forgotten for thirty-five years, and only rediscovered at the turn of the twentieth century. By that time cytology (cell-research) had advanced far enough to be able to explain some of the processes in conception and heredity. Science had discovered the chromosomes in the cells, but could not yet explain how nature could manage with only 46 chromosomes (until 1956 they were believed to be 48) when there are 40,000 hereditary characteristics in the human individual. It was only after science had gone much further in microcosmic research (by another forty degrees of intensity) that these questions could be answered—when the giant molecules were discovered which form the cells of every living creature.

How these discoveries were made can be only outlined here. The most important studies were those made on those strange phenomena which already before the turn of the century physicians called "viruses," also identified as "toxins" because they were assumed to be toxic and contagious. But nothing more was known about their nature. During the first quarter of the twentieth century "filter-passer" viruses were discovered. Finally an important proof was made with the discovery of the tobacco-mosaic-virus, a border case (as it were) of life; this is a form of life which can appear in crystalline form (that is, as an inorganic substance) but which, when in contact with living cells, can multiply itself by using the cell-ferments, and then behaves as if it were alive. Virology and molecular biology (by devious processes revealing as much fantasy as modern art) have now led to a completely new understanding of the dynamic power within the cell. This smallest unit of life now presents itself as a completely self-sufficient production machine, a factory (so to speak) containing everything necessary for production: (1) a technical head which regulates the "production machinery" and tells it what to produce from the available nutritive substances (energy or forms of albumen which are necessary for the construction of cells); (2) messengers which transmit and sort out orders; (3) catalysts or ferments which stimulate certain processes in the cell without undergoing any change themselves. This smallest living structure appears as a complete, self-sufficient sphere of action which takes its orders from a single "archive"; the latter must remain intact if the cell is to live. The "archive" consists of a giant molecule called DNA (Desoxy-Ribo Nuclein-Acid). Orders are given by a kind of Morse code contained in the DNA. Certain orders which are filed in the DNA may be blocked for a while and then released when needed. The cell has a good capacity for adapting itself to different environmental conditions; in fact it defends its life at any price.

The virus, the extreme border cases of life, may play the role of a wolf among the sheep. Through a process which in the old inorganic chemistry would have been called "affinity," it seeks out the cells which are useful to it, forces its own DNA into the production machine and upsets the control-system, monopolizing for its own purpose the enzymes or ferments which the cell had produced for its own life. It superimposes its own technical direction, so to speak. The products which result no longer have anything in common with the original aims of the cell; they help to produce fresh viruses instead. This is particularly evident in the case of a group of viruses called bacteriophagi (bacillus eaters). These bacteriophagi succeed in injecting their own DNA into a bacillus (leaving their empty protein sheath behind); after a time during which apparently nothing happens, the so-called "eclipse," the bacillus bursts open and a whole number of new bacteriophagi, each one covered with a protein sheath ready to start the game all over again with a new host, appear. During the "eclipse" the intruder had been exploiting the host-cell for his own benefit. The amazing thing is that these new viruses have no enzymes or ferments of their own. They have to look for other cells the ferments of which they can exploit for their own use. Another amazing thing is that these viruses not only succeed in producing protein (with the aid of the host-cell), but even impart their own characteristics to that protein. Here we have an excellent example of what we call heredity.

In fact, it seems as if genes and viruses are, if not identical, at any rate very closely related. Their close relationship is proved by their capacity to modify cells, and also by the fact that they are not actually alive but, as molecular particles, need a cell in order to assume the appearance of life. The word "gene" was introduced in 1909 by the Danish biologist Johannsen. It denotes "that part of a whole hereditary disposition which determines the inherited characteristics." The sum of all the genes constitutes the genotype. After what has been said, it is easy to guess where to look for the gene: in the nucleus of the parents' reproductive organs, and there in those colored bodies which already at the turn of the century were called "chromosomes" because of their color. By a process now known to every schoolboy as *meiosis,* these chromosomes in the embryo-cells divide up so that each parent-cell contains only half the number. It is only when conception takes place that the divided cell-nuclei complete the normal number of chromosomes. In the new cell the control by the genes has a twofold consequence: after each division the gene controls the structure of the new cell, and in the resulting cell-agglomeration it serves as a differential organ of control. It ensures the formation of cells of different kinds which appear more clearly after each division. A living creature emerges from this shapeless agglomeration of cells, and develops as it grows: limbs take shape, epidermic, nervous and osseous cells form, color-patterns are fixed, organs appear and develop their characteristics (often including the organic weaknesses of the parents). When this development is complete (which for the human being takes nine months in the mother's womb and many times as long afterwards) there is the finished creature—a mixture of its parents' characteristics, often modified by some (recessive) genes of the grandparents or of some unknown ancestor.

Logically this process would lead to a rigid repetition of the same fixed pattern. All children would inevitably be a sort of cross section of the characteristics of their ancestors. For a long time, however, we have known that this is not so. There is always some variation, some arbitrary innovation, which has nothing to do with the previous generation. These are called "mutations" and are explained by the fact that somewhere in the hereditary disposition the control-pattern of a gene (or group of genes) has been upset. A change has occurred in the sequence of the four basic genes inside the DNA-molecule, which forms the actual code determining the inherited characteristics. The result is a new pattern which in turn becomes hereditary. In extreme cases this mutation may render the new creature unfit for life (lethal mutation); in others the new creature may live, but with certain deformities. So we speak of hereditary deformities or congenital diseases; these may take the form of mental diseases (schizophrenia, feeble-mindedness) or nervous diseases (Huntington's chorea or St. Vitus' dance), of physical defects (congenital hip-weakness or muscle-dystrophy) or merely a tendency to certain defects or weaknesses. This is probably the case with diabetes and tuberculosis.

The Prospect of Biological Salvation

It must be made clear at the outset that none of the hereditary processes is subject to an absolute law like that of gravity or to the laws governing a magnetic field. And there is a reason for this. According to the thinking of Teilhard de Chardin, there are in this world not one, but three "infinites"—the infinitely small (the atom), the infinitely vast (the universe, the galaxies, the nebuli), and "the infinitely complex." That is what life is like; the possibilities of variation increase more and more as more variants come into the picture. In the case of very complex beings like man, the number of possible variants is already tremendous. That is why one cannot simply apply to man the results of experiments made with viruses or bacteria.

The biological research which concerns us here has three essential goals:

1. Research into harmful mutation and the possibility of preventing it. If they occurred frequently, certain deformities might constitute a real danger to society, or might even destroy it. If these harmful mutations occur in excessive numbers, they might one day make man's social existence impossible, as for instance would happen in a civilization where the majority of people could live only with the help of some technical aid or artificial limb. There are already signs of this tendency today.

2. Research in the field of diseases caused by viruses or bacteria, and attempts to combat them. Priority here would certainly be given to the fight against cancer, a disease which may well be caused by a group of viruses.

3. The theory that man in his traditional form, as part of a very slow evolutionary process, may already be outdated in his genotype and in urgent need of improvement, which cannot wait thousands of years but must be achieved within a few generations. In other

words: search for a Superman who would be better adapted to his own civilization than man is at present. This change could be obtained only by human interference with the embryoplasm.

The problem of hereditary diseases caused by mutations is certainly one of the most discussed and disputed questions today. We have seen what damage can be caused for a whole nation when a small minority tries to apply a merely materialistic "biological" theory of "pure genetics" for political and national purposes—without clearly defining for what purpose, and from what influences, this hereditary strain should be kept "pure." This "biological" ideology misled millions of people to such an extent that they lost all sense of humanity, all sense of responsibility and all their Christian convictions. As a result of this experience, the pendulum has now swung in the other direction: today we are shutting our eyes to the problem of hereditary disease. It continues to exist, however, and demands the attention of biologists, physicians, and theologians. It is not so much the simple question how to detect certain hereditary diseases, which were already recognized as such forty years ago, such as schizophrenia, feeble-mindedness or physical deformity. Much more complex is the problem whether in modern civilization (particularly in the industrial welfare state) there has not appeared a negative form of social selection, due to the fact that people with hereditary diseases are protected by doctors, by medical insurance and ultimately by the whole of society. The problem is still further complicated by the fact that in recent years genetic research has discovered that certain deformities or weaknesses which were hitherto regarded as hereditary defects are not due to mutations but are what biologists call "phenocopies"; in other words, nature has copied some aspects of a hereditary disease, but in reality the invalid could produce perfectly healthy children. If he is sterilized, his intimate life is damaged with serious legal and sociological consequences, without bringing any socio-medical improvement. Here a wide field for research still remains to be explored. The complex problem of "hereditary diseases," however, with its manifold implications (sterilization, euthanasia in cases of gross deformity, the question whether such decisions should be entrusted to the public authorities or whether special genetic centers should be set up) can no longer be kept out of public discussion. Theologians must also face this problem; it cannot be evaded.

The second question, the struggle against the causes of disease, looks like a purely medical one and might therefore seem to be outside the scope of a biological paper. But this view is a mistaken one. Already in the thirteenth century (under Frederic II) in Europe the physicians and the pharmacists were separated into two distinct professions. In the nineteenth century, pharmacists gradually allowed the pharmaceutical industry to take over the development and production of medicines. The pharmaceutical industry in its turn placed more and more importance upon biochemical and biological research. It also enters into commercial competition in accordance with the law of free enterprise. In this way, personal control has lost its influence in another very vital matter, and the consequences are already being felt. Obviously, as drugs become increasingly effective, their noxious by-effects also become stronger, and in an increasing number of cases some powerful drug has proved to be very dangerous for society. There are evidences of this in a variety of fields, not only in human medicine. Certain products for plants, called pesticides, may produce larger harvests; but they may have devastating by-effects on man's environment. Antibiotics are not merely "wonder-drugs"; they tend to produce dangerous side-effects which may cause permanent injury (as in the case of tetracyline where, as the result of early treatment, babies have been crippled and thus made useless, sociologically speaking, for the rest of their lives). There are other dangers in this craze for wonder-drugs in our time. Teratogenic and mutagenic damage occurs as a consequence of drugs being taken by pregnant women; the first type of drug causes deformities; the second type causes permanent mutation of the genotype.

One outstanding example of the tremendous implications of these drugs for modern life are the contraceptive drugs ("Enovid," anti-baby pills, and the like). The procedure is well-known, but the effects are still unforeseeable. These pills provide almost 100 per cent protection. But some of their side-effects must be mentioned. At present no doctor or biochemist can say with accuracy whether these hormones, taken regularly over many years, will not eventually cause malignant tumors (cancer of the womb). Moreover, the mechanical use of these pills leads to a completely new mental attitude toward sex. It degrades sexual intercourse into a material affair—on the same footing as other forms of business in our modern, commercialized society. (One buys sex, as one buys a dress, a car or some canned goods.) These are dangerous consequences which may have repercussions on the whole of society and which, on the rebound, influence every individual member of society (repression, guilt and anxiety-complexes). Statistics show that an enormous group of sexually mature women are withdrawn from the social economy of a nation and are put into the category of young girls or older women. Abandonment of all discipline by the younger generation, overindulgence in sex because no risk is involved, aversion, disgust and attitudes even more dangerous to society are the consequences that are to be feared. Here again, the question arises whether man, now intellectually able to control "natural" events, will be able also to control the far more difficult ethical effects.

This leads to the third question: is it wise or even necessary to interrupt the natural evolution of man by means of biochemical controls and to force him into a new phase of evolution? The question to be considered is not only whether this is possible at all. One must also ask what is the purpose of such interference, and if there is any proved necessity for it. There is no certain answer to any of these questions which would be scientifically satisfactory. This field is a kind of "No Man's Land" open to all sorts of ideological and emotional speculation. Here one can no longer speak of science, in the strict sense of the word, where results are recognized as valid only if they have been thoroughly tested and proved. Instead, we are flooded with ever-new biological "gospels of salvation" or gloomy predictions urging us to take urgent action. A tremendous superstition is developing under our very eyes, sponsored by certain specialists who may be masters in their own field, but who are complete amateurs in every other sphere. It is good that the churches are examining this ghost soberly in the light of the whole picture of man.

An English biologist suggests the biological regulation of whole nations by means of contraceptive hormones. After having temporarily sterilized all the women in a nation (or even a continent) by means of pills, only those women would again be made fertile who were likely to produce the "best" descendants. The venerable Nobel Prize winner Muller (U. S. A.) postulates enormous deep-freezes in which would be kept the sperms of those men who seem best fitted to assure a stronger human race.

Jean Rostand, a leading French biologist, declares man to be "the weakest link" in the chain of evolution, a "blunder in construction" who should be replaced by a Superman, scientifically engendered. According to Lederberg (another American Nobel Prize winner) the greatest danger for man lies in his incapacity to control the forces that he has released, thus destroying himself. Lederberg's solution is to create a new man with a superbrain who would be able to think things out better, thanks to his greater intellectual capacities. This reminds one of the technical research in the field of computer-construction. His American colleague Melvin Calvin (also a Nobel Prize winner) speculates about the possibility of increasing the number of cerebral cells to the tenth degree. Roger and Colette Vendrely foresee a possibility of the "synthesis of living matter." According to them, this new matter too would be submitted "to the strict order of unchangeable plans," that is, the artificial creature would continue to procreate according to the old system of cellular division and the DNA-register.

The biologist Weitzel (of Tübingen, Germany) calls for a campaign to "abolish all diseases" and explains that his aim is "to discover effective forms of therapy for every disease within a few decades"—as if "disease" were a static concept and not a complex psychosomatic process which is different in every individual instance. He is the author of the striking statement: "The declared aim of natural science is precisely to create a world with less suffering," whereby he reduces even the concept of "suffering" to a quantity. Another British biologist, Sir Julian Huxley, strongly supports such efforts and advocates that the man of the future may feel "happiness" by means of electric currents which will stimulate sections of the brain. The emphasis is placed on making people "happy." The claims of the new science of biology were never expressed more clearly than by W. M. Stanley at the 1955 conference of Nobel Prize winners held at Lindau: "This development might eventually place the embryoplasm of the world in the hands of the chemist, and thus the power might be transferred from the nuclear physicist to the chemist." This statement unconsciously reveals the struggle for power and status between the nuclear physicists and the biochemists.

Sociologically it is interesting to note that a kind of trauma, an inferiority complex, has developed in biologists and biochemists, which drives them to make increasingly audacious statements. Biology, being the youngest of the major sciences, has not been able to establish a professional code that would safeguard their professional status (as that of the medical profession, which has been built up over thousands of years, is safeguarded). In biology there is as yet no etiquette as to what should be said in public, and what would better be left unsaid.

Side by side with the sociological (and psychological) findings of a science, which today already concentrates considerable power in its institutes and laboratories, arises the anxious question, Which of these suggestions is really practicable? The answer, "Certainly not all of them, and certainly not as some biologists believe," is not adequate. Admittedly many scientists oppose these utopias. The development of the atom bomb has made many of our contemporaries suspicious, and this leads us back to the questions that we mentioned before: Even if these suggestions are practicable, what is their purpose, and why should we necessarily carry them out?

Overlooking Humanness

The purpose of these biological experiments is to produce a superior type of human being—but it is extremely uncertain whether they would prove successful. To be sure, we shall have to take steps to counteract what is called the "negative effect of science" (that is, the deterioration in the genotype owing to the survival of the "unfit"). But in an age when technology is constantly changing, it is impossible to predict anything about future generations. Man will always have to adapt himself to his own technology, and this adaptation will cause suffering. The attempt by means of genetic control to create a new type of man, who would be better adapted to the technological age of the future, is as difficult as the attempt to hit an aeroplane with an anti-aircraft gun, only far more so. In the case of anti-aircraft defense there are only a few possibilities of either hitting or missing. In the case of human adaptation, the possibilities of variation are infinite. So far nobody has mentioned the simpler solution—namely, to adapt technology better to the spiritual and intellectual development of mankind. But it is this simpler solution which will certainly have to be adopted, and this will mean rethinking many aspects of the problem. It may also be permissible to draw attention to the pure mathematical fact that man (regarded as a logical system) cannot adequately define himself. This supports the fact that genetic regulation of the "biogenotype" for technical purposes is not only unethical; ultimately it is bound to prove abortive.

The question about the necessity for carrying out these suggestions must be understood psychologically. Man will always feel the need for "necessities" without which he cannot live. Yet the greatest lesson of these past distressing years has been that there are no absolute values in this field. The thinking of many biologists today expresses a philosophy of "well-being," a longing for immanent "happiness" and "security," on the altar of which other values are to be unconditionally sacrificed. In creating a new world controlled by biology, the consumer-mentality has far more influence than ethical considerations or personal moral decisions. Admittedly it has been characteristic of all utopias (ever since Plato's *Republic*) to be preoccupied with "the happiness of the greatest number" and to be willing to pay the price in the form of a little inconvenience. That is why utopias remain utopias, that is, patterns, warnings, attempts at orientation. But today the biologists want to make their utopia a reality, and are already beginning to impose their concepts with gentle force.

How shortsighted much of their thinking is, becomes clear when we look at some examples. There are the biological contraceptives which can be bought on the market and which are being used by millions of women—not in the continents where the population-explosion really presents a problem, but in civilized countries where the birthrate is already low. What will happen when these contraceptives are used on a worldwide scale, under the auspices of a biological Master-Plan? It is only the consequences of sexuality that will be removed, not sexuality itself, the control of which has always been part of man's ethical achievement, part of his humanness. Age-old, necessary taboos without which no human society could prosper will slowly disappear, because they can be dispensed with. But with them man's moral stamina will also disappear. There will no longer be any need for that "personal asceticism," which was formerly the basis of western civilization. Yet, at the same time, by controlling the hormones of the masses, the biologists propose the production of "a new and better human race." The truth is more depressing: the biological cybernetic expert no longer regards other people as his fellowmen but as genetic strains of certain viruses or bacteria which can be enlarged or reduced at will on an artificial form of nutrition.

The anxious question whether "man can adapt himself to his own technology" betrays the same uncertainty in thinking. The argument is quite transparent; technology will conquer the whole world. Since it is rational, it will create an optimal, uniform, worldwide technology which in turn will need a special type of "technician" to be produced in advance through genetic control or manipulation. Variety will disappear; that is another part of man's nature that must be sacrificed on the altar of the machine. What will be left is precisely *l'homme machiné*. This recalls the thinking of the eighteenth century. For it is there that the roots of this rationalism are to be found—not in the twentieth century. The exaggerated importance attributed to the intelligence quota, which biologists regard as one of the major factors in the development of the new type of man, fits in with this rationalistic thinking. Though admitting that the I.Q. is very helpful in measuring certain intellectual qualities, it must be remembered that man is not merely a computer. Man is not an intellectual being, but a moral one. This is another example of an arbitrary, naïve distortion of the meaning of life. Man no longer lives in order to discover the meaning of his existence; instead, he is to be forced into a crude "mold."

At the dawn of western scientific history, the astronomer Johann Kepler wrote his famous phrase, "The Creator gave man his reason so that he could perceive the marvellous order in nature and then use this perception as the basis for ordering his own condition." Some 350 years later the British mathematician and philosopher Bertrand Russell announced the contrary: "Away from human passion, away from the lamentable facts of nature, generations of men have slowly created an ordered universe where pure thought can dwell as in its natural home, and whither one at least of our nobler impulses can take refuge from the sad exile of the real world." Russell's view is probably typical of the radicals in modern biology today. They too dream of a man-made universe. Johann Kepler, on the other hand, regarded Nature as "a sublime game," and the scientist as a man who was privileged to perceive its rules: "First the Creator played, and then He taught Nature to play the game which He had played before it." But modern biology is trying to lay down its own rules for the sublime game. Perhaps this is why its methods break down in face of the "infinite complexity" and lead to illusion?

A very young science cannot cope psychologically with the wealth of insights that have poured into it for decades, because it has fixed its own methods in a static and biased form, and imagines that its own limited sphere is the whole world. This is certainly not true of all biologists. The great accomplishments of biology in our time are beyond dispute. But if critical thinking and direction from the realm of reason and faith are to influence these developments before it is too late, philosophers and theologians must understand more about modern biology—not only about its findings, but also about the methods, ways and impulses of this powerful science. For "only when the spirit hath learned to contemplate (*betrachten*) what God hath made," says Johann Kepler in his wisdom, "will it learn also to do what God hath commanded." The old meaning of *betrachten* includes the idea of becoming deeply absorbed in something, and learning about it. This is where the nonbiologists must share the guilt, because they trust the findings of the experts blindly and without justification.

15

THE CURATIVE COMMUNITY

by ERNA M. HOCH (Switzerland) [1]

MARTIN HEIDEGGER stresses repeatedly in *Sein und Zeit* [2] that what we commonly know as the average, the customary, the self-evident, may be exactly that which conceals the true nature of what we meet. It may be what makes things appear as what they essentially are not, while whatever is useless, defective or inappropriate, whatever is missing or lacking, whatever is experienced as irrelevant, redundant or obstructive is more likely to call attention to the structures of meaning that constitute a "world" than any smooth, unhindered functioning of that which we take for granted in its unobtrusiveness.

If we accept the biblical statement that man was created "in the image of God" (Genesis 1 : 27) and that, with all other creatures, he was found, on the sixth day of creation, "to be very good" (Genesis 1 : 31), we may well discover that it is not so much the individual human being, whatever his shortcomings and distortions,

---

[1] Circumstances have placed me in a position to view the problem of "man as a person in community" more or less from the outside. I have been living for eight years in cultural surroundings in India very different from those in which I was born and brought up; moving almost entirely among people of a non-Christian religion and temporarily withdrawn from the usual interactions between individual and society. I am also accustomed to work with mental patients, in other words, with those whose manner of thinking and behaving deviates from the commonly expected and accepted norms to the extent that they are often regarded as "alienated," as outcastes, or as human waste and wreckage.

[2] M. HEIDEGGER: *Sein und Zeit,* Niemeyer, Tübingen, 1957.

that is "useless," "irrelevant" or "defective," but that on the contrary, the kind of community to which he is expected to adapt does not take account of his true nature and needs. Psychiatrists, psychologists and even sociologists question the adequacy of concepts that take man's "adaptation" or "adjustment" to the society in which he lives as a criterion for "mental health" or "normalcy." A recent publication leaves the impression that the experts are at a loss to characterize "mental health" in a way that would hold good in every society at any phase of its development.[3]

Thus, while the close connection between mental illness and the norms and demands of society are recognized, a new understanding is also emerging of the responsibility and concern which the community should feel with regard to those who cannot find their optimum fulfillment within its framework. It finds expression in the demand that the old mental hospital system be replaced by "community care" for the mentally ill. At the same time, interest in what is called "social psychiatry" is booming, though, again, many experts might be at a loss to define how this "social psychiatry" differs from what has hitherto simply been called "psychiatry," that is, the art of diagnosing, classifying and healing diseases of the mind.

Furthermore, as soon as mental illness is no longer regarded as due to possession, or as hereditary, or as a merely physical disturbance of the brain-structure, of the hormones or some metabolic process, but as the result of a faulty interaction between man and community, we face the urgent necessity to re-examine what man really is, what community should be and do to help toward man's fullest development. We must also ask what philosophy and theology can contribute to the building of a valid foundation for a new science of man and society. Philosophers and theologians may have to revise their formulations in order to do justice to the newly emerging concepts derived from the study of the mentally ill.

---

[3] K. Soddy: "Identity" and "Mental Health and Value Systems, *Cross Cultural Studies in Mental Health,* Nos. 1 and 2, published by World Federation for Mental Health.

Psychiatric Views on Man and Community

In the past, though with variations according to different cultural settings, there have been people whose behavior set them apart from the customary norms of their time and place, and whose condition was usually attributed to possession by evil spirits, which conveniently played the role of the scapegoat. The question of deriving any views about man as a person in community from the problems of mental illness hardly arose. Lunacy was regarded as an irruption from a dimension outside the system of coordinates within which social life was supposed to take place. The social awareness of a dimension of this kind, however, created a legitimate sphere within which a mentally deranged person could move. Treatment consisted in some magic performance, some act of exorcism, which brought the person, thus contaminated and defiled by mysterious forces, back to the common human level and to his ordinary function in society. In certain periods of history, it went to the length of barring him completely from society; he was expelled or put to death on a charge of witchcraft.

In India one still encounters "primitive" beliefs in possession by evil spirits and the corresponding healing practices, which are not so unreasonable, fantastic and cruel as one might imagine. They even lend themselves to quite "scientific" interpretation in the light of more recent psychiatric thought and they are certainly based on some vague though fundamental insight. Those who established these practices were forced to express them in terms that could be understood and accepted by their contemporaries.

This need to speak the language of one's time has determined psychiatric thinking to a great extent. As man took to investigating, measuring, analyzing and controlling his material surroundings, it became only natural that mental disease too should be regarded as a consequence of certain derangements in the physical sphere. We find the beginnings of a "science" of this kind not only in the writings of the old Greek physicians, but in the ancient medical systems of the East. During the Middle Ages, however, these views were mostly forgotten in Europe. When later on theories about "vapours," "miasms," "humours" as causes of mental illness began to be formulated, they went little further in defining the responsibility of man and the community than those evolved by people who had believed in possession by ghosts. Therapeutically, such physical theories led to certain new practices which nowadays one would regard as almost as cruel as the old rituals of exorcism: flagellation, being burned as a witch, expulsion from the community were replaced by bleeding, purging, being turned in a rotation cage, sudden showers of icy water, branding and other painful practices.

That the insane are not entirely indifferent to their surroundings, that a pleasant environment, human concern, even encouragement to engage in some work can do more to reclaim them than all these drastic cures or than mere "custody" in conditions hardly worthy of human beings, was only gradually discovered. "Moral treatment," a term coined by the great French pioneer, Philippe Pinel, in 1801, then became the fashion, and the mental hospital atmosphere gradually began to change.

Till then, care for the mentally sick in asylums and hospitals can hardly be said to have sprung from a spirit of Christian charity, but rather from a fear that the presence of lunatics in society might be in some way contaminating and at least embarrassing; and the mentally ill person himself became a kind of scapegoat.

The more humane approach, which recognized in "lunatics" human beings with a need for recognition, understanding and sympathy, enabled the physicians who dealt with them to collect valuable information, on which further therapeutic advances could be based. At the same time, medical science began to discover more and more connections between physical disturbances and mental derangement. The first concepts that could be called scientific in the modern sense took the brain and the nervous system as the substratum of mental activity and tried to establish correlations between anatomically or functionally disturbed processes of brain activity with symptoms of mental illness. Later, mental deviations were attributed to changes in the body fluids and the hormonal secretions.

But even Sigmund Freud, with his discovery of the role of the "unconscious," could still maintain, right up to his later years, that the only two facts really known about the human psyche are its physical organ and scene, the brain or nervous system, and a person's conscious acts. His theory represents the human soul as a lifeless apparatus, combining various parts and functions, something in which one could localize different levels and layers, as in a spatially well-defined structure. His "unconscious" was a kind of dark cellar below the house of the conscious mind; his "libido" resembles the driving power of a machine; such terms as "projection," "transference," "repression," "complex" can easily be recognized as borrowed from the natural sciences.

Though man was thus viewed as being determined in his thinking, feeling and acting by a kind of "psychic apparatus" that functioned according to exact inherent laws, it was admitted that the inhibitions, conflicts and complexes by which the functioning of this machinery could be disturbed had their origin in the social environment, in particular in early childhood and the relationships with significant figures—above all, the parents and siblings.

Mental illness and emotional distortion ceased to be something that "just happened," due to some mysterious causes, and it became possible to discern the same subtle influences and processes behind normal everyday behavior, as well as in the bewildering labyrinth of dream-life and the confusion and extravagance of the insane.

Though Freud's formulations fell short of his achievements as a therapist, they had the power to inspire new approaches even in the treatment of delinquents. (See, for instance, the work of August Aichhorn.)[4] Society began to recognize that it had some responsibility for its rebels and outcastes.

Some of his followers later demonstrated that the almost obsessive importance of sex in Freud's psychoanalytical system was determined by the prudish moralism of the particular setting—Vienna at the turn of the nineteenth to twentieth century—from

---

[4] AUGUST AICHHORN: *Verwahrloste Jugend,* 4 Aufl., Huber, Bern, 1957 (English title, *Wayward Youth*).

which his patients came. But the essential point was that every society has both its accepted values and its interdictions, its "taboos" or, in other words, a particular pattern of revealing and concealing, to which its members are expected to conform. It was Alfred Adler who demonstrated that the area of conflicts, between an individual's own need for fulfillment and the necessity to follow the demands of the group from which he expects security, livelihood and companionship, need not necessarily be sex, but may just as well be the need for "power," with all its problems of social rivalry and competition.

In his "superego," Freud had visualized some kind of moral authority, a censor and judge. This superego, however, mainly had the function of opposing the "id," of balancing man's animal nature with his social functions and higher aspirations. It was regarded more as a derivative of the moral standards prevailing in society and less as an individual monitor that could have called man to anything beyond "social adaptation."

Freud's dualistic approach: man as a more or less calculable and predictable psychic apparatus, driven by instincts and based on physical mechanisms, on the one hand, and his environment, "the outside world" with its conditioning, molding, limiting and obstructing influences on the other, seems to have necessitated the fixing of a firm ceiling between these "realities" and any supreme power that might have transcended both: the inner and the outer world, the physical and the mental, the individual and the community.

Among Freud's associates, C. G. Jung was the first to be profoundly disturbed by this limitation in his master's formulations. As his recently published autobiography [5] shows, even more clearly than the works that appeared in his lifetime, he had a lonely struggle, which took him through a deep mystic experience, and which forced him into breaking the bonds of what was conventionally regarded as "respectable science," and to sense that ultimately,

---

[5] C. G. JUNG: *Erinnerungen, Traüme und Gedanken von C. G. Jung*, Aniele Jaffe, ed., Rascher, Zürich, 1962. (English edition: Collins, London, 1963.)

there can be only the oneness of the "Self," in which all contradictions are solved, all opposites united; in which there is neither a "below and above," nor an "inside and outside," no "black and white," no "good and evil." This, in contrast to Freud's "secular" system, called for the inclusion of the divine, or, as Jung himself prefers to call it, "the numinous." Freud's teachings could simply be ignored or refused by the Christian theologian as belonging to a level that did not really concern him, but Jung's formulations contained an alarming challenge (for example, in *Antwort auf Hiob* [6] and the autobiography); and they provoked indignation and controversy among theologians.

Though we may say that it is not for a psychiatrist to dabble in theology, we must give Jung credit for having done his utmost to clothe in comprehensible language, often that of myth and allegory, experiences and insights that approached a quite different level of reality, for which forms and formulations can never be an adequate expression. We are inclined to seek the truth of Jung's thought in these very formulations, which he would probably have regarded only as "emergency solutions" for the purpose of communicating what ultimately eludes all definition and structure. An Indian psychotherapist, A. U. Vasavada,[7] who is thoroughly acquainted not only with Indian philosophy, but with Jung's work, believes that Jung's merit is in having had the courage to dissolve concepts and formulations, to approach the eternal realm of the unmanifested, the unchangeable, the unstructured, which plays so enormous a role in eastern thought. It was not what Jung had *said,* but what he dared to leave *unsaid* or merely hinted at as a mystery that brought him closer to truth than any of his predecessors in this field.

It is clear that an approach of this kind, in search of an ultimate, inward reality, would attach little positive importance to the social influences to which a person is exposed. The stress is on inward

---

[6] C. G. JUNG: *Antwort auf Hiob,* Rascher, Zürich, 1952.

[7] A. U. VASAVADA: Several unpublished essays on C. G. Jung and his work and one publication in Hindi, "C. G. Jung ka vislesanatmaka manovignan," Chowkambha Vidya Bhavan, Varanasi, 1963.

realization of the self, which transcends all mere social adaptations. The "persona," the mask through which we usually communicate with our environment, is seen as a precarious defense which can petrify man and cut him off from the stream of life. The circumstances of outward life are merely the raw material from which we have to distill the "elixir of life," the dust which we have to transform into the incorruptible gold of wisdom. Communication with the inward forces, with the so-called "collective unconscious," the treasure house of human experience at all times and in all ages, which may present itself in the form of the "archetypal" figures, is held to be more important and "real" than the daily interactions with people in the actual surroundings. Still, the problems of social involvement are taken as a welcome stimulus and starting point in the search for the self. The "outward" may appear first, and lead the way toward recognizing inner reality, and the inward truth, arrived at perhaps through dreams or an intuitive process, will gradually bear fruit also in the "outward." Both "inward" and "outward," however, are just different aspects of the one fundamental Reality.

One should add that Jung himself saw his theories and the therapeutic methods based on them as more applicable to the second half of life than for youth. In the same way as the traditional Hindu system of the four "asramas" recognizes the need for contact with the material world and human society in all its forms, at a first stage of "pravritti" (rolling, moving on, activity, progress, exposing onself), before the process of turning inward, the phase of "nivritti" (nonrevolving, cessation, abstention) can profitably begin, Jung affirms that the stage at which we take this material and social world for the real one and in which we have to shape and harden ourselves into a consistent "persona" by friction and interaction with it, is a preliminary necessity. Ultimately, however, the available forces have to be withdrawn from these outward forms, from obsession with material prosperity and success. Jung senses the danger of seeking security in firm structures, in that which is generally recognized and approved.

Though Jung's analytical psychology has contributed little toward the solution of social problems or toward defining the place of man in community, it has opened the field of psychiatry and psychology to a recognition and appreciation of eternal forces that go beyond a mere mechanistic functioning of a psychic apparatus and its interactions with a conventionally established social group. Community may serve as a kind of "matrix" that holds and nourishes the individual during his first stages of growth; but if, at a given point, its hold cannot be shaken off, it may block the way toward individuation and may suffocate the "self."

Modern Existential Thought

This ambiguous aspect of community, as a supporting and nourishing mother and as destructive, devouring monster, emerges even more clearly in modern existentialist thought, in particular in the work of Martin Heidegger, who has provided a powerful stimulus for a new orientation in psychiatry and psychotherapy.

Limitations of space and of the author's capacity preclude any exposition here of the teachings of *Daseinsanalytik* [8] and their application to psychiatry and psychotherapy. We can only indicate what Heidegger's philosophical thought implies for the relationship between man and community.[9]

But perhaps we may not even speak of a "relationship," in the sense of something to be established between two separate, closed entities. For Heidegger and his pupils, man can never be understood as an apparatus primarily enclosed in himself and only transcending his limits in a secondary approach to his environment. Man, on the contrary, exists primarily and originally "outside himself," "in-the-world." He is his relationships with the things, creatures and fellow human beings that come within the sphere of his

---

[8] "Dasein" is difficult to translate. It means, literally, "being there." This implies that "being" cannot be thought of as an abstract concept, but that at any given moment it has its particular "there." At the same time, however, "being there" constitutes a world, a sphere of light, within which all other creatures and things can find their place or "there."

[9] M. Boss: *Psychoanalysis and Daseinanalysis,* Basic Books, Inc., New York and London, 1963.

existence. This sphere, in its turn, is to be understood as man's openness to the world, his power of illuminating and bringing into its very being that which he encounters. This again presupposes an immediate and primary awareness of "being-ness" [10] as such.

Based on this primary awareness, human existence is capable of "disclosing the world," of understanding and elucidating things as they are.

This "being-in-the-world" as the primary awareness or the lighting of Being-ness, exists only as all the different concrete modes of man's behaviour in his world and as his relating to the things and fellow men whom he encounters. In other words, the very essence, meaning and content of every single concrete human relation to a particular being is the disclosure of this particular being.[11]

According to his mood at any given moment, man will disclose "quite different qualities and meaningful connections of the things he perceives in these respective moods. . . . All particular beings 'need' the luminating nature of man in order to be. . . . However, as things cannot be without man, man cannot exist as what he is without that which he encounters." [12] Above all, "Dasein" understands itself through its encounter with particular beings; it "always falls prey at first to the particular beings it encounters . . . losing itself, so to speak, to them." In particular, instead of accepting and appropriating all his life possibilities to be a free, authentic self of his own, he risks being caught "in the narrowed-down mentality of an anonymous, inauthentic 'everybody.' " [13]

From this possibility of misunderstanding and failing to distinguish itself from somebody else and through something else, "Dasein" can be released.[14] At such moments of crisis, during which man may have to pass through extreme darkness and intensive

[10] In India, I have found it useful to avoid the ugly translation of "Sein" or, as Heidegger prefers, "Seyn," as "Being-ness" or "Be-ness," and to use instead the comprehensive Sanskrit term "satta," "the possibility or potential of being," or even "Mahasatta," "the great or supreme potential or source of all being."

[11] Boss: *op. cit.*, p. 40.

[12] *Ibid.:* p. 41.

[13] *Ibid.:* p. 47.

[14] *Sein und Zeit, op. cit.*, p. 277.

anguish, he may hear the voice of his conscience calling him to his responsible task of being "servant and shepherd of Beingness." [15] In contrast to other, more nihilistic formulations of existentialist philosophy, Heidegger's teachings stress the concept of "care" as a central concern of human existence. In a manner which has much significance for the work of the psychotherapist or of anyone who helps human beings in their growth, he distinguishes between "intervening" care, which simply takes over the other person's actual, immediate load or problem, and "anticipating" care, which seeks to prepare him for responsibly assuming his own burden and to make him free for the "care" which his own existence implies.[16]

The call to a responsible assumption of this "care" is, however, frequently missed, ignored or misinterpreted. Escape from this central task of caring and of carrying out one's world-disclosing possibilities lies at the root of all guilt-feelings, no matter how trivial and how definitely attached to one particular life-situation they may appear to be. The problem that leads to mental disturbance may thus be one of remaining behind one's possibilities; but it can also be one of having been pushed or having ventured to climb beyond the possibilities that are open at a particular stage of maturation.

This concept of "care," of assuming responsibility, not only illuminates many problems of the mentally or emotionally disturbed, but gives the psychiatrist a well-grounded motivation for his activity: To help others, as a psychotherapist, to grow into their true being is only a particularly excellent and explicit way of fulfilling one's general human task.

In the existentialist view, to talk of "social psychiatry" or of man as a "social being" is a mere pleonasm. By its very essence, man's existence is one that can be thought of only as "being with," as moving in a "fellow world" of beings endowed with similar possibilities. This "fellow world" is the indispensable complement to man's own power of disclosing, understanding and caring. The

---

[15] M. HEIDEGGER: *Über den Humanismus,* Klosterman, Frankfurt (Main), 1947, p. 29.
[16] *Sein und Zeit, op. cit.,* p. 122.

question, however, is whether he allows himself to fall a prey to what he meets, whether he succumbs to the attraction of the indiscriminate masses, whether he is blinded into mistaking that which is "common," "usual," "self-evident" for the true essence, or whether he awakens to the insight that the "average" is more likely to conceal than to reveal and that if he wants to fulfill his existence, he has to rise to the authenticity of his own, unique existence.

This short summary may serve to show that for Heidegger and such writers as Boss, Ludwig Binswanger, and Victor Frankl, as well as for Jung, man's living in community is a double-sided situation: He needs his fellow world, as the nourishing, protecting "matrix" or even as the indispensable complement or condition for his very existence; but this very "matrix," in the same way as a too-concerned and pampering mother will prevent her child from growing into a man, may keep him back from realizing his individual self, from fulfilling his own responsibilities, and from following the call of his conscience, which reminds him of his task of being "the servant and shepherd of being-ness."

Though Heidegger carefully avoids any formulations that could be called "religious," in particular any reference to a personal God, one cannot help noticing how close some of his ideas come to certain passages in the New Testament. Equally, though he has, as far as I know, no close acquaintance with eastern philosophy, his line of thought can easily be reconciled with many of the concepts of ancient Hindu philosophy. But before attempting to show how, for myself, Heidegger's work has opened up new paths of understanding of the New Testament, and provided a promising approach in psychiatric work, we have to consider briefly some trends in present-day psychiatry, which seem to go in the reverse direction.

The work of Jung and of the existentialists brought the spiritual dimension back into medical psychology. But at the same time, a very strong psychiatric school developed which still seeks the causes of mental illness exclusively at the physical level. On the one hand, we find that certain diseases, which till recently were regarded as strictly "physical," can be understood as being due to emotional strain, as representing a "bearing out in the physical sphere" of an existential problem. On the other hand, the scientists in histological, biochemical and biophysical laboratories triumph over their discoveries which have brought them—as they think—very near, not only to explaining all psychic phenomena—thinking, emotions, individual character traits, and the like—in terms of molecular structures and subtle chemical and electrical processes, but even to being able to "create" life itself. They regard their fields as the "basic sciences," which are likely to discover "the foundations" of all human needs, abilities and strivings. They confidently expect that ultimately nothing will have to be left to the vague hypotheses of the philosopher or even of the psychologist, but that all will be sufficiently explained by concrete structures and processes that can be observed and reproduced in any well-equipped laboratory. Correspondingly, many psychiatrists rely for the treatment of mental disease and emotional trouble entirely on physical methods like electro-shock, narcosis by injections and gases, insulin-coma, sedatives and, above all, the host of modern tranquilizers and stimulants. The availability of all these chemical and physical aids greatly reassures not only many restless, depressed and anxious patients, but their doctors as well: It saves them the trouble of penetrating to the truly "fundamental" questions; it enables them to avoid responsibility for their own and the patient's true growth and to shift the burden onto those who invent and produce the wonder-drugs and magic gadgets. But unless some truly human concern is invested even in applying these therapeutic aids with discriminating wisdom, the result would appear to consist merely in resettling the patient in his social and personal rut from which he must risk being removed if he is to turn again into a "useful member of society." We need not ask what kind of society this may be and whether the patient's disturbances may not have concealed a legitimate conflict between simply "adapting" to this society and growing into his own, authentic existence. It would be too embarrassing a question, requiring one to revise one's own attitude and to give up many convenient "certainties" and immediately effective shortcuts.

Thus modern medical science, in particular what are wrongly designated as "basic sciences," assumes a strangely ambiguous character: Man has gained the power of disclosing the mysteries of living matter and of relieving human suffering and even of saving lives to a quite unprecedented degree. But the very ease with which the secrets of matter and energy can be illuminated by the human mind makes one forgetful of the fact that this power of illumination is in no way explained by the structures it discloses and that ultimately it must be drawing its light from a source that resists all scientific explanation.

The "scientific approach" is at best one of the many moods or modes in which man can open himself to the world; but it excludes and obscures many other possibilities. As "science" is now the fashionable, respectable and profitable avenue, man risks falling a prey to it just as blindly as he may succumb to the attraction of the anonymous mass. In either event, he is narrowed down rigidly to a small sector of his life possibilities and he contracts an enormous debt with regard to the unfolding and responsible assumption of his full and authentic existence.

Insights Gained Through Transcultural Psychiatric Experience in India

I do not know whether my skepticism with regard to the positive role of society and to the omnipotence of science would have developed to the same degree had I not spent the past eight years in India, a country whose culture—and with it the whole traditional social order—is undergoing rapid and profound transformation.

In any country sufficiently different from one's own land of origin, one naturally begins to question one's values: the customary, self-evident aspect of one's own background can suddenly no longer be taken for granted. There are, on the other hand, conditions and practices that strike the newcomer as strange, if not impossible, which are part of unquestioned, everyday life for the inhabitants of the host-country. Beyond this, however, as gradually I encountered some of these strange new influences—not least of all by the study and daily use of an Indian language—my thinking and experience underwent some more specifically Indian modifications or even revolutions.

It soon became obvious that where western man has a tendency to regard the individual as a primary unit, closed in itself, and assembled or organized only secondarily into social groups or "*root* organizations," Indians, not only in their traditional philosophy, but in their spontaneous behavior, still see their original *roots* in a "universal self," a fundamental oneness, a supreme consciousness, of which individual human existence is only a tiny spark. The formless, the unmanifest, the unborn, the unstructured, is the primary and fundamental reality; all forms and structures are only the result of a secondary and temporary flocculation or grossification, in which this primary, supreme reality occasionally allows itself playfully to engage. What western man regards as his strength —his firmness and consistency as an individual—is to the wise Indian a somewhat embarrassing limitation and separation, which he hastens to overcome by meditative and ascetic practices that will help him to merge again in the universal self. The concrete structures of this world, in which western man tends to seek his "security," are, according to the ancient Indian scriptures, treacherous mirages from which one should detach oneself, in order to find one's truly safe abode in that which is without form and without limits. Though yogic practices, if taken seriously, require that the aspirant should first become conscious of himself as an individual and should even build up a resistance by attaining control over body and mind, Indian life never laid much stress on forming what modern western psychology would call "ego-boundaries." If there are any firm limits, they are rather those that are drawn round the circle of the joint family or even round a caste or religious community. Within these confines, a people of similar needs, gifts, interests and aspirations are held together in a "congenial" [17] atmosphere. Whatever passes in and out, between the members

[17] The origin of the word shows its appropriateness: "congenial" literally means concerning or belonging to "those that have been born together" or "that come from the same family stock."

of a unit of this kind, is so similar that there is little need to build up an individual "membrane" for one's defense, for keeping one's own together, for detoxicating and transforming into one's own substance whatever touches or penetrates one from the "outside."

The old social order in India, with its strict caste and joint family system, seems to have been deliberately set up to provide this congenial or "iso-osmotic" [18] environment to the majority of the people, who needed this security of being embedded among "their own" and protected from any "strange influence." Only the specially gifted, destined by their fate to become heroes, could rise beyond this collective order into individual consciousness and fame. In other words, this old social order provided plenty of security and stability, but little social mobility and hardly any stimulus toward individual emancipation.

Nowadays, as most of the old social structures are crumbling, people who have never been encouraged to build up strong individual traits through experiencing their separateness in coming up against frustration and resistance, are suddenly thrown into an open society. In it, they are exposed to many strange influences, to the necessity of withstanding competition and of holding, on their own merits, positions which previously had fallen to them as a birthright or by their merely advancing in age.

Observing the anxieties, doubts, depressions and psychotic breakdowns that result from such precipitate and enforced individual emancipation, I came to realize how closely mental illness is associated with the problem of emerging from a primary symbiotic-empathic union into the conscious existence of a responsible individual; and the tension that arises between a person's

[18] The term "iso-osmotic" refers to chemistry: two solutions, e.g., one inside a cell, the other one the surrounding fluid, are called "iso-osmotic," if they contain the same quantity and quality of dissolved, ionized substances; in this case, the two solutions are balanced, i.e., nothing that passes through a separate membrane can change the composition of either solution. If the "osmotic values" are dissimilar and there is a permeable membrane between them, the higher "osmotic pressure" invades the lower, in an attempt to establish equilibrium. Subtle processes of a similar kind are probably going on between people living in a certain social setting and may be "influencing" us more than many a conscious and deliberate communication.

aspirations toward individual growth and the limits which his society imposes on him or between the call of his conscience and the rigid wall of defense which he himself has allowed to form round his living core. But, while in the West most of the conflicts seem to arise from this latter situation of being confined by a social mask, my Indian patients appeared more often to suffer from lack of a protective "shell" than from an excessive individual crust.

Western psychology has recognized that a state of being merged in primary empathy exists for the new-born baby with regard to the mother during the first months of life. Only quite recently certain authors [19] have pointed out the persistence of an empathic oneness of this kind, an inability to distinguish between a "private world" and a "common world" in certain abnormal types of behavior in children, which can later develop into adult schizophrenia. My own studies on so-called "autistic" (self-centered) children,[20] but also experiences with adult Indian patients, led me to conclude that the gradual growing out of the initial state of empathic-symbiotic oneness leads through the following stages:

One first step from empathic oneness to differentiation between a "private world" and a "common world" leads to a level at which this "common world" is perceived and understood as a kind of liberal mother, from whom one can take without having to ask or to thank. It is easy to recognize that this stage often persists, even in people who regard themselves as quite grown up. Many forms of what one calls "psychopathy," and of addiction, criminality and psychosis, are characterized by "autistic" behavior of this kind. In a milder and more subtle form, at least isolated traces of it are to be observed even in quite responsible and mature people. Our dream-life is an example of it: in dreams, we "take" features from our fellow beings, we "use" them to stage our own little internal drama, without taking account of the true being of these people, without asking them for permission or thanking them

[19] G. Bosch: *Der frühkindliche Autismus,* Springer, Berlin, 1962. (Heft 96, Monographien aus dem Gesamtgebiet der Neurologie und Psychiatrie.)

[20] E. M. Hoch: "Autistische Entwicklung indischer Kinder," as yet unpublished, and "Indian Children on a Psychiatrist's Playground," manuscript to be published by Indian Council of Medical Research.

and without feeling any obligation toward them. Many people act in almost the same way in their waking life: their fellow world is of use to them only as a convenient object for exploitation, as a mirror in which to reflect their own glory, as a scapegoat for their own shortcomings.

At the next stage there is a growing awareness of the existence of fellow human beings who are equally alive and who have the same needs and rights as oneself. Many people—in particular, again, certain mental patients—can break through into this second stage only by first experiencing the living resistance which another person can offer to some aggressive act. This happens normally to a certain degree in the phase of spitefulness of the three- to four-year-old child and again during the rebellious phase of the age of puberty. Once this stage is reached, a person assumes the character of an individual, and can approach his fellow human beings as equal to himself; he lives in a kind of "brother world" and he keeps up a fairly well-balanced exchange of taking and giving between his "private world" and the "common world." Even then, plenty of defenses and filters will be built in, so as to guard himself both against exploitation and against letting his antisocial impulses leak out into the "common world." If defenses of this kind become too rigid and permanent, they may impose themselves as neurotic symptoms.

This is the stage of many of our western societies, with their stress on equality and fraternity and on following "the golden rule." It also seems to have been the spirit of the early Christian communities, though there the element of competition, which is so prominent in our modern worlds, was less obvious.

At a final stage, a human being would arrive at an openness which, without any defenses, allows the stream of life and love to pass through him from eternal sources to his fellow human beings, without expecting anything in return.

At this stage alone, free from any ambitions and aspirations of his own, man can be entirely receptive to the needs and problems of his fellow human beings without bringing in his own distortions. In the light of the purified consciousness of a person of this kind, others will then be able to grow into what they are meant potentially to be, and not merely into poor distorted products of the pressure of an imperfect society.

It would be an attractive task to follow up this theme further, to relate it to Christian teaching, to modern existentialist thought, as presented by Heidegger, and also to the ancient Indian scriptures, which contain very lucid references to the last two stages of the development I have sketched out, with perhaps some illustrations from psychiatric case histories.[21]

Community as Escape from Authentic Existence

Some time ago, I had an interesting discussion with a Hindu surgeon, among whose tasks it is occasionally to perform the brain operation called "leucotomy," by which one hopes to calm the anxiety, doubts and excitements of mental patients and to bring them back to a "useful" function in society. I as a psychiatrist, more inclined toward patient, psychotherapeutic methods, and this mature and responsible surgeon were convinced that this irreversible operation, though many doctors maintain that it is completely harmless, damages what is perhaps most human in man: it may turn him into a docile social animal, but it permanently cuts him off from "becoming," from realizing his future in a creative manner and from aspiring to more penetrating and more subtly illuminating states of consciousness. During our talk, this surgeon remarked: "There are five types of leucotomy: through surgery, through drugs, through alcohol and other addictions, through society and through organized religion." That is to say, there are other situations and agents, besides an operation, which successfully blind man from seeing, and which paralyze him in his essential task of becoming himself, of responsibly carrying out all his potentialities.

---

[21] E. M. Hoch: "The Christian Church as Community, Seen by a Psychiatrist," paper written for a Consultation on the Christian Church as Community in North India, Christian Institute for the Study of Religion and Society, Rajpur, U. P., India, 1963. Published in *Religion and Society*, Vol. X, No. 4, Bangalore, Dec., 1961.

The first three "conscience-killers" will be understandable to most readers, and the fourth society has already been presented in its ambiguous aspect of a mother that nourishes and a monster that devours. But what about religion? Is it not blasphemy to liken it to a mutilating operation?

It might be reassuring to some to answer that it was "only a Hindu" speaking, and that a religion which allows "idolatry" must surely be crippling. Such a remark, coming from a Christian, would exactly prove my friend's claim, that affiliation to any organized religion bears in it the danger of stagnating, of closing oneself to the call of one's conscience, of banking on a guaranteed security instead of deriving from one's faith the courage to remain open and defenseless.

Just as society can promote or block a man's growth, so religious faith, if adopted simply in conformity, as a convenient, ready-made solution to the problems of this life and a kind of insurance for a possible beyond, can keep a man in existential blindness, while religion as a personal spiritual venture can truly enlighten him and lead him to his fulfillment.

It seems that anything that provides the security and shelter necessary for human growth is inherently also a potential danger, something that can lead to lethargy, to stagnation, to passive settling down or even to regression into childish dependency.

Among those who are in the best position to understand this sinister threat in its full meaning are the psychotherapists: if one wants to help a person whose growth has been stunted or distorted into a fuller realization of his possibilities, the first requirement is that the patient should feel secure and comfortable with his therapist. He must be allowed to relax, even to "regress," which means to go back to being a child, so that he can gather up all the possibilities that may have been left behind in the course of an inappropriate upbringing. But this very permissive attitude also implies the danger that the patient will misuse it, that he will stagnate, remain fixed, refuse to grow any further. The therapist has constantly to watch out for the point at which creative regression risks turning into destructive stagnation. Often he has to move on a razor's edge between permissiveness and frustration, if he really wants to promote the patient's growth and not merely to give him temporary relief.

A psychotherapist who at any given time is entirely tuned to the needs of one individual patient, with whose problems he is thoroughly acquainted, may be able to afford such truly human care. But what about an organization or institution that has to cater for the many, for people who may have arrived at quite different levels of maturity and who have widely varying needs and problems?

It is at this point that "community" in most of its forms, be it a politically defined society, a cultural or racial group or even a religious body, reminds one of the old Greek tale of Procrustes and of the conditions on which the traveler could use the bed.

Wherever people are catered for in masses, be it with the commodities of daily life, with education, with social security and legal provisions or even with religious dogma and ritual, there is a tendency to reduce all the varied needs to one common level or at best to a few "models." If this level is put low, if, for example, a society is built up on the assumption that most of its members will prefer stable conditions and that there is not much aspiration for social change, those who have it in them to grow beyond their environment will feel tied down, and their courage and resistance may be weakened. Meanwhile, those who are well protected will decline in lethargy. But if a government allows free social mobility and gives equal opportunity to all for education, the ambitious will find their road open; while the weak and unfit may also be encouraged to rise and find themselves carried to positions which they cannot hold on their own.

Similarly with any organized religious system: the dogma is strict and narrow, those who seek security in conformity will be well provided for. Overprotection and the demand of blind obedience may, however, prevent growth into personal responsibility. Only the person who has a strong urge to undertake his personal spiritual venture may dare to break loose, possibly to become an outcaste, while a less forceful and independent nature will be torn by doubts. But if the religious approach emphasizes a high degree of personal reflection and individual choice, those who can thrive only under close guidance will feel lost or will overstrain themselves in attempting what is beyond their capacities.

It is impressive that in Hinduism many different ways are open to the faithful: from simple worship of a figure that symbolizes a particularly familiar aspect of God, and which in some instances may simply be a stone,[22] to the highest mystical experience and unitive knowledge. Similarly, the Roman Catholic Church, in spite of the apparent rigidity of its official dogma, provides for a variety of tastes and levels of understanding. Many of the Protestant denominations, however, seem to expect that everyone will enter the church through the same door and proceed toward his salvation on the one common road.

Religious teaching cannot be much more than a pointer, a road sign. Whether, in what manner and how far the "faithful" will venture on the path of personal experience will be largely a matter of individual disposition and level of maturity and possibly of the wisdom of one's spiritual guide. All too often, however, we find the situation which Alan W. Watts formulates so delightfully in *The Wisdom of Insecurity:* "The common error of customary religious practice is that one mistakes the symbol for reality, that one only looks at the finger which points out the way and then prefers to suck it comfortably instead of following the direction it indicates."[23]

[22] It is a frequent misconception among western people that the Hindus "worship idols" in the crudest sense. Among my Indian patients, who came from all walks of life and all educational levels, I have not found a single one who would not have answered the question about the object of his worship first with "Bhagavan," namely, "the Blessed," "the Adorable," "the Divine." Only on my specific asking would the name of a particular deity, through whose image this one God was approached, be mentioned.

The old Hindu scriptures recognize that some people need a concrete symbol, through and in which they can worship what ultimately is formless. But the more concentration is turned inward, the more all possibilities are assembled in the self, the less will there be any need for such outward representations. During this process of inward realization the images gradually lose their attributes and finally disappear.

[23] A. W. WATTS: *The Wisdom of Insecurity,* Pantheon, New York, 1951. German edition, *Weisheit des ungesicherten Lebens,* Otto-Wilhelm-Barth: München, Planegg, 1955. Quoted from p. 22 of German edition.

This dilemma, between having both to provide shelter and indicate a direction and to stimulate individual spiritual growth, is one which any organized religious community has to face. We must therefore examine to what extent and in which way Christ's original teachings solved this problem and whether and how the tradition of the Christian church has succeeded in transmitting it.

An Attempt at Defining a Christian View

The term "ekklesia" which one finds in certain passages (for example, Matthew 16 : 18 and 18 : 17), even more so if taken in connection with verses like Matthew 24 : 31 or John 15 : 19, indicates that the "chosen" are in no way to be called *into* the shelter of any organized community, but rather *out* of their customary attachments and securities, *out* of the world.

To follow Christ was to be venturing *out* of tradition, *out* of the "consensus of opinion," *out* of any comfortable settling down in the shelter of the anonymous mass.

> To be called *out,* to have to leave one's attachments, one's securities, for something as vague and intangible as "Spirit," "truth," "light," is very threatening. Most people hate to be "out of things," "out of contact with events," "out of date," "out of fashion," "out of a group," "out of a job." One cannot bear to be suspended in the uncertain, unlimited and formless, but hastens to precipitate oneself into some concrete structure, whatever it may be. If nothing else is offered as a shelter, the "structure" may be a neurotic defense. Instead of being "*out* of everything" one may choose to be at least "*in* trouble." This human tendency to seek security in the concrete and tangible is something we certainly have to keep in mind if we try to understand the development of the Christian church out of what is given in the gospel.[24]

In other words, a truly Christlike life would consist in having the same courage to discover and fulfill one's own mission, even if it carried one against the stream of fashion and public opin-

---

[24] E. M. HOCH: "The Christian Church as Community . . . ," *loc. cit.*

ion and perhaps into situations "whither we would not" (John 21 : 18). It is an ironical paradox, particularly in the age of advertising and rapid mass communication, that anything that is an individual venture into new land has immediately, as soon as it becomes known, to be "consolidated," brought down to a common denominator and made fit for mass consumption by a process of predigestion. The very spirit of the venture, which was precisely intended to lead away from the conventional average, perhaps into loneliness, into hearing the silent voice of one's own conscience instead of listening to the blaring loudspeakers of public opinion, is killed. Is it perhaps that "truth" and "spirit" can best survive, not if they are shamelessly revealed or exposed, but if they are given shelter, hidden in silence or in the mystery of a symbol or parable, an unseemly seed which can come to growth only in the depth of the individual heart?

How then are we to reconcile Christ's challenge that "calls *out,*" with the need of the many who, for their growth, need to be taken *into* a secure fold?

The solution of the problem may well lie in the stages of development sketched out above: the slow growth from being merged in a primary oneness toward being able to open oneself to a "common world" in a gesture of pure giving or rather of passing on the fullness of life and love, which one has learned to draw from eternal sources. It will be noted that the description of the final stage would come very close to being really "Christlike." People who attain to that stage have always been rare, and have more frequently arrived merely at splendid isolation in self-sufficiency. They will, however, be exposed to, and be defending themselves from, the claims which their fellow human beings will expect them, often at a very material level, to meet. As I have suggested Christ himself met this same situation:

People, instead of being receptive to his spiritual teachings, expect from him to be fed, to be cured of their physical ailments, to get advice for their everyday problems, to gain worldly positions or even access to a heaven of their own imagination. It is indeed one of the amazing features in the gospel to find with how much versatility and intuitive understanding Christ meets all those who claim his help on the very level and in the very manner which is adequate and meaningful to them. But one cannot help feeling that even Christ at times inwardly rebelled against this exploitation, against having to give, not at the level at which he was unique and that was closest to his spiritual being, but to bend down to the needs of those who could understand love only in terms of material, physical ministration. This readiness to meet one's neighbour at the point where he can understand and appreciate our concern for him, seems to me to be one of the mysteries of "incarnation." To live in the Spirit, to have one's security beyond the material world, should not make one shrink back from getting involved in worldly matters, but, on the contrary, it should render one free to incarnate oneself again and again in the form, the living parable, which to any one of one's human brethren will be meaningful and revealing. In other words, the "impersonations" or "integrations" or, if one likes, the "roles" which one assumes at any given moment are no longer determined by one's own needs, ambitions, fears and inclinations, but by the needs of our neighbours and God's will that we should minister to them. This is perhaps what some of the Roman Catholic authors (e.g. De Caussade and John Chapman[25]) call "the sacrament of the present moment." [26]

This supreme openness in love, which is actually the message of the New Testament, is, however, possible only when it has been preceded by a phase of limiting and gathering, of "individuation," as we find it expressed in many of the stories of the Old Testament, not only with regard to individual characters, but also with regard to the setting apart of a "people of God." Only in contrast to the discipline of the law, building up on it and transcending it, can this oneness be conscious and willful and distinct from the indiscriminate merging of a primitive chaotic state.

Though thus to follow Christ in the deepest sense presents a challenge to a most personal venture in faith and love, the message that by him and in him even the weakest and humblest are accepted, understood and forgiven, that they can come to him just as they are, equally assures a safe shelter and opportunities for

---

[25] Dom. John Chapman, O.S.B.: *The Spiritual Letter,* Sheed and Ward, London, 1935. Père de Caussade, S.J.: *Letters* and *L'Abandon à la Providence divine,* quoted in J. Chapman.

[26] E. M. Hoch: "The Christian Church as Community . . . ," *loc. cit.*

growth to human beings at any level of development. Even the best shepherd needs his flock. Only the presence of those entrusted to him enables him to be what he is and wants to be, to fulfill his mission of true care. Thus, in the ideal Christian community, not only can each find his own natural place, but he can also grant a place to any other member whom he can thus enable to appear in his true being. Each one can be open for the neighbor's needs, as he himself is safely enfolded in the love of God.

A Christian community cannot and should never be just a choice group of advanced and mature people with high spiritual aspirations. As in Christ's time, the teachings of love, forgiveness and respect for the humble will attract and sustain believers from all walks of life and from all levels of development and with the most varied motives. "Young churches," in particular, who are still drawing new members from non-Christian groups, may find it difficult to organize a community which provides a place and a suitable climate for spiritual growth for each of the widely differing aspirants. It is easy to understand how the presence of members who are at the level of interpreting Christian love and acceptance in terms of the satisfaction of their material needs or worldly ambitions will force the community into adopting a worldly structure. This is the more inevitable when (as was and to some extent still is the case here in North India), new converts, by the very act of joining the Christian church, are debarred from the material privileges and social securities which their former groups provided. This necessity, however, carries in it the danger that the spiritual nature of the kingdom of God will be obscured by wrongly regarding the church as a "universal provider" for all human needs. It is a situation, too, that involves two main risks: the loosening of social barriers, and the opportunities for higher education and social advance, which the new Christian finds in the group that he joins, may drive him into social and educational ambitions for which he is not ready (a danger which I have had plenty of opportunity to observe in India); and the security of the "mission compound," the certainty of finding all one's needs provided for, may cause other types to "settle down" in complacency and lethargy.

These risks, however, are encountered not only in "young churches," they are inherent in any Christian group that has to constitute itself in any concrete form. The Spirit may "blow where it listeth," but if it has to be communicated, it needs a form, it has to be incarnated in a body. But the denser and more concrete this body, the more the Spirit risks suffocation.

Here the secularity of modern states may offer great possibilities: the more that certain tasks, for instance, in present-day India, are taken over by the state, the more free will the Christian community become to develop its spiritual dimension. To be in the world yet not of it is easier and more obvious in a social order that relieves a religious organization of its worldly tasks.

This does not mean that, as individuals and as a community, Christians should cease to express their concern for suffering and underprivileged human beings through action in the field of education, medical aid and social welfare. On the contrary, they ought to feel freer than ever to do so: if they are no longer compelled to attend to these needs of their neighbors because no one else does so in the hope that by the mere establishment of such services, Christian prestige will be increased, then the way is open toward a charity that really comes from the heart. If such services are no longer a monopoly of Christian groups, like Christian missions in an "underdeveloped" country, there will be a new challenge to make them truly Christian, no longer by their name, but by the particular spirit which devoted individual workers or groups can infuse into them.

There may then be more adequate scope for the beneficial climate which the Christian spirit of acceptance and forgiveness can provide for human growth. The unique certainty that we are accepted in Christ as we are gives us the shelter *and* the freedom within which each of us can afford to grow according to his own speed and capacities. An atmosphere of this kind, in which no one need strain to go beyond what he can do and yet in which the assurance of being enfolded in the love of God and of those whom it inspires is guaranteed, even if one rises beyond one's original environment, must surely be one of the most valuable contributions which the Christian church can make within present-day open society, with its rapid change and feverish competition.

16

WHOLENESS IN ART, WORK AND LEISURE

by MARVIN P. HALVERSON (U. S. A.)

Search for Wholeness

SEVERAL years ago *Life* magazine published a pictorial graph designed to show the levels of American taste in art, music, literature and food ranging from lowbrow to highbrow. Some of us had a good deal of fun using it to test our friends. I remember that I myself found particularly amusing and appealing an item in the lowbrow category—a pillow stuffed with pine and balsam needles with words embroidered on the cover reading: "I pine for you and balsam." But though this chart was intended as a humorous commentary on the confusion and distortion of taste in this country, it was sobering to realize that it described the actual situation.

Fundamentally, however, the problem is not one of good taste or bad taste, although the dichotomy between highbrows and lowbrows suggests the serious split in modern life between high culture and popular culture. The issue is really the question of man and the meaning of his life. For the current confusion of taste and general disregard of art is a symptom of the loss of man's relationship to himself, to his fellows, to nature and to that ultimate reality we call God. We have lost the sense of the whole in personal existence and in society. Thus man is involved in a search for a lost wholeness.

"Wholeness is no mere desired goal," said Waldo Frank in *The Rediscovery of America,* "it is the origin and the end of all our creative being. Wholeness is one in life as in letter with holiness and health. Wholeness must be both personal and social in order to be either. Individual man cannot achieve his health unless he lives, consciously, within a Whole that holds all life." [1] The sense of the whole once bound the world in a living tether. But this awareness of the ground and ultimate fulfillment of life no longer undergirds and overarches the life of modern man. He stands as a lonely individual in an alien society. He is no longer a person in community. The universal is not disclosed in the particular, and the eternal is not realized in the moment. And this is our loss.

"Where is there a whole man?" called out Ralph Waldo Emerson over one hundred years ago; and his plea can be multiplied a hundredfold today. The *Vitruvian man* of the Renaissance, the *animal rationale,* whose ideal proportions gave measure to the arts and the whole of man's activity, has vanished. Instead we have the image of man as a toolmaker, the fabricator of useful things who derives his diminished dimensions from the triumph of technology and scientism. But man is more than a toolmaker. His activity as artist demonstrates this. Perhaps more than anything else artistic activity, whether of a child or a Picasso, breaks the fetters of such a limited conception of man, his nature and his destiny. Ernst Cassirer has contended that man is fundamentally *animal symbolicum,* a being who is both a symbol maker and a symbol user. The art of primitive man, which we have come to know only recently, argues that man was an artist working in a world of symbols before he was ever a successful toolmaker. This would not deny the rational idealism of the Renaissance but embraces an even wider apprehension of man's powers and relationships. And as we begin to think of man's life in terms of symbols, new possibilities of renewal in religion, art, work and leisure emerge. For art, like religion, is fundamentally a relational expression of man in terms of the whole. In the Old Testament, man was regarded as a unity.

---

[1] George Braziller, Inc., 1958.

For instance, the Hebrew belief that the soul was carried in the bloodstream was a symbolic attempt to say that man, unlike Gaul, is not divided into three parts, but is one. He is a whole being.

But as the uniqueness and wholeness of man was lost in our modern world, man himself became expendable. Thus as mechanization and automation take command, man is displaced from the center of the stage, and becomes a shadow of the machine he has created. It is only in a world which had made itself vulnerable by disintegrating the whole man that the tyrannies of our time could thrive. The loss of freedom, not only in the lands of the dictatorships, but also within our own borders of alleged freedom, is symptomatic of a larger loss—the abdication of the human personality itself.

A recent article in the Sunday *Times* (London) "Abundant Leisure Under Automation—Experts want to prepare for an age of culture," was written on the assumption that given forethought and planning we were on the threshold of a new renaissance of culture. I cannot imagine that this expectation is similar to the excitement that prevailed among the *cognoscenti* of Florence when they realized the beginning of days and the freshness of rebirth in the air. Nonetheless there is a stirring within the older cultures of our present world and a restless anticipation of the future among the younger nations which presage something new.

My apartment in New York looks out on an asphalt square bounded on one side by a row of century-old houses, on another by a public library with a small art gallery and gymnasium and on the other two sides by giant buildings which house the increasingly automated machines for lithographing and box making, which work night and day. The square provides a recreation center for people from blocks around, and a playground for the nearby vocational high school and grammar school. In the summer bathers cavort in the big outdoor pool. The other day as I was starting to write boys were flying their kites in a stiff breeze, a group of older men were playing *boccie,* an Italian form of bowling on a clay court, several adolescents were shooting baskets and a baseball game appeared to be shaping up.

This panorama of automation and leisure viewed from my window struck my consciousness with great force as I was reflecting on work, leisure and the arts. Perhaps nowhere else in the world could the scene be duplicated, and yet it seemed to me to symbolize some of the problems we experience today and will confront even more acutely tomorrow. How is work related to leisure and leisure related to work, and both to the realm of art? *Laborare est orare et orare est laborare.* In this assertion of the unity of work and prayer St. Augustine and the Benedictine order struggling to bring order out of the disintegrating empire established a norm for the Christian life in the West. It has become a franchise for the gospel of work, especially among Protestants. Protestantism has been notoriously effective in fostering the notion that work is more worthy than leisure and superior to art. Christians who have long been wedded to the notion that work is one of the highest virtues are increasingly perplexed by the coming world of leisure. The economic needs of earlier centuries which made work a social utility ratified by religion are vanishing rapidly as we move from an age of production into an age of consumption. We are in transition from a world of enslavement to work to a promised land of freedom from work, and we are bewildered by it.

In the midst of the unbridled expectations of Victorian England, Ruskin wrote, "I could smile at the hopeful exultation of many at the reach of science and worldly effort as if we were at the beginning of days. There is thunder on the horizon as well as dawn." We now have heard that thunder in our own ears. Automation portends both peril and promise. If only to maintain social peace, it will be necessary to share the economic dividends of automation far more radically than we have dared to think. Not only shall we require imaginative social planning transcending the thought of Marx, the fears of Von Mises and the hopes of Keynes, but all religious institutions which once provided a rationale for the accumulation of capital will be challenged to interpret the religious meaning of leisure and art as opposed to work. This will be particularly onerous for those Protestants who found little difficulty being at ease in Zion but stretched every nerve while in the world.

The ordinary hymnal demonstrates the penchant of Protestantism to ascribe to work a spirituality it finds difficult to associate with leisure or art. We shall need a "theology of leisure" and a "theology of art" for the plenitude of time without work which will thrust to the heart of personal existence and our common culture. But one of the problems is that time without work is far different from leisure.

Several years ago Joseph Pieper, a German Catholic layman, wrote a reflective and prophetic essay which he called "Leisure, the Basis of Culture," in which he said: "Culture depends for its very existence on leisure, and leisure, in its turn, is not possible unless it has a durable and consequently living link with the *cultus*, with divine worship." Western society, however, is dominated by the assumption that "one does not work to live; one lives to work." The popularity of hobbies and the do-it-yourself cult in the United States argues our need to keep busy. Modern man invests his hobbies with the intensity he previously gave to his work. It is no wonder, contends Pieper, that the face of modern man, and especially of the intellectual worker and the organization man, bears the mark of strain and tension. Long ago Goethe observed that "perpetual activity to the exclusion of all else ends in bankruptcy."

Leisure, on the other hand, is not simply the absence of work but is characterized by fullness, inner silence rooted in the confidence one calls faith. "Have leisure and know that I am God," Pieper translates Psalm 46 : 10, for it is in leisure rather than effort that love comes, and contemplation which to him is the highest form of knowledge. Pieper calls attention to the way in which St. Thomas speaks of contemplation and play in the same breath. Because leisure and contemplation are bound together by their very nature, the divine wisdom itself in Proverbs 8 : 30–31 says: "I was with him forming all things: and was delighted every day, playing before him at all times; playing in the world; and my delights were to be with the children of men."

Play—and I believe this is equally true of art—is basic to man's life. Play generally precedes laws, liturgies and customs but sometimes derives from them and represents their residue. For instance, children's games often preserve tradition and ritual, as a study of Breughel's paintings reveals. In other instances, children's play is astonishingly open to the new and prophetic of what is to come in the adult world. The speed with which children incorporate the new into their play is remarkable. For instance, not until November 25, 1936, did the British public learn through the newspapers of Edward VIII's romance with Mrs. Simpson; but before Christmas thousands of British children were singing a carol parody:

> Hark! the herald angels sing,
> Mrs. Simpson's pinched our King.

The internationalism of the world of children's play is demonstrated by the immediate appropriation of the couplet on the American side of the Atlantic. But because the word "pinch" no longer means "swipe" to American children, there was some confusion!

Roger Collois in *Man, Play and Games*—an important contribution by the editor of "Diogenes" to the growing body of cultural analysis of the forms of leisure activity—argues that man's play can be classified in four categories: Agon (competition); Alea (chance); Mimicry (simulation); and Ilinx (vertigo). In each category there are differences as games move from the primary power of joy and improvisation, which he calls *paidia,* in the direction of gratuitous difficulty which he calls *ludus*. The general tumult and agitation found frequently among young children move toward the patience required by kite flying, solitaire and crossword puzzles. In this connection it is interesting that although children's games are often remnants of cultural history, they represent even more the evolution of highly developed rules out of those sorts of play which seek intoxicating vertigo. It is no less significant that out of the industrial revolution came the contraptions of our amusement parks and carnivals which create vertigo by mechanical means.

Technological Culture

The hobby, a form of play for leisure time especially characteristic of our industrial and technological civilization, betokens the need for compensation for personality injury arising from bondage to meaningless work. There are instances of worker-turned-artisan making complete scale models of the machines to which his work indentures him, thus avenging reality in a positive and creative way. But hobbies are not limited to making gadgets which will improve the home, make life easier for mother or take vengeance on the machine which has usurped man's role as craftsman and artisan. More and more they are moving in the direction of high culture.

"They laughed when I sat down at the piano." Do you remember that delightful illustration of derision turned to confusion as the man in the advertisement proved he could play? Thirty years ago—or was it longer?—advertisements encouraged the musically untrained to enroll for piano lessons and surprise their friends by unsuspected "cultural" attainments. What began as an appeal to status achievement has grown to a flood of enticements to become familiar with great music, great painting and great literature. Even the grossness of the mass media does not seem to stanch the appeal. In fact the mass media serve as the vehicle for advertisements luring men to the arts so they may rise above the mass media! Such is the irony of a mass culture!

We can glimpse the contours of the coming technological culture in the new patterns of life and cultural expressions already among us. For example, perhaps three hundred persons knew or had seen the work of Titian during his lifetime. Over a quarter of a million people saw the works when they were shown in the summer of 1960 at the Tate Gallery in London—the largest number of visitors in its history. Thanks to photography and modern techniques of reproduction (what Malraux terms "the museum without walls"), man's knowledge of other cultures through the arts has enlarged unbelievably. We know more about the past and the present than was ever possible before. And art is able to demonstrate its truly international character. For example, Le Corbusier, perhaps the greatest architect of the twentieth century, of Swiss Protestant ancestry, designed a world-famous chapel for the Roman Catholics at Ronchamp in France and also planned the new capital of Chandigarh in Punjab! The works of past and present-day musical composers are more widely known than was ever imagined possible; the music of African tribes and the Gregorian chants of the Middle Ages are equally accessible to all.

Despite the fears of some critics that there will be no art in a mass culture, we shall undoubtedly have more "art" than we had in former generations. But art, like everything else, will be "processed"—the rough edges will be knocked off and the marks of individual idiosyncrasy removed. For in a mass culture art becomes a commodity and so must be made immediately appealing. "To hell with culture," quotes Sir Herbert Read from an essay by the late English Catholic sculptor, Eric Gill. "When will revolutionary leaders realize that 'culture' is dope, a worse dope than religion; for even if it were true that religion is the opiate of the people, it is worse to poison yourself than to be poisoned, and suicide is more dishonourable than murder. To hell with culture, culture as a thing added like a sauce to an otherwise unpalatable stale fish." In other words, Gill and other artists who stand in judgment on contemporary society remind us that culture is not the decorative icing on a cake which has fallen. Rather, culture is the fabric of society, and religion and art are its warp and woof.

Art—A Universal Medium

What is art? For many people it is those objects which have no utility in themselves, in contrast to machines and buildings. At one time, however, the word "artist" was not limited to those who painted pictures or carved statues. "Art" referred to a craft or specialized form of skill. Graham Carey has drawn upon this older usage in asserting that art is "doing well that which needs to be done"; and Cocmaraswamy, in contending that "the artist is not a special kind of man, but every man is a special kind of artist." Such attempts to rehabilitate the words "art" and "artist" do not seem fully cognizant of the developments of the last three centuries by which technology has become an alternative to art. The exaltation of things and the denial of art are a consequence of this split in our life. In the face of "thingification," art points to the unique character of man as a personal being rather than an economic or technological unit—or thing. Having this in mind, Denis de Rougemont defines art in this way: "As distinct from all other products of human action, *the work of art is an object of which the raison d'être necessary and sufficient is TO SIGNIFY, organically, and by means of its own structure.* Whether it consists in a structure of meanings, or forms, or sounds, or ideas, the work of art has for its own specific function the bribing of the attention, the magnetizing of the sensibility, the fascinating of the meditation, the ensnaring —and at the same time it must orient existence toward something which transcends sounds and forms—of the words so assembled. It is a trap but an oriented trap . . . *a calculated trap for meditation.*" In the words of Picasso, "Art is a lie that makes us realize the truth."

For this reason there is a sense in which all art is religious. Certainly this may be said of the works of outstanding artists of the twentieth century who are concerned for truth rather than beauty. Preoccupation with beauty as beauty arose in the Renaissance with the return to late Greek ideals, and paralleled a decline in the religious depth of art. This coincidence should not be surprising, for the Bible is singularly unconcerned with beauty. Biblical religion is more concerned with the beauty of holiness than with the holiness of beauty; and great art is more concerned with inner reality than with surface reality, for the artist is dealing with truth about man and his inner vision.

"All art is sacramental in its nature," said P. T. Forsyth in *Christ in Parnassus,* one of the few efforts by a Protestant theologian to deal with religion and art. "The artist has a . . . vision, which he embodies in a certain material form, with the object of conveying to . . . me the same vision or the same mood. The outward is used by his inward to rouse a like inwardness in me. But his sacramental use of the outward is more than memorial. . . . He incarnates his vision, he does not merely suggest it." To do this the artist does not employ the language of science or economics. He must use to fulfill his aims allegory, the parable, the myth, the dream. In other words, the artist works in symbols which in pointing to an ultimate reality thereby participate in it.

Art possesses revelatory power. Once given form, it exhibits an authority and a life of its own which denies manipulation by man for his own ends. Consequently there has been tension when any institution, whether state or church, has sought to force art into conformity. There must be freedom for the spirit to do its work. But it is a freedom conjoined with discipline. The discipline to which the artist must subject himself as he seeks to bring his inner experience into aesthetic form is analogous to the *askesis* of the dedicated religious life. Religion cannot dominate art, and art cannot dominate religion. The temptation of the artist is represented in Shelley's assertion that the poets are the unacknowledged legislators of the world. And the temptation of religion is to judge a work of art by canons of morality or sentiment or utility as a teaching device. Whenever religion has done this, bad art has been enthroned in the name of religion. Not only has art been denied: religion has been weakened.

To judge art religion must not only recognize its nature but must also understand the vocation of the artist. When it does so, the artist will be recognized as a strong ally of religion. As a consequence of a long estrangement, churches have tended both to romanticize the artist and to deny the artist. The two responses are, of course, directly related. But one of the results of a *rapprochement* between the church and the artist will involve an awareness that the artist serves religion as a judge, seer, and advocate. The artist is not an isolated being. He is modified by the milieu of the culture and the character of the age. Thus the vocation of the artist today reflects his perception of the nature of our times. The artist today appears to be more of a prophet, judge and seer than an advocate, more of a John the Baptist than a Paul the Apostle. He makes straight in the desert of our civilization a highway for our God. His work constitutes a *preparatio evangelium.* The artist himself is not so much an advocate as one who prepares men for the disclosure of an answer which is yet to come.

Paul Gauguin was not a Christian in the sense that the church understands it, but a short time before his death he wrote in a letter about a work he had completed:

> Before I died I wished to paint a large canvas that I had in mind and I worked day and night in an incredible fever. They will say that it is careless, unfinished. It is true that it is hard to judge one's own work, but in spite of this, I believe that this work not only surpasses all my preceding ones, but that I shall never do anything better or even like it. If anyone should tell Beaux Arts pupils for the Rome competition: The picture you must paint is to represent "Who are we? Where do we come from; and where are we going?" what would they do? So I have finished a philosophical work on a theme parallel to that of the Gospel. I think it is good. If I have the strength I will copy it and send it to you.

The painting about which Gauguin wrote was entitled "Who are we; where do we come from; where are we going?" But though Gauguin thought of it as a philosophical parallel to the gospels, the painting does not give the ultimate answer. Instead it poses ultimate questions. In this respect it is characteristic of modern art. And this quality of modern art which makes us uncomfortable may well be regarded as the divine vocation of the contemporary artist whose art probes deeply into the heart of present-day existence.

But the artist not only poses ultimate questions: he also proclaims an answer. This is true in a large measure of the great religious art of the past made in an age of faith. The church no longer stands astride the times giving form and substance to the culture. The powerful symbols of the Christian faith are no longer a common language which the artist can employ in the knowledge that he is reaching a vast community of faith. Often when an artist does turn to traditional Christian inconography his work does not exhibit as much penetration as when he employs secular themes. Gauguin—like other artists of more recent times—asked the question, but he was unable to give an answer.

But the artist today is often a prophet to the churches. For art not only reflects the spirit of the age in which the artist works: it also brings judgment. It conveys truth about the human situation more pointedly and more profoundly than the words of preachers, sociologists and scientists. Until 1913 what we call modern art was relatively unknown in the United States. In that year, however, an artistic bomb hit America which ended an era and ushered in a new period of artistic activity. In the Armory Show in 1913 (at that time there was no museum of modern art nor were the established museums prepared to house the exhibition which was installed in an armory!), the first large showing of modern art was presented to the American public. It was exhilarating to some. It was shocking to most. It was reported that a visitor, looking at the Van Goghs, and particularly the Duchamps, the Picassos and the Matisses, cried in shock and dismay, "There is something wrong with mankind." A year later, the First World War started, providing some justification for this comment on the human condition. But he implied that art, too, was ailing.

The truth is that art is not sick, but rather it is our age which is sick and the times which are out of joint. Since art in all periods of man's history has reflected the fundamental character of the age, it is to be expected that the serious art of our times—the paintings, the novels, the plays and the poems—will mirror the world of the twentieth century. But modern art does more than reveal the human and cultural situation: it often discloses a wholeness beyond brokenness.

Not only the courage of the artist in confronting meaninglessness, but his ability to take fragmentation and brokenness into his own being and out of this encounter to achieve order and form in a work of art, is testimony to the spirit. Modern art is not limited to the themes of disruption which we see, for example, in Picasso's *Guernica,* painted in 1936 as a protest against the first mass bombing of a city during the Spanish Civil War. It also displays a lyricism which in color and rhythm celebrates the goodness of creation and the joy of play.

We have forgotten the art of play. We must find anew for our time the unity of art and work and leisure in terms of nuclear physics, interplanetary travel, the laboratory test tube and automation. It will be difficult. In the past, leisure was aristocratic privilege rather than democratic fact. We not only inherit these presuppositions about leisure, we are also burdened with untenable assumptions about work. We have been estranged from art and we bring inexperienced eyes, untuned ears and uninstructed minds to our encounters with the great art of the past and the statements of the present. But this makes our efforts to achieve new unities all the more urgent.

When Matisse commenced the design and decoration of the Chapel of the Rosary at Vence, he was charged with undertaking this task in repentance "after sixty years of producing a hedonistically pagan art." But, "in my own way," said Matisse, "I have always sung the glory of God and His Creation. I have not changed." And in paintings like those of Mark Tobey, Morris Graves and Paul Klee we find that mystical apprehension of the whole and the realm where joy, love and peace reign.

On all levels of fulfillment, therefore, art points beyond itself and enables man to participate in the whole more fully than in most of the other experiences of life. The search for wholeness is a perennial one, and is deeply personal. Yet since we discover our identity through another and fulfill ourselves as persons in community, the search for wholeness takes on added urgency and pathos in our time. Ours is not a society which recognizes wholeness as the ground and goal of life. For the togetherness of women's magazines, Madison Avenue and superficial religious fellowship bears little resemblance to that wholeness whereby our very being is grasped by the ultimate in such a way that we are sustained and renewed. It may not be ours to experience the fullness of the whole in this disordered and broken time, but we can have intimations of the reality of which we speak. And here art, whether we be makers or beholders, can bring us to the perimeter of the whole and enable us to gaze in wonder and joy at what we shall yet behold.

17

THE "POSITIVE" IN MODERN LITERATURE

by Heinz Flügel (Germany)

Contradictions in Existential Writings

In critical discussion of modern literature from a Christian point of view people often ask, with impatience and reproach: where is the positive element? Max Picard seems to have given the best answer, when he remarked paradoxically, in a conversation on existentialist literature: "The missing element is overwhelmingly present." To call for something positive—whether interpreted as the proclamation of divine grace, the overcoming of evil or the teaching of traditional morality—would betray a fundamental misunderstanding of the condition in which literature exercises its intellectual and social function today. Indeed, openly to express despair, to doubt where doubt seems to have been resolved and to challenge, even in the point of blasphemy, what has been taken for granted, may be a sign of high literary and moral merit. Think, for example, of the nihilistic variant of the Lord's Prayer in Ernest Hemingway's story "A Clean, Well-Lighted Place." In it, the waiter, who is overcome by St. Paul's worldly grief and by the emptiness of existence, replaces all the essential terms and expressions of the prayer—father, heaven, bread, earth—by the little word *nada*—"nothing." In this way the missing element is much more prominently and convincingly present than it could be in a pious, so-called "positive" treatment of the subject. We must not, of course, underestimate the problems to which Sören Kierkegaard draws attention, namely, that the power of creative writing, which stands for the sinister mysteries of *all* words, "is being bought by the writer for a small mystery"—by which Kierkegaard means the devil being driven out by Beelzebub. Even if we are not prepared to draw the suicidal consequences which Manfred Hausmann assigns to the artist in his novel of conversion, *Der Überfall*—the unavoidable fact remains that the writer has to make common cause with atheism in order to remain a respectable writer. Neither the formalist preoccupied with aestheticism nor the moralist working within the theological framework can do justice to the contradictory fact which Gottfried Benn pinpointed poignantly, if blasphemously, when he wrote: "God is a bad basis on which to form a style."

Explaining this view—admittedly in a seemingly frivolous manner—Gottfried Benn maintains that his situation as a poet, belief in a given metaphysical truth, places him outside the material in which he works: belief corrupts the style. Today, however, priority must be given to syntax. Therefore the poet has put the whole vigor of the nihilistic sentiment into the formal constructive elements of the spirit. Austerity of style is grounded in metaphysical asceticism. Further, insofar as style is self-subsistent, skepticism is favorable to its formation.

Indeed, Benn's provocative formula recommends itself to the Christian observer of literature as a focal point, especially since he is inclined to judge literature chiefly by its missionary value, in order that he may achieve an objective appraisal of modern art. In this he might be aided by a verse from Eduard Mörike's "Ode to an Antique Lamp," although it originated in a very different climate of feeling: *"Was aber schön ist, selig ist es ihm selbst"* ("But what is beautiful is blessed in itself").

Equally, Gottfried Benn affirms this belief again in his essay on art: "this phenomenon wants only to exist." Later in his writings he may even intimate that the eternal seeps through everywhere. We should adopt this style-forming skepticism all the more strictly, since experience teaches us that an exaggerated willingness to confess his faith has more than once played havoc with an author's artistic vision. Usually such missionary zeal strangles the literary discipline, which demands—again quoting Gottfried Benn—a certain skeptical inaccessibility: "Animals which generate pearls are closed up."

Occasionally Benn also speaks of the need for the artist to "immure" himself. Here we are touching on the problem already mentioned, and I am even inclined to detect a certain tragedy which, incidentally, was touched on in Oskar Söhngen's address on the occasion of the poet's death in 1956, when he took as his text the word from the prophet Jeremiah, selected by the deceased himself: "He has walled me about so that I cannot escape" (Lamentations 3 : 7).

Looking on lyrical art, with Gottfried Benn, as a laboratory for words, the poet would find himself in a situation analogous to that of a man in the field of technical experiment. Undoubtedly life today is of an experimental character: the marks of the age are nonmetaphysical realism, profane exactitude, intellectual honesty. We should be careful not to append, from a pious reaction, a negative symbol to this decided secularism of modern man and to condemn it as such. We should, rather, recall Dietrich Bonhoeffer's theological speculation, whether it is not God himself who is showing us that we have to live as those who contend with life without God. Similarly, we should drop any Christian indignation over Berthold Brecht's icy statement in *Flug der Lindbergs:* "When I fly I am a real atheist." What is true in the technical and scientific sphere generally, that man experiments *"etsi Deus non daretur,"* is equally true of Gottfried Benn's laboratory of words.

On the other hand, it could well be the special task of literature to become creative precisely by going through this problematical situation. Unreflected unbelief, confessional atheism, are just as much a basis for today's literature as unreflected faith. The *homme de lettres* is the man who is driven to writing because he senses the problematical tension and reacts seismographically to the spiritual structural changes which the tension causes. In experimenting with language he seeks to give adequate expression to connections and events which in that particular manner had not existed before, and he thus has to probe thoroughly into the possibilities of language. This is at bottom not just an aesthetic and artistic venture—although literature is certainly often used as such. Rather, we should evaluate what it means for man when huge areas of his world and existence are essentially inarticulate. *"Ich lernte traurig den Verzicht, kein Ding sei, wo das Wort gebricht"* ("I sadly learned to resign myself to the fact that no thing is there, where the word is lacking"), as we read in the late Stefan George (who gave the statement, however, a magical meaning). A whole world of unspoken and unspeakable things surrounding us would constitute a factual threat. Looked at in this light, literature today should be understood in its existential seriousness, and especially when, in frigid understatement, it is called a laboratory for words. Gottfried Benn described himself literally as an experimental type, and as such he was fully aware of his problematical position, mainly borne out in his attitude at the beginning of the Hitler dictatorship. In the same way as the lyric artist experiments primarily with words, the prose writer experiments with ways of existence and patterns of fate. The novels of the Swiss author, Max Frisch, provide some good examples in this respect which reward discussion. They demonstrate a modern anthropology, to be studied with profit even if the manner of presentation is traditional and often playful. He makes the experimenting narrator of his novel, *My Name is Gantenbein,* say: "I try on stories like clothes." Exactly in this way, by trying out experimentally the most diverse variations of destiny, he escapes being tied down to an immutable fate and fixation on a responsible personal mode of being. Here we meet man as a bunch of possibilities, as a protean changing design. He himself can no longer be grasped. There is no mistaking the risk of losing humanity which this continuing experiment brings with it, when we seek to cling to the concept of humane man living his life as one for which he has to account, as something which he has himself to create from a secret center outward. Max Frisch is essentially an engaged author, involved with existence at a deep level, even if he may have relented and enjoyed himself with pure fantasy in *Gantenbein.* But with the inexorability of an almost archaic logic he leads *ad absurdum*—in his earlier novel—the irresponsible existence of *Homo Faber* who has undertaken to live "without death," without the metaphysical dimension. For the technician Walter Faber, life is merely a sum of additions which, he thinks, you can calculate. He is not interested in mystery, in what is incalculable: time, for him, is of purely mathematical importance. Nobody will deny that in the conditions and framework of a technical process, mathematical exactitude is more important than a metaphysical shudder. This observation is almost a platitude. Our question is, rather, how far the method of the technician, of *Homo Faber,* can be valid. How far has man already adapted himself to the experimental character of the world which he has "humanized"—at the cost of his true humanity? How far has the experimenter become the subject of his own experiments? We cannot, I believe, afford to minimize this process of adaptation, as some "churchy" Christians, who are afraid of not appearing modern or positive, are apt to do. The reproach leveled at literature: "Where is the positive element?" could therefore stem from the mediocrity of mind of those who do not want to be disturbed in their urge to conform and, conforming, to live comfortably. Over against this, literature impels us to rebellion and despair, because obviously literature is essentially nonconformist. It is a specially outstanding feature of the literature of French existentialism that it is resolute in taking seriously—and to the point of despair—man's position in a world which is forever tempting us into subjection to the dictatorship of sociological and technical experiments. We cannot deny that existentialism, impelled here by the love of man, is driven to contempt of God—which is the cardinal sin with which the Jesuit philosopher Le Blond charges it. This is, however, simultaneously acted out with tragic consequence, which in turn cannot be denied, and which shocks all the more deeply, when Albert Camus is able to rebut the reproach of Christian criticism with the counterclaim that Christians, in order to save the absolute, are abandoning man.

Presence of the "Missing" Element

Jean Paul Sartre, after having dispensed with God in the interests of human freedom, by no means does away with the discussion with him. Max Picard's comment, that the missing element is overwhelmingly present, is borne out quite as accurately in the pessimism of this French thinker, who undertakes to define man without, or rather, against God. We can hardly maintain that in doing so, he has made man's existence easier. On the contrary, he weighs man down with the terrible burden of his metaphysical loneliness, for he has "burnt his boats." With nothing but himself to rely on, man has to endure to the end the terror of this immutable freedom: "If I exist, I do so because I feel the terror of existing. I myself extricate myself from the Nothing!" (*La Nausée*).

We should not underestimate the extent of the sense of the terror and of strength which, in spite of peripheral frivolities, are equally balanced in Sartre as to their moral significance. Nor should we ridicule the absurb postulate of extricating oneself from the Nothing by pointing to Münchhausen's humorous tale in which the lying baron saves himself by pulling himself out of the quagmire by his own hair. Reinhold Schneider was surely right in observing that where tragedy is no longer taken seriously, Christianity too would soon go the same way. Is it not true—as Sartre has explained and demonstrated, both as philosopher and as dramatist—that human life begins beyond despair, when zero has been passed? It would of course be an illusion to assume that beyond zero, faith would arrive almost automatically on the scene. Passionate loyalty to humanity may mean for a radical thinker the loss of faith. The same honesty that forbids us to reduce faith to an act of obedience, bids us respect the thinker who sees the ground of human liberty in the absurd. The only chance— and a great one—for a discussion between believers and nonbelievers, Christians and existentialists, seems to lie in the endeavor, on the Christian side, to understand the abyss of the absurd. Should the Christian have any advantage over the nonbeliever, it might well be his readiness to be solidly with him, even up to the point of being forsaken by God.

To defend the strange "god of the flies," who, in J. P. Sartre's Orestes play *"Les Mouches (The Flies)"* is made into a caricature of the divine and then despised as such, would serve neither God nor man: one might perhaps identify that "god of the flies" with the devil. But the spirit of responsibility which makes Orestes willing to give account of his bloody deed, after having executed his mother with her accomplice Aigisthos, shows man as God's potential partner, even if the partnership is expressed in terms of despising God. As Orestes is unable to acknowledge any judge other than himself before whom to give his account, his way has to end in prison, in the dungeon of his own self which constitutes justice. Again at this point we may recall Gottfried Benn's immured attitude, which is caused by his aesthetic postulate, an attitude that later in life began to worry him because of its prison-like characteristics and which he expressed when he wrote: "You are escaping behind bars which nothing now can open." The theme of captivity, which we encounter in innumerable variations in modern literature, seems to derive in the first place from modern man's existentialist interpretation of existence, which does not mean that the writer is in every instance committed to upholding philosophical existentialism. Here we are dealing with an elementary experience.

In his *Confessions* St. Augustine has described this experience with astonishing precision when he analyzes the spiritual state in which he found himself after the loss of his dearest friend: "And I was left alone at the fateful place where I could not stay and whence I could not depart." Whereas Max Frisch allows his Anatol Stiller to make the attempt—repeated by Gantenbein with less seriousness but with greater literary elegance—to escape from the fixation of that "fateful place" into a fictitious life, Jean Paul Sartre accepts this "fateful place" with the fortitude of the atheist thinker by interpreting it as the place of his freedom. Sören Kierkegaard's sentences in *Either-Or,* used by Max Frisch as a motto for *Stiller's Diary in Prison,* could also serve as an introduction to J. P. Sartre's hell-framed one-act-play *"Huis Clos (No Exit),"* one of the most radical, dramatic paraphrases of man's destiny to be presented in an existentialist perspective. "Look, that is why it is so difficult to choose oneself," runs the passage from *Either-Or* which Max Frisch quotes, "because in this choice absolute isolation is identical with deepest continuity, because through this continuity every possibility of becoming something else, or rather of rewriting oneself into another self, is entirely excluded." Sartre's unconditional personalism, which permits man no refuge but himself, does not lack cruelty, and thus hell proves to be the best place in which to demonstrate the moral postulate: here man is handed over to himself as his judge and executioner for all eternity. There is no longer any authority in the beyond which could correct man's choice, once it has been made by an act of grace. The existence to which man, in making his choice has condemned himself, is unalterable. For, as Sartre says in the play *"Le diable et le bon Dieu* (Lucifer and the Lord)," "if God does not exist, there is no longer any means of escaping from man." A better illustration of Kierkegaard's statement than Sartre's *"Huis Clos"* can hardly be imagined: the play is of immense importance as a piece of negative theology. Sartre is, no doubt, a moralist of extraordinary and, as I have already remarked, cruel severity. At some points in the play it is possible to discern undertones of a longing for the God who for the sake of absolute humanity, has been deposed (as when Garcin, for instance, shut in with the two women in the obscure hotel room of hell, sighs: "If only a soul could believe in me I should be saved"). But because and as long as this authority, which alone could save man from being shut into himself does not exist outside this closed room, man, who condemned himself, has nothing left but the unceasing circle, the hell of total autonomy. In his "speech of the dead Christ from the building of the world (*Rede des toten Christus vom Weltgebäude herab*)," Sartre called this terrible vision of a world without God "finiteness chewing its own cud." Existentialist thinkers of the rank of Jean Paul Sartre or Albert Camus have sought to win precisely from this terror the strength for a humanism cleansed of all illusion. For Albert Camus, Sisyphos who in the classical myth rolls his rock unceasingly from the abyss to the summit, is a quasi saint in absurdity. "His rock is his cause," we read in the essay inspired by his image, and this essay reaches its height in the proud confession or, if we prefer it, in the desperate paradox: "We have to imagine Sisyphos as a happy man." We could also use a composite expression of Sartre's and call Sisyphos "a desert of pride"; and in "The Flies" it is even said, of the freedom which Orestes won, that it "bears a little likeness to death."

Making Sense of Existence

In the discussion with atheist existentialism we should, however, be treating it too lightly if we used—or even abused—such formulations in order to prove that man cannot live without God. In doing so, we should be degrading God into a stopgap and confirming Gottfried Benn's statement: "God is a bad basis on which to form a style." Nor does the assertion hold good, that without faith in God there could be no true morality, because it lacks transcendental foundation. Conversely Jean Paul Sartre is convinced that we have to dispense with God in order to lay the foundation for the freedom and the nontransferable responsibility of the individual before himself, his evaluation, his identity. The principle of his humanism reminds us of Kant's maxim in the foundation of the Metaphysics of Morals: "One can choose only that value which one desires at the same time to see become a general law (Is existentialism a humanism?)."

But the question arises, what is there to guard man against undertaking with impunity, in his desperate attempt at self-justification, at making sense of his existence through his freely taken choices, the most inhuman of experiments? Thus, on the stage of Sartre's existentialism, Götz, in *Le diable et le bon Dieu,* arranges, in the spirit of despising the divine, a gigantic experiment, in this case a comedy of the Good in order to prove that Good and Bad are human inventions. In Camus' play "Caligula," Caligula too, in the place of the deposed god, experiments with men. Yet Camus' horror at these excesses of human wickedness is not less than his indignation in the face of the injustice of God, of the suffering imposed upon the innocent. That man, *l'homme révolté,* who rebelled against the injustice of God, has lost again the freedom which he won from God and has surrendered it to men who now play the part of God, to the dictators, the hangmen and the nihilists in the course of history—that, for Camus, is the tragedy of our age. Whereas Sartre undeviatingly maintains that even a valid proof of God could not save man from himself, Camus suffers the tragic dilemma of being compelled by the same intellectual and moral honesty to rebel against God on the one hand, and against the unbelieving nihilists on the other. In the conflict between faith and nihilism, between grace and the sword, he defends his moral spiritual position—not without sincere sympathy for the upright Christians to whom he said (in a memorable speech at the Dominican monastery in Paris in 1946): "I feel the same horror of evil as you do, but I do not have the same hope." It is remarkable that in his works too the situation of captivity emerges several times as one which is representative of human existence: Thus, in *La peste* (*The Plague*), a state of emergency is proclaimed for the plague-stricken city of Oran; and in the macabre story, *La chute* (*Der Fall*) the judge Clamans resided in the hellish quarters of the canals ("Grachten") of Amsterdam, the place of his self-condemnation. When readers who expect literature to provide in the first place consolation, and especially Christian consolation, encounter the works of Albert Camus (fatally injured in an accident in 1960), that impatient and intolerant call for something positive can be heard. Could it perhaps be that the unbeliever is putting the believer to shame, because the mystery of wickedness obviously troubles him much more deeply than it does the saturated church Christians who sometimes regard their indifference as a state of redemption? Could it not even be that the rebel, the blasphemer (who expressly says of himself that the man who revolts challenges rather than denies), has the greater spirituality? Is there not an infinite sadness, a heartbreaking sense of grief at being forsaken by God, in this passage from the essay on Sisyphos?: "The certainty of a God who gave meaning to life is much more attractive than the power to do evil with impunity. The choice would not be difficult. But there is no choice." For a man whose spiritual and mental integrity seems to deserve the love of God, God's absence is, I admit, a grave and painful problem. Simone Weil, that Jewess who was so wholly filled with the spirit of Christ, could well have had in mind an unbeliever like Albert Camus—who later published her writings in the Collection *Espoir*—when she wrote: "Of two men without the experience of God, the one who denies him is nearer to God," nearer, we may perhaps add, than the one who in his forced piety imagines himself to have experience of God, and nearer than the one who, out of obedience or convention, claims to have such an experience.

The encounter with the unbelievers, represented by Albert Camus, presents us indeed with an enigma of great theological weight. The idea of a "saint without God"—and Albert Camus certainly never thought of himself in that way, but, rather, as a rebel—as we see in *La peste,* relates to a spiritual constellation which Robert Musil, in his universal novel *The Man Without Qualities* (*Der Mann ohne Eigenschaften*), using an almost identical phrase, "saint without religion," analyzes with penetrating accuracy. Conscious that we are living in an epoch of revolutionary transition, which he already saw approaching in the years before the First World War, Robert Musil suspects the image of the personality that tries to fix man in an ideological frame. By letting the "Man Without Qualities" speak, he is choosing a tentative, improvised mode of being which does not permit of "highfalutin plans," but only of partial solutions, of hypotheses. Again we encounter the theme of captivity; for, as the prisoner waits for the opportunity to break out, so we today can exist only in an "active passivism," in readiness and openness for new, still unthought-of possibilities. The world, in Robert Musil's view, is a laboratory where we have to try out human existence. For that reason we must beware of everything that threatens to put us, hastily and finally, into a fixed frame. And for Musil this also applies to conventional religious faith which is taken for granted. Have not "the visible successes of scientific thought," asks Ulrich, "become possible only since man 'avoids God'?" Again, we might point to Dietrich Bonhoeffer. Yet Musil also wonders whether this "ungodly," "godless" thinking may not be the way to God in our day? What is generally held to be faith is compared to the impotent, pitiful attempt of a chicken to fly. True religion, as Musil understands it, is mankind's most difficult adventure and is still before us. Anyone who asks for something "positive" would have the best chance of finding it here, where belief is denied insofar as it is only a historical tradition and therefore left behind, something ordered and administered by the church, even if, or rather because, Robert Musil's "Man Without Qualities" cannot believe that God has already been. Through his unbelief we can glimpse the outlines of a new, not yet definable faith, related to the impossible, filled with the intuition that perhaps it is God himself who, in this incomprehensible laboratory, experiments with men. With Robert Musil we can but know that man is in no way "complete," and that each one of us is only an attempt, a "potential man." But if we ponder in this, then, beyond the prison wall of a world without God there arises the dimension of hope.

PART V

TOWARD A SECULAR SOCIETY?

18

CULTURAL UNITY AND PLURALISM

by Arend Th. van Leeuwen (Holland)

Unity and Pluralism

The question of cultural unity and pluralism is vast and complex. The terms used in defining the subject are so vague and general as to have little meaning. First, what is culture? If we accept the identification between culture and human existence presupposed in cultural anthropology, culture may be defined as that mode of being which is typically human and which distinguishes human nature from the rest of nature. Second, does the concept of culture include the totality of human self-expression, or is it to be understood as a particular department of social life, as distinguished for instance, from politics and economics? Third, does our subject pertain to culture in the singular or in the plural? Culture as an essential activity of man is part of human existence in all periods of history everywhere in the world. But at the same time a great variety of particular cultures, more or less distinct from one another, have developed throughout history and spread around the world and, although it is difficult to set limits and dates for each culture, together they unquestionably form a pluralistic complex.

We shall approach the concept of culture not in terms of a study of the philosophy of man, but as an actual fact in the course of history. Every man is born into and leads his life within the framework of a particular culture or at the crossroads of various cultures. In modern times, we are all caught in the dynamic interaction between various cultural trends and traditions, all contributing to the main stream of a developing world culture which in the long run is likely to embrace the whole of mankind. But even this world culture is not identical with the abstract anthropological concept of culture as human self-expression, but is a process of formation that is taking place in the twentieth century.

In every society there is a tension and, in some circumstances, a conflict between, on the one hand, the necessity to maintain the basic unity which prevents chaos and anarchy, and, on the other, the essential need to preserve the freedom of every individual and group to follow its own way of life and to make its own spiritual choices. Can this tension be resolved? Can the well-being of all be reconciled with the deepest interests of each individual? Defined in this way, the problem is reduced to finding the middle course between the extremes of individualism and collectivism, the one overstressing the value of individual existence and the other the necessity for corporate cohesion.

But in the course of history and in spite of tensions and clashes, failures and frustrations, most cultures have, on the whole, achieved a certain equilibrium between individual and social demands. Though the golden mean is difficult to attain, it is possible at least to approximate it. At a deeper level, however, the basic question is not how to reconcile individual and collective needs, but how to realize at the same time, and within the same precise context, contrasting and mutually exclusive concepts of the role of the individual as well as of the meaning of collective unity.

Some Essential Features of a Pluralistic Society

In a pluralistic society no concept of the total structure of society has a monopoly. There are at least two, and probably more concepts, each of which claim with greater or lesser urgency to offer the final solution to fundamental human problems. Since it is impossible for any of these concepts to overrule or cancel out its rivals through a process of long-term education, an experimental attitude evolves which enables people to live with competing ideals and ideologies, and which results, in practice if not in theory, in a penetrating process of relativization which affects all groups and their respective concepts and ideals.

Second, such a society presupposes open-mindedness on the part of the various groups which belong to it; a pluralistic society is essentially an open society. This openness goes deeper than a mere insight into the relativity of any concept or into the impossibility of achieving a monopolistic position. Open-mindedness means a fundamental break with the tendency, inherent in the individual as well as in the group, to mold its ideas into closed concepts, to become imprisoned in a self-sufficient vicious circle.

A pluralistic society is a dynamic society in which no group is allowed to remain isolated, and in which all positions and interests are directly or indirectly subordinated to an overruling process which in principle draws the whole social structure into the stream of progressive development.

It should be realized, however, that these three conditions for a pluralistic society can function only in a setting which forces its component groups to work upon one another. It would be too much to call this setting an organic whole, for that would presuppose a unity of a basically biological character. It belongs to their particular qualities as summed up above, to break through the laws of organic life; their cohesion differs from the fixed synthesis which characterizes biological organisms.

A pluralistic society of this kind is admittedly a rare phenomenon, perhaps even only an ideal type which does not really exist. It is certainly easier to point to societies where this pluralism is absent than to those where it is found.

One type of nonpluralistic culture is the tribal type. Basic to any tribal society is a comprehensive pattern, often discernible only after close analysis, which holds the whole tribe together and which tolerates no serious rivals. Societies of this type can exist only in geographical and spiritual isolation. In the event of conflict with neighboring societies, its only alternatives are to maintain its predominant pattern in the face of foreign influences or to surrender it and finally break down. The coexistence of contradictory or mutually exclusive patterns within a society is beyond its cultural horizon.

A second type is what has been characterized as "oriental despotism." This term is open to misinterpretation and comprises a wide sweep of social patterns. Nevertheless, it indicates a basic quality which lies at the root of the traditional cultures of Asia. One of the decisive features of such cultures is the absence of effective checks by society: it is impossible for independent centers of authority to counterbalance the power of the central regime.

In his discussion of traditional Hindu society, the Indian scholar, K. V. Rangaswami, defines genuine absolutism as "a form of government in which all the powers must be vested in the hands of the ruler, there being no other concurrent and independent authority habitually obeyed by the people as much as he is obeyed, and which lawfully resists him or calls him to account."

However, experience has shown that a despotic regime may in many instances permit some autonomy, not only of its individual subjects but also of certain secondary groups. But this does not lead to genuine autonomy. In China and in India the government traditionally permitted the kinship group to settle its own internal affairs in accordance with family laws, but this posed no political threat to a normally functioning despotism. The villagers of imperial China, though less strictly controlled than those, for instance, of India and the Near East, were inescapably tied to an operational system that served the interests of the government rather than their own. The guilds in this type of society were permitted a certain autonomy not because they were strong politically, but because they were irrelevant.[1] The status of religious minorities in the Islamic Near East was strictly limited by the "millet" organization. In traditional China Buddhism made headway during a period of imperial disintegration, but harsh persecutions and

[1] WITTFOGEL has analyzed the role of secondary religions, which he discusses in the particular light of Islamic society and traditional China: *Oriental Despotism,* New Haven, 1957, p. 125.

careful supervision by the government prevented it reaching more than a secondary position. In traditional oriental society, the dominant religion was integrated in the power system of the government, and independent religious power had a chance to arise.

This does not mean that under a despotic government it was impossible for a variety of cultural and religious trends to develop. On the contrary, history gives ample evidence of the ability of these societies in various periods of their development both to bring forth and to absorb a wide range of spiritual movements. Two outstanding examples are the hellenistic period of the Roman Empire and the cultural synthesis of medieval Islam under the Abassid Caliphate, both of which gave magnificent proof of the richness of cultural and religious life which can be tolerated or stimulated within the framework of a politically centralized society. It would, however, be a serious misinterpretation to regard these as pluralistic societies. The decisive fact in this cultural and religious diversification is that it never runs contrary to the basic concept which underlies the whole society. Like a tree which develops its many branches solidly supported by its one trunk, the unitary politico-religious concept which conditions the dominance of the central government, remains the foundation of a variety of cultural expressions which, however, never attain more than secondary relevance. Unity and variety are not contradictory, but complementary aspects. This may be illustrated further from two other worlds, Hinduism and Islam.

Professor Radhakrishnan has argued that Hinduism accepts all religious ideas as facts and arranges them in the order of their intrinsic significance. The bewildering polytheism of the Hindu masses and the uncompromising monotheism of the classes are the expression, at different levels, of one and the same force.[2] The Hindu and Buddhist religions recognize some degree of truth in every form of faith, "with the doubtful result that all sorts of foreign culture and superstitious beliefs are to be found within the pale of these religions." [3] The whole range of religious perception is

[2] *The Hindu View of Life,* 8th imp., London, 1949, p. 32.
[3] *East and West in Religion,* 2nd imp., London, 1949, p. 52.

interpreted as different forms of worship of the one Absolute. Hinduism accepts the fact that mankind seeks for God at various levels and in various directions, and feels sympathy with every stage of the search.

However, this boundless hospitality in no way contradicts a fundamental unity. For the Hindu the most perfect self-expression of the Absolute is embodied in the Vedanta, to which every form of Hinduism in every stage of its growth is related. Indeed, it is even more than that! It is "religion itself in its most universal and deepest significance." [4] Although admitting a graduated scale of religious perceptions of the Absolute, Hinduism enjoins a strict code of behavior. "The theist and the atheist, the sceptic and the agnostic may all be Hindus if they accept the Hindu system of culture and life." In this practical respect also unity and variety go together. "In the interests of spiritual freedom, Hindu society regulated the most intimate details of daily life, and they are the rules of dharma." [5] Hindu Dharma is at the same time one and manifold, being different in all parts of the country and in all periods of Indian history and yet held together by the all-embracing unity of Hindu society.

In a completely different fashion, Islam can be understood as the final synthesis of diverse religious trends. One of the most successful advocates of modern Islam [6] describes Muhammad's mission as "being destined not to the Arabs alone, but for all mankind to the end of the world." "The same causes which led to the appearance on the shores of Galilee, in the reign of Augustus Caesar, of a Prophet whose life is a tragedy, operated with greater force in the seventh century of the Christian era." For the beginning of the seventh century was an epoch of disintegration—national, social and religious. Everything pointed to the need for a more organic revelation of divine government than that attained by Judaism or Christianity. "Never in the history of the world was the need so great, the time so ripe, for the appearance of a Deliverer."

---

[4] S. Radhakrishnan: *The Hindu View of Life,* p. 77.
[5] *Ibid.* p. 80.
[6] Syed Ameer Ali: *The Spirit of Islam,* new ed., London, 1946, p. 18.

In a later chapter the same author traces the tragic course of Islamic history during which the original unity was split asunder by political divisions and schisms.

> Had the followers of Muhammad marched on the lines of the Master and adopted the character of the early Caliphs, the empire would have been still more vast and more durable than that of the Romans. But the greed of the Ommeyyade, the unruliness of the Arab, and his spirit of individualism . . . caused the overthrow of the stupendous fabric which the heroism and devotion of the early Muslims had raised.

This did not spell the end of unity, however. Though the republic fell, the faith lived. "It was the outcome of ages of evolution. It represented the latest phase in the religious development of man; it did not depend for its existence on the life of empires or men. And as it spread and fructified, each race and each age profited by its teachings according to their own spiritual necessities and intellectual comprehension." [7]

These two religions thus present their claims, widely different and yet analogous, to offer mankind, in the midst of bewildering contrasts and contradictions, the glorious and all-embracing unity of the true and unique religion.

Unity and Pluralism in Modern Nation-Building

The unifying forces within a society are not always capable of upholding their claims in the face of strife and conflict or of holding together different traditions which have been thoroughly alienated from one another. The claims of Hinduism and Islam to possess the ultimate answer for the whole of mankind cannot fail to make their coexistence within the framework of one culture and society extremely difficult. The most tragic illustration of this is the partition between India and Pakistan. Here the idea of a genuinely pluralistic society has been frustrated, not by a predominant unity but by the incompatibility of two contradictory concepts, each raising the banner of finality and all-inclusiveness.

---

[7] P. 292.

An eloquent advocate of the Indian view of the problem [8] believes that no country in the world is as clearly marked out by sea and mountains to be a single whole as is India. This geographical wholeness explains a central feature of Indian history: the urge to political unification, in defiance of vast distances and immense difficulties of transport and communication. Prior to the application of science to transport no empire endured for many centuries in India, but the centripetal forces, buttressed by cultural homogeneity, were irrepressible. All history, he concludes, shows that especially since the mechanical revolution there is room in India for only one political system. To call the Hindus or the Muslims a separate nation is to use the term in the unusual sense of a religious group, and in any event it does not follow that nationhood coincides with statehood. The confusion between the two has been one of the chief sources of disquiet and frustration during the last century and a half in Europe. We need to remove the political sense from the whole concept of nationality, and to give up the idea that those who feel themselves to be a nation should necessarily constitute an independent state.[9]

The pluralistic concept of unity is assumed in this line of thinking. First, it implies a secular interpretation of India's history which has developed under the impact of modern technology and civilization. Second, the religious and national communities are dissociated from nationhood in its ethnic sense and statehood as expressed in political organizations.

Gandhi supported this argument in a letter of September 15, 1944, to Jinnah:

> I find no parallel in history for a body of converts and their descendants claiming to be a nation apart from the parent stock. If India was one nation before the advent of Islam, it must remain one in spite of the change of faith of a very large body of their children. You do not claim to be a separate nation by right of conquest but by reason of acceptance of Islam. Will the two nations become one if the whole of India accepted Islam?

---

[8] Beni Prasad: *Indian Hindu-Muslim Questions,* London, 1946.
[9] *Ibid.*, pp. 79ff.

Gandhi's appeal for India's unity differs from that of Beni Prasad, whose presupposition is based on common interest. Gandhi, on the other hand, introduces the idea of the Indian "parent stock" which supposedly formed a nation before the advent of Islam.

He did not have to wait for the Muslim counterargument, for Jinnah's reply arrived within two days:

> ... We maintain that Muslims and Hindus are two major nations by any definition or test as a nation. We are a nation of a hundred million, and what is more, we are a nation with our own distinctive culture and civilization, language and literature, art and architecture, names and nomenclature, sense of value and proportion, legal laws and moral codes, customs and calendar, history and traditions, aptitudes and ambitions: in short, we have our own distinctive outlook on life and of life. By all the canons of international law, we are a nation.[10]

This two-nations concept denies the existence of a pluralistic unity. Jinnah and Gandhi confuse the modern nation-concept with the traditional bounds of their respective religious communities. To a considerable extent the British colonial setting which introduced this secular nation-idea, was responsible for blurring the issues.

The late builder of modern India, Jawaharlal Nehru, never doubted that the old Indian culture was to succumb to "a new and all-powerful opponent—the civilization of the capitalist West. It will succumb to this newcomer, for the West brings science, and science brings food for the hungry millions. But the West also brings an antidote to the evils of this cut-throat civilization—the principles of socialism, of cooperation, and service to the community for the common good." However, he vigorously resisted the British interpretation of modern Indian history, which claimed that the British transformed India into a single unitary state, engendering among Indians a sense of political unity and fostering the beginnings of nationalism. He gives the British credit for having first opened India's window to the West and bringing her one aspect of western civilization—industrialism and science. But having done

---

[10] Quoted from Hector Bolitho: *Jinnah Creator of Pakistan,* London, 1954, p. 149.

so they throttled the further industrial growth of the country till circumstances forced their hand. India was already the meeting place of two cultures, the western Asia culture of Islam and the eastern, her own product. The third impulse, from the modern West, could have solved many of India's problems, but the British, who had themselves helped to introduce it, tried to arrest its influence. "The political unity of India," Nehru wrote, "was achieved incidentally as a side-product of the Empire's advance. In later years, when that unity allied itself to nationalism and challenged alien rule, we witnessed the deliberate promotion of disunity and sectarianism, formidable obstacles to our future progress." [11]

It would be an oversimplification, however, to hold the colonial power responsible for the way in which the modern nation-concept developed in India. The Indian historian, K. M. Panikkar, stresses the radical newness of the Indian nationalism which developed as a result of European contacts, as compared with traditional Hindu patriotism. Yet, there was also "the acceptance of the doctrine of a national personality, of an identification of all the people within the territory with the individuality of the State, of the belief in a kind of mystic brotherhood of the people that constituted the nation. Indian nationalism emphasized the Indian-ness of their people, of their common bond of history, civilization and culture, mystically united to the land of Hindustan." [12]

Modern Muslim nationalism is another illustration of national development based on a special ethos. Wherever nationalism has arisen in the Muslim world, and in whatever form, the "nation" concerned has been a Muslim group. No Muslim people has ever evolved a national loyalty to or even concern for a community that transcended the bounds of Islam.[13]

A remarkable instance of the modern attempt to reinterpret Islamic history is Dr. al Faruqi's presentation of "Urubah" or Arabism, as the genuine expression of Islamic unity.

---

[11] Jawaharlal Nehru: *An Autobiography,* new ed., 1947, pp. 433ff.
[12] K. M. Panikkar: *Asia and Western Dominance,* London, 1953, pp. 491f.
[13] Smith: *op. cit.,* p. 77.

Conceived as an offspring of western nationalism, with similar or identical character, Arab nationalism is of recent origin and certainly new. But conceived as pursuit of "Urubah," Arabism is as old as the Arab stream of being itself, since it is the spirit which animates the stream and gives it momentum. "Urubah" is that which agitated the Arabs to seek their liberty and unity in the twentieth century as well as to press northwards towards the Fertile Crescent to give its people their language, culture and religion, in four succeeding waves: as Muslims in the seventh century A.D., as Arameans in the fifteenth century B.C., as Amorites in the second and third and as Akkadians in the fourth millennium B.C.

In contrast with western nationalism, Arabism means an "open" society, a community which anyone can enter, regardless of race, color or sect. "Whereas the idea of the anglicization or of the germanization of a billion colored people would be repulsive to the English or German nationalist, the idea of the arabization of the universe would fill the heart of the Arab 'nationalist' with joy." [14]

Christian Participation in Nation-Building

In an outstanding study of Christian participation in nation-building, which reflects the thinking of leading Christians in India,[15] the secular democratic nation-state is conceived of as a self-evident foundation of Christian social philosophy.

The attempt to unify the nation through the domination of the State by one religion (Hinduism), one culture (Aryan), one language (Hindi), over the nation-state and through it the whole nation will destroy not only democracy but also national unity, by strengthening the separatist tendencies of the other religions, cultural and linguistic groups. The aggressiveness of any one of them feeds that of the others, and what is destroyed in the conflict is the unity of India.[16]

It is argued that in a land like India, with many different religions, the establishment of the "secular state" is the essential

[14] Dr. ISMA'IL RAGI A. AL FARUQI: *Urubah and Religion,* Amsterdam, 1964, pp. 1–3.

[15] *Christian Participation in Nation Building,* P. D. Devanandan and M. M. Thomas, eds., Bangalore, 1960.

[16] *Op. cit.,* p. 39.

anchor to national unity: it stands for neutrality between religions, for separation of state and religion, and for freedom of religion as a fundamental human right. The secular state is also defended because of the Christian understanding of religion itself. Christians, runs the argument, should be critical of every attempt on the part of any religion, whether Christianity, Hinduism, Islam or Paganism, to discover the unity of all things and to manifest it in a religious synthesis of society. No religious system can ever reflect the true complexity, order, freedom, truth and righteousness of God's order. Secularism is welcomed as a protest against this sacrifice of the fullness of life to man-made unity. "True religion gives society an abiding faith in that ultimate unity of all things which eludes its own grasp, and gives motivation to society to seek it and develop itself in the process." In the Indian social situation, where religion has led society to stagnate in a static unity, a large measure of secularization, and even of the separation of society from religion, is advocated as a necessary condition for a more dynamic society.[17]

In discussing this view, Paul Abrecht has asked whether these Indian Christians have sufficiently realized the basic incompatibility between this concept of a new, individualistic, responsible and national order of life and the traditional cultural patterns. Can the concept of the autonomy of state and society, which is rooted in the Christian understanding of man, be made compatible with ideas and customs which express views of man held in other religious systems? Will the Christian participation in efforts to create the basis of a secular society weaken the Christian witness regarding the true foundations of all social order and nation-building? "At this point the problem of rapid social change becomes very existential for the church." [18]

These questions raise the fundamental problem of the basis on which the church can realize its responsibility to participate in the growth of a genuinely pluralistic society. Neither the ideal of na-

---

[17] *Ibid.*, pp. 155f.

[18] PAUL ABRECHT: *The Churches and Rapid Social Change*, New York, 1961, pp. 201ff.

tional unity nor hopeful prospects for cultural and social renewal can hide the invincible paradoxes inherent in the ideal of a pluralistic society. This ideal strikes at the roots of all religious systems; it is a product of western Christian history; it is presented by the Christian church as a universal human right; it demands an ongoing process of secularization which undermines the very certainties on which the church builds its own witness; it points to a unity which will evolve only in the distant future and it defends the disorder of conflicting trends and powers which is characteristic of the modern technological world.

The Biblical Perspective

The story of the tower of Babel in Genesis 11 may provide the best perspective for an interpretation of our subject. This story may be characterized as a repetition of the Paradise story in the setting of world history. Unity and plurality are the two ends of the axis on which the story turns. The whole earth was one people, and they united their efforts in building the temple tower, the religious center of Babylonic society and a universal symbol of what I have called elsewhere [19] the "ontocratic pattern" which underlies the great civilizations of Asia. This united human attempt to link heaven and earth is revealed as original sin and is judged by the Lord. Mankind is scattered over the face of the earth; and the city, with its tower, is left deserted, a symbol of frustration and disorder. Then follow without interruption the generations of the sons of Noah, the line of the descendants of Ham which ends with the appearance of Abraham, the founder of a great nation.

It is evident that the "nation" which is to descend from Abraham is the exact counterpart of the "people" which built the tower of Babel. For the "people" which was identical with the whole of mankind, the Hebrew word "am" is used, whereas in Genesis 12 "goy" denotes the "nation" that will be the descendant of Abraham. This terminology is remarkable, for throughout the Old Tes-

---

[19] A. TH. VAN LEEUWEN, *Christianity in World History*, London, 1964, pp. 165ff.

tament "am" is used for the elected people of Israel, whereas the surrounding Gentiles are called "goyim" (plural of "goy"). In other words, the nation of Israel has vicariously to represent the original unity that was lost when mankind was scattered over the earth.

Later the same theme is reiterated when the nation of Israel itself is judged by God, and scattered, becoming a "diaspora" in the midst of the Gentiles. And finally, in the New Testament Jesus Christ sums up in his own life, death and resurrection the theme met twice in the Old Testament. On the Mount of Olives, the eschatological center of God's universal rule,[20] Jesus tells his disciples that they will all fall away because of him, for it is written, "I will strike the shepherd, and the sheep of the flock will be scattered." It sounds like an explanation of the Passover which they have just celebrated, in which the blood of the Covenant "is poured out for many." [21] But Jesus adds, "But after I am raised up, I will go before you to Galilee,[22] and it is from there that Jesus sends them out to make disciples "of all nations." [23] Jesus, who on the cross bears the judgment of the scattering of mankind and particularly of the people of Israel as representative of mankind, brings the whole earth into the unity of his coming kingdom under his authority as the risen Lord.

It is against the background of this biblical theme that the question of a Christian understanding of cultural unity and pluralism is to be approached. There is a lesson to be learned:

The lesson is that unity is not to be reached
- on the basis of any religious or ideological concept which claims that it is the only system through which a plural society can be realized,
- nor on the basis of the belief in a "holy nation."
- nor within the setting of a "Christian" society and culture.

---

[20] Cf. Matt. 24 : 3.
[21] Matt. 26 : 27–32.
[22] Vs. 32.
[23] Matt. 28 : 16–20.

But, on the other hand, we may hear a positive lesson too: in the first place, it is the Lord himself who has designed the unity of mankind and who will fulfill his promise at the end of history; no religion or ideology can replace this God-given unity. Second, though a religious or ideological nationalism comes under God's judgment, the secular goal of nation-building can lead toward a genuinely open and pluralistic society which may reflect, within a limited setting and for the time being, the historical goal of universal unity. Third, the church as the body of the crucified and risen Lord of the whole world does not need the support of a "Christian" culture, nation or empire. In the midst of a non-Christian world the church proclaims the good news of the coming kingdom which will restore that pluralistic unity which the Lord has been preparing throughout the course of human history. When this proclamation is heard and understood, the result will be a true open society and there will be room to do the great things which the Lord is doing for mankind.

19

DYNAMICS OF A PLURALISTIC SOCIETY—THE INDIAN EXPERIENCE

by C. I. Itty (India)

Cultures everywhere are faced with an unprecedented crisis. The British historian, Arnold Toynbee, writes of "Civilization on Trial." The Indian historian, K. M. Panikkar, finds "Hindu Society at the Crossroads." The Muslim leader, Mohammad Iqbal, has called for a radical reconstruction of Islamic thought and culture.[1] President Kwame N'Krumah of Ghana points out the critical need of African culture for a new cohesion and synthesis.[2] This crisis in culture is most acutely felt in the lack of unity and inner cohesion. The genius of any culture is its configuration, its pattern of wholeness, and when these are threatened, its very essence is called in question.

One of the main factors that has contributed to the loss of cultural unity has been the emergence of a pluralistic society. Pluralism is not a new phenomenon: it has been a characteristic of all cultures and societies.[3] Every society consists of many men, groups and institutions engaged in preserving and fostering many values,

---

1 *The Reconstruction of Religious Thought in Islam,* Oxford, 1934.
2 *Consciencism,* London, 1964.
3 H. Richard Niebuhr: *Christ and Culture,* New York, 1951, p. 38.

often dissimilar and disparate. A certain measure of pluralism is essential for the freedom and dignity of individuals and groups within a society, and also for the richness and growth of the culture itself. A culture that does not have a certain measure of pluralism becomes rigid and oppressive, and tends to be static and stagnant. The inner conflicts and tensions of a pluralistic society often supply the dynamism for growth.

Every living culture moves between the two poles of unity and pluralism. Therefore a concern for culture should always involve a concern to keep those two poles in balance and in tension.

In modern societies, the cultural balance has been weighted heavily toward pluralism, and the resulting variety of value systems, social relations, institutional patterns, modes of thought and means of communication has enriched culture immensely. "Culture is richer and more powerful than ever before. But it lacks the genuine proper style, a unifying faith, the inner confidence in its own validity. It has no standard of truth, no harmony, no real dignity and divine serenity." [4]

The issue of pluralism deserves serious attention because it is affecting not only all cultures and societies but also human existence and survival at all levels—personal, communal, national and universal. On the other hand, it offers the greatest opportunity that mankind has ever had for developing a fuller, richer, more creative and wholesome personal and corporate life.

It is not possible to present here a comprehensive analysis of the worldwide problem of cultural unity but only to outline briefly the problem in one society.

Traditional Cultural Unity in Indian Society

India has one of the most complex pluralistic societies of our time, made up of people belonging to a variety of religious, ethnic, and linguistic groups. Though the majority of Indians are Hindus, there are large minority communities of Muslims (India has the

[4] J. Huizinga, Quoted by Hendrik Kraemer: *World Cultures and World Religions,* London, p. 346.

third largest Muslim population in the world), Christians, Buddhists, Jains, and Zoroastrians. Hinduism itself is a pluralistic religion comprising various types of beliefs and practices: polytheism, monotheism, monism, syncretism and even materialism. Besides these ancient religions, there are also several new faiths such as theosophy, communism, secularism. Indian society is divided into many caste and subcaste groupings affecting mainly, though not exclusively, Hindus; and economically it is a complex class society consisting both of the traditional classes based on caste and of new classes originating in a capitalist economy. The people of India are also divided on racial and ethnic lines: the Indo-Aryan (mostly in the north), the Dravidian (mostly in the south), the Mongolian (in Assam), aboriginal communities known as hill tribes and a number of small but significant communities such as the Parsees (of Persian origin) and the Anglo-Indians. The linguistic differences cut across religious, ethnic, caste and class groupings and complicate further the cultural pluralism. India has fourteen major languages and a large number of minor languages and dialects.

This pluralism has existed in India for centuries, and yet Indian society has maintained a measure of unity. This social equilibrium was maintained by absorption and coexistence. Through absorption the Vedic religion of the Aryans and the indigenous religion of the Dravidians were merged to form the Hindu religion; Buddhism, which originated in India as a secular protest movement, was soon absorbed so completely by Hinduism that it was practically nonexistent in India for centuries. Sikhism originated as a Hindu attempt to absorb and reconcile itself with Islam. In later years Indian culture became even more composite by absorbing a variety of cultural patterns contributed by Arab traders and European colonizers. "The genius of India has ever been the reconciliation of opposites. The natural bent of the Indian mind, as witnessed abundantly in her religion and philosophy, is to understand and incorporate rather than to reject and discard." [5]

---

[5] FREDERICK V. MOORE: *Christians in India,* Delhi, 1964, p. 48.

Whenever the Indian society found it difficult to absorb new cultural movements it followed the method of peaceful coexistence. This attitude was adopted by various religious communities toward each other. The Syrian Christian community and the majority Hindu community have lived together for more than fifteen centuries, giving an excellent illustration of this spirit of tolerance and respect. The relationship between Hindus and Muslims in India, was also generally cordial and tolerant until it took a violent turn during the period of political agitation for the dividing of the country and the establishment of Pakistan.

A combination of absorption and coexistence is apparent also in the way Hindu society held together various caste and subcaste groupings. By providing a religious sanction for the caste structure it maintained the various caste groupings within the larger framework of Hindu society, but without either social intercourse or cultural conflict between them.

However, in the past, social unity and cultural integration have largely been confined to caste, language and religious groupings: people have seldom had a sense of belonging to the Indian society as a whole. Though the different cultural groupings had much in common— their attitude to life, sense of values, societal structures, historical heritage—there was very little awareness and appreciation of this. On the contrary, each cultural grouping tended to emphasize its own uniqueness. It is not difficult to see the reasons for this. Indian society was never united into a single nation until the achievement of independence in 1947. Second, until the establishment of British rule, the various Indian cultures had hardly felt any impact from an entirely foreign culture, which would have challenged them to see their own similarities. Third, until the introduction of English as a common language, at least among the educated, and the achievement of a measure of social mobility, people belonging to one part of the community had scarcely any possibility of knowing those in other parts.

The most important characteristic of the traditional cultural unity of India has been its religious orientation. Hinduism has supplied the basic norms, beliefs and values underlying Indian culture; it has shaped its family system and social structures and relations; it has been the major factor in determining the character of Indian art, music, literature and architecture. For many people, Indian culture is synonymous with Hindu culture. Religion, society and culture were so integrated that they were hardly considered as separate entities. The fact that Hinduism has remained solely an Indian religion—with the exception of Nepal and Bali—has reinforced its character as an Indian, ethnic-cultural religion.

The invasion of Islam and the introduction of Christianity did not seriously challenge this basic religious integration of Indian culture. In fact, the growth of these foreign religions among Indian people led the majority Hindu community to reinforce the religious orientation of its culture, in self-defense. The Muslim and Christian communities were also led to discard their Indian cultural heritage and to pattern their cultures after those of the lands from which these religions came. For example, the Muslim community in India rejected the Hindu code of ethics and introduced instead "sharia," the Muslim law. They rejected the Devanagifi Script and introduced Arabic script for the Indian language. In short, they developed their own culture on the basis of Islam, claiming to be a people totally different from the Hindu Indians, and later demanding to be recognized as a separate nation, Pakistan. The other important minority community—the Indian Christians—also developed a culture largely based on their religion, though they did not carry this as far as did the Muslim community. In spite of the introduction of religious pluralism, Indian culture maintained its religious unity of culture, this time in the form of a plurality of cultures all patterned and integrated by the religions concerned.

During the last five centuries, as Indian society has become religiously pluralistic, a process has been initiated to develop a composite Indian culture made up of the various religions and cultural strands within society as a whole. Moreover, these religious and cultural groupings have influenced one another even as they developed separately. However, this modern cultural evaluation has received conscious recognition and support only in recent years, as Indian society has developed a sense of nationhood.

The leaders of the freedom movement and the architects of the Indian nation-state have obviously envisaged building on this trend to usher in a new era in Indian cultural history.

The Present Crisis

To what extent can the traditional unifying factors be operative in India today? Is it possible and desirable to expect "religion" to continue to be the primary basis of cultural unity? Can cultural unity be confined to the narrow limits of village, region, or linguistic area, or caste or religious community? Does the unprecedented dynamism of the present-day pluralistic Indian society permit the traditional methods of absorption and coexistence to operate effectively?

First of all, the new political situation in India today requires that the context and contours of cultural unity be widened to encompass the entire national society. India today for the first time in her history is a nation-state, and therefore cultural unity has become for the first time a political necessity. Political integration requires an emotional integration of people, based on shared social goals and cultural values.

But precisely at this period when cultural unity has become an urgent necessity for the political development of the nations, the pluralistic groupings within Indian society have emerged with new dynamism as divisive forces. The national struggle and the attainment of independence have awakened the various religious, linguistic, caste, and regional groupings to a new self-awareness and sense of individuality.

It may be argued that the present resurgence of cultural groupings is more in keeping with Indian history than the attempt to build a single state based on territorial nationality, and that what is required is a recognition of the cultural groups as separate nation-states. This view is held by political parties like Dravida Munnetta Kazhagam in South India. This issue cannot be dealt with in detail here. Suffice it to say that a breakup of Indian society into various sovereign states each consisting of a single cultural unit is not feasible due to lack of clearly defined geographical limits for such units and to their vast number. The major linguistic areas alone offer a certain possibility, but even that does not offer a practical solution. The will of the people as expressed so far has been definitely in favor of one "nation-state." One school of thought, though not a significant one, advocates the development of existing cultural groupings, not as separate nations, but to function like other interest groups in a democracy through their bargaining power.[6] This is a realistic approach considering the growing influence which cultural groupings have on their adherents and the power which they already exercise. However, it is hard to believe that such a process which encourages competition between many narrow group loyalties would not lead to national disintegration and anarchy. The only feasible course seems to be to weave a national culture from the various strands contributed by the newly awakened cultural groupings.

The traditional methods of absorption and coexistence seem to have serious limitations in the present situation of dynamic pluralism. Religiously based cultures do not lend themselves easily to absorption by one another, although certain factors contributed to such a merging in India of Buddhism and Hinduism. The major minority religions in India, such as Islam and Christianity, have put down their roots in Indian soil; they have a long history of separate existence and a large following who would resist absorption, and they have international connections to give them a sense of strength and identity. However, there is evidence that Hinduism, with its genius for absorption, may be able to incorporate within itself various elements of these two religions. But it is yet to be seen whether this process will continue, and if so how long Hinduism will be able to resist a radical change in its character. But the fact remains that the Muslim and Christian communities in India have come to stay, and there is no possibility of eliminating them by absorption.

Coexistence is also running into serious difficulties in the in-

---

[6] MYRON WEINER: *Politics of Scarcity,* Asia Publishing House, Bombay, 1963.

creasingly dynamic Indian society. Modern means of communication have opened the closed societies and brought them into intimate contact with each other. Growing urbanization and industrialization have shaken traditional patterns of community and society. The introduction of democratic political institutions and new economic organizations, and a new sense of human values in all the traditional cultural groupings, and a dynamic interpenetration of cultures and societies and increasing personal relations across traditional groupings have made the static formula of coexistence unworkable and undesirable. Static coexistence is giving way to dynamic cooperation between and within groups more and more in terms of common humanity and common citizenship, rather than on the basis of common membership in a caste, religion or village.

The crucial factor in present-day pluralism is not the traditional cultural groupings but the impact of western culture which is not confined to any identifiable group. It has initiated three simultaneous revolutions in Indian society: the scientific, which is altering the ways of thought; the technological or the urban, which is changing the mode of life; and the secular, which is transforming the "mood" of man. It manifests itself in entirely new cultural values, family structures, interpersonal relationships, categories of thought, patterns of community, means of communication, and cultural media. The traditional cultural and social structures including the joint family, the caste and the village, have been shaken. This new cultural force cannot be easily resisted, absorbed, or accommodated. It is spreading like a potent virus in the entire culture.

The greatest challenge that the Indian culture faces today is to its religious basis. The traditional unity of religion and culture is being shaken by revolutionary changes in the political, economic, social and religious realms. The establishment of a secular state has meant a complete separation of the state and religion, recognition of the equal status of all citizens irrespective of their religion, and the initiation of a process of secularization of politics, law and education. Besides, by accepting its responsibility for establishing economic and social justice, the state has moved into the realm of social structures, relations and customs which functioned traditionally under religious sanctions.

Recent economic changes have also weakened the religious control of social structures and cultural values. Industrialization has challenged the traditional division of labor along caste lines maintained by religious sanctions. Urbanization has destroyed the joint family system. Science and technology have brought a new attitude toward nature, history, and secular life, quite different from traditional religious concepts. Nature is desacralized. History is seen as linear rather than a cyclic process. Life here and now takes on new meaning and significance. More and more areas of life are gradually freed from religious and metaphysical control. The traditional integration of culture and religion is heading for a final breakdown.

However, many people in India would question this claim. Several arguments are offered in support of their view. One of these points out that studies in cultural anthropology have clearly shown that religion was essential to cultural integration and survival in the past, and therefore it cannot be otherwise in the future. But an increasing number of anthropologists and sociologists are of the opinion that "the spaceless and timeless generalizations about the 'integrative functions of religion' are largely, although not of course entirely, derived from observations in nonliterate societies." [7] Since the breakup of medieval unity and the religious divisions resulting from the Reformation, the cultural unity of Europe has been based on a common intellectual heritage and a classical tradition rather than a common faith. In a religiously pluralistic society, no one religion is able to integrate the whole culture; in such societies, the different and even contradictory value systems of various religions often act as divisive forces working against the development of a unified culture. Other factors may also oppose the integrative role of religion. Professor Milton Yinger lists five of these: when the "established expectancies" of the members of society are frus-

---

[7] MILTON J. YINGER: *Religion, Society and the Individual,* New York, 1957, p. 62, quoted from Robert Merton, *Social Theory and Structures.*

trated; when social change reduces the ritual and belief questions; when mobility from society to society is great; when society is sharply divided into classes or other hierarchical divisions; when outside pressures split a society.[8] If this analysis is correct, then it is quite clear that the religious unity of Indian culture is doomed as all the factors mentioned above are present and growing in Indian society today.

Toward a New Culture and a New Basis for Unity

What does this analysis of India's cultural crisis imply for the future? What is the role of the various religious communities in reconstructing Indian culture on a new basis?

First of all, the religious communities must accept the historical inevitability and practical necessity of a secularized culture. Second, the various groupings must cooperate to evolve and disseminate a common outlook and ethos conducive to the development of an integrated national community. Third, all religious groups, separately and together, must make a supreme effort to supply a spiritual basis for the secularized culture and national values.

I. *A secularized culture.* The historical inevitability of secularization is evident in the movement of society everywhere. "The revolutionary history of the West up to the present time is rightly held to have been a continuous ongoing process of secularization which nothing has been able to halt, let alone reverse." [9] Now, largely due to the impact of the West, the nonwestern societies are caught up in this historical process. It is both the precondition and the consequence of a technological civilization. The desacralizing of nature and culture is inescapable in a technocratic era. In the Indian situation, secularization is necessary not merely to prepare the ground for a technological civilization, but also to provide the basis for common humanity and citizenship in a culturally heterogeneous society.

First of all, the secularization of culture means its liberation

---

[8] *Ibid.*, pp. 67–69.
[9] AREND TH. VAN LEEUWEN, *op. cit.*, p. 331.

from religious and metaphysical control. This liberation helps to remove the most important barrier to cultural unity in Indian society. It also helps to de-absolutize and demythologize culture, so it is seen as relative, provisional and open to change and dynamic growth. Second, secularization of culture implies a new emphasis on life here and now, on the world and history as a whole. The religious orientation of culture has often been the primary factor curbing such an emphasis in Indian life and thinking. This change in attitude is a precondition for the growth of the scientific outlook and technological development. Third, secularization means an increasingly differentiated society which encourages freedom and creativity, provides an opportunity for social relations, and permits the realignment of society on functional terms with a consequent breakdown of the traditional walls of separation between the cultural groupings. Fourth, secularization means that certain areas of life and thought become more and more autonomous; that is to say, they are governed by their own built-in code of ethics and behavior. People belonging to different religious groupings who are involved together in some particular sphere of life can adopt common attitudes, values and styles of life dictated by its purpose and function rather than by their religious traditions. In short, secularization helps to destroy the traditional barriers between religious cultures and provides a new opportunity for developing a common culture.

By what means can a secularized culture be developed in a country like India, and how can the various religious groups help in such a process?

Secularized sociopolitical institutions are both a means of developing a secularized culture and an expression of it, and these should be established and strengthened. Foremost among such structures are state, law, educational institutions, welfare agencies and community organizations. India has already initiated the secularizing of these agencies and institutions, but this process needs the wholehearted support of the people, including the various religious organizations and groups. According to the Constitution, the state gives no preferential treatment to any particular religion, and guarantees freedom of religion to individuals and groups; it forbids discrimination on grounds of religion, race or caste and prohibits state taxation for any religious purpose.[10]

The establishment of a secular state has meant the secularization of politics at the local, regional and national levels. The majority of political parties in India today are secular in their composition and outlook. However, religiously oriented communal groups bring strong pressure on these secular parties; and some communal political parties do exist. Religious groups in India have a particular responsibility to fight against such communalism.

In the past religion has exercised a great influence in the field of law. Custom, under religious sanction, dictated not only personal morality but also social relations. As customs varied according to religious and caste groupings, a number of legal systems developed, causing enormous difficulties in intergroup relations. There was very little room for new concepts and ideas on human rights to find legal expression. But the situation is changing. Law is being increasingly liberated from the rigid control of religion. Universally valid human rights are incorporated in the Constitution. The state is working out codes of law applicable to all citizens irrespective of religion or caste. The new laws concerning marriage, inheritance, the rights of women, and so on, incorporated in what is called the Hindu Code Bill, are excellent examples of these. Religious groups and especially the majority Hindu community have a responsibility to further this process of secularization of law and to help people to see its validity and desirability.

Eucation plays a key role in developing a secular culture. Secular educational institutions are essential to free scientific inquiry, and to the development of a national community. Schools and colleges run by religious groups often tend to perpetuate religious prejudices and to prevent the development of open communities. Universities, which claim to be centers of culture, must be pioneers in the development of a secular outlook. Welfare agencies must also be recognized as effective means for developing a secularized cul-

---

[10] *The Constitution of India*—Articles 15, 25, 26, 27.

ture. In the past, most of them were run by religious organizations with religious motivations, in the interest of one community; the new situation requires that they be secularized, that service be rendered for its own sake, and that it be given to all those in need irrespective of their religious affiliation.

The concept of community is a new one in India, especially among Hindus. The only community they knew was the primary groups of family, caste and village. Rapid urbanization and industrialization have destroyed these traditional community structures and are forcing the development of new forms. But in this period of transition, there is a vacuum, and religious groups ought to engage in a common effort to evolve new patterns of community and social organization.

Traditional Indian culture, art, music, dance, painting, sculpture, architecture and literature have been very much under religious control. If such a pattern were to continue it would be very difficult to evolve a national culture in a pluralistic society. These media must be secularized and helped to express the common concerns of all people and to mediate the composite cultural heritage.

II. *A national culture*. The secularization of the various cultures in a pluralistic society is one step toward providing a new basis for unity. Religious walls which keep cultures apart are destroyed, and possibilities for interpenetration are opened. But such interpenetration does not take place automatically; it depends largely on the effort by the religious and cultural groups to develop common values and ethos based on their common nationality.

There is a strong possibility of evolving a national culture in a pluralistic society if the people share a common heritage from the past, a common involvement in the present and common goals for the future. The various cultural groupings should try to see their own traditions as part of a composite heritage which is shared by the whole society. They should also face together the tasks and challenges of today. The national struggle for independence gave a clear example of how persons and communities belonging to different religious and cultural traditions can establish a united front. In fact, it was in that common struggle that the present Indian national community was born. The danger is that now that self-government has been achieved the people will return to their narrow traditional loyalties and allow the national community to die. They need to see that their common struggle has not come to an end with the establishment of self-government, that in fact the more exacting struggle has only begun. It is not a struggle against outside forces but against internal threats: the threat of poverty, illiteracy, disease, social disintegration, economic injustice, spiritual bankruptcy, and other social evils. The various cultural groupings must see these social evils as national problems whose solution will require a concerted effort by all people. It is in a common struggle against the demonic forces within society itself, that the young national community will grow in strength and evolve common goals and values which will give it a sense of purpose. The preamble of the Indian constitution states that the goal of the nation-state is "to secure to all citizens (a) justice, social, economic and political, (b) liberty of thought, expression, belief, faith and worship, (c) equality of status and opportunity." However, the people as a whole need to share these principles, to translate them into action, and to evolve a common ethos and cultural values in the life of society at every level. In this task, the adherents of historical religious and secular ideologies have a common responsibility:

They have a duty to be involved together in the process of transforming India's cultural traditions and to evolve a common outlook and ethos conducive to the development of a responsible state and society. In this common task they must enter into conversation with each other with the aims in view. First, to understand one another's cultural traditions and the truths about God, man and the world underlying those traditions; second, to study new trends in philosophy, art, and religion in India, with a view to defining the living issues of Indian culture today; and third, to discuss in common these issues, each bringing to the common pool, the best possible critical and constructive cultural insights. It is through such a common search that citizens of India in this generation and the next can help in the development of a body of insights about man, the structures of social existence and the nature and destiny of his freedom and also of a common cultural life embodying the insights and influencing the thoughts, emotions and the spirit of the nation.[11]

III. *A culture based on spiritual foundations.* All cultures—even those which are secularized—require spiritual foundations. Without such a basis, a secular culture will have no firm roots, no emotional power, and no sense of direction. A secular culture is a culture open to influences from within and without which keep it dynamic and growing. But should this be indiscriminate openness? If so, will this not lead to a lack of direction and confusion? If not, what should be its frame of reference for judgment and selection?

Such a criterion cannot come from within the secularized culture itself, as it would then be part of the culture that it seeks to judge and change. It must come from outside and transcend the culture and yet at the same time be related to it. This is precisely the realm of spiritual values. A culture which is not open to the spiritual experiences and values of man becomes a closed culture and betrays its true secular character; secularization then becomes secularism, an absolutist ideology.

Perhaps the necessity for a spiritual basis for a secularized culture can be seen most easily in the personal life of men and women. In a differentiated society man lives as "one man in many worlds." He plays different roles and lives in a diversity of spheres. Each sphere in which he plays a role seems to be a world in itself, with its own autonomy, built-in authority, code of ethics, modes of behavior, and cultural ethos. These different and often contradictory worlds compete for his time, loyalty and interests, with a resulting loss of wholeness and integration of personality. He becomes a "bundle of functions tied together by the fiber of the body and the brain." Only a spiritually based inclusive cause or a transcendental common frame of reference can help him recover personal wholeness and integrate his various worlds. To insist that a secularized culture also must have a spiritual basis does not mean to restore religious domination. On the contrary, it is the right

[11] P. D. Devanandan and M. M. Thomas, eds.: *Christian Participation in Nation Building*, Bangalore, 1960, pp. 263–264.

spiritual basis that encourages secularization and preserves the freedom and openness of culture. The spiritual basis is not intended to absolutize and invoke religious sanction for social structures, but rather to preserve their genuine secular character, their historical provisional, relative, functional, and experimental nature, and at the same time permeating them with spiritual values. "However well ordered it may be, the secular can only be delivered from frustration and brought to fruition, as it is vivified and transmuted by the forces of religion." [12] This implies not only a new relationship between religion and culture, but also a renewal of the spiritual and ethical character of religion. "The hope of an ethical society is bound up in the possibility of restoring ethical integrity to religion and religious dynamic to the moral effort." [13]

The crucial question is, Will the religions of India, and especially the dominant Hindu religion, be able to provide an adequate spiritual basis for a secularized culture? A number of western Christian thinkers believe not.[14] They argue that the scientific secularized culture originated from within Christian civilization, and that only the Judeo-Christian faith can offer an adequate theological basis for a secularized culture. There is a good deal of truth in this. However, to deny that non-Christian religions could offer a spiritual basis and a theological framework for a scientific and secularized culture is to go too far. Students of Hinduism can point to various instances of secular forces, movements and schools of thought emerging from within Hinduism. Buddhism, and to some extent Jainism, were originally secular movements which emerged from within Hindu society. The Lokayata system or school of thought in Hinduism was essentially a secular philosophy of life. Kautilya, the author of "Artka Sastra" the Hindu classic on government, is often spoken of by Hindu politicians as the Indian Machiavelli. Hinduism's fourfold duty consists of artka, kama,

---

[12] Philip Arthur Micklem: *The Sacred and the Secular,* London, 1948, p. 16.

[13] Reinhold Niebuhr: *Does Civilization Need Religion?* New York, 1941, p. 242.

[14] Paul Abrecht: *The Churches and Rapid Social Change,* London, 1961, pp. 197–207.

Arend Th. van Leeuwen: *op. cit.,* pp. 349–365, 399–422.

dharma and moksha, in other words, economic, sensual, moral and spiritual values. It is also true that the folk literature such as Panchatantra, Hitopedesha and Kathasaritsagara, stresses the artka tradition, the values of this worldly existence. Perhaps the most important argument in favor of Hinduism's claim to provide a spiritual basis for a secular culture can be drawn not from its history or traditional theology but from the resurgent Hinduism of the present time. As Dr. Devanandan wrote, "Merely to indicate that Hindu metaphysics does not justify the contemporary Hindu concern for life here and now, does not help. The fact remains that modern Hinduism is tremendously concerned with all that life in our world today means, and ought to mean to modern man." [15] The beginnings of this new secular outlook can be found in the renaissance movements which were inspired by a long line of Hindu reformers, starting with Raja Ram Mohan Roy in the early decades of the nineteenth century and reaching to Swami Vivekananda at the close of that century. This movement gathered momentum in this century through the efforts of leaders like Gokhale, Gosh, Tagore, Gandhi, Bhave and Radhakrishnan. They reinterpreted Hinduism to take into account the reality of this world, the significance of the secular life, the value of genuine humanism, and the importance of science, technology and social and political organization. The Gandhian Sarvodaya movement is an excellent illustration of this understanding of Hinduism. Though the movement itself is confined to a small section of Hindu society, it has a profound influence in the entire Hindu society and the nation as a whole. It may well be claimed that the dynamic of the new secular faith which provides the drive for national planning and concern for international affairs can be traced to the Gandhian emphasis underlying the Sarvodaya ideal. It is also true that the essentially secular Gandhian view of life has become a fundamental of faith in contemporary Hinduism. The emergence of this new secularism points to the possibility of a new era in the development of Hindu culture and social ethics.

---

[15] P. D. DEVANANDAN: *Gospel and the Hindu Intellectual,* Bangalore, p. 22.

It can be argued that this secularist trend has been forced upon Hinduism by historical necessities and is largely a result of the Christian impact. But as M. M. Thomas points out, "After all, secular movements and historical necessities have in the West played no small part in bringing churches to an appreciation of open secularism. The realization that it accords with the Christian fundamentals came afterwards."[16] Even today, this realization is not shared widely by Christians in the West where over a period of years secularization has gone a long way. The fact that Hinduism has only recently come to appreciate secularization cannot be taken as evidence of its inherent inability to accept a secular culture. Though it may be true that the Christian impact has been either a direct cause or a catalytic agent of the new resurgence in Hinduism, its leaders hold that its main source is in Hinduism itself. In any case, this new Hindu movement is making a bold attempt to provide a spiritual basis for a secularized culture.

Similar movements are afoot in the Muslim community in India today. The Ahmadiya movement is an excellent example of resurgent Islam, presenting itself as a progressive rationalist religion well adapted to the modern scientific world. Various Muslim leaders have attempted to interpret Islamic theology, law and customs to suit the modern age. Cheragh Ali Khan, the founder of the first Muslim college at Aligarh, tried to show the fundamental concord of Islam and science. The greatest Muslim reformer of this century was Mohammad Iqbal whose famous book, *The Reconstruction of Religious Thought in Islam,* is a bold reinterpretation of Islamic thought for the modern way of life. However, the Indian Muslim leaders are still struggling to find in Islam a spiritual basis for a secularized culture.

The Christian Contribution

The Christian community in India comprises only about 2 per cent of the total population. In spite of this minority situation it

---

[16] *Religion and Society,* Vol. IX (No. 1), 5, Bangalore.

has a significant part to play, out of proportion to its numerical strength.

It cannot be said that a concern for the unity and reconstruction of Indian culture is widespread or profound in the Christian community. Certain Christian groups, mainly among the intelligentsia, share this concern, but the Christian community, by and large, is quite indifferent. The first great need is to help them recognize their responsibility in this matter as part of their Christian obedience. Culture is an area of human life which comes under the Lordship of Jesus Christ and the church's witness to the redemption of Christ must inevitably include the message of the renewal of society and culture.

However, the real difficulty lies in discovering how a Christian concern for cultural unity should be expressed in actual situations. Richard Niebuhr has pointed out that "the Christian perplexity in this area has been perennial, and that the problem has been an enduring one through all the Christian centuries." [17] It is the task of Christian individuals and groups in each place and time through practical obedience to find an answer to this problem in their own situations.

In India today the Christian community has the responsibility of practical obedience in three main areas: the secularization of culture, the development of common values and ethos for the national community and the building of a national, secular culture on spiritual foundations. In none of these areas is their task very different from that of other religious communities. However, their minority position, their Christian heritage and theological insights enable them to make a unique and significant contribution.

In the secularization of culture, their main responsibility is to strengthen those sociopolitical forces and agencies that further the process. In this respect, their minority situation is not a disadvantage. As Prof. D. E. Smith has pointed out, minorities are natural guardians of the secular state, and have played a signifi-

---

[17] *Christ and Culture,* p. 2.

cant role in its evolution in the West and also in India.[18] The presence of a large Muslim minority and other significant minorities, including the Christian, helped the Indian society to accept a secular rather than a Hindu state. They must continue vigilant in maintaining the secular character of the state and politics, abandoning any idea of organizing their own religious political parties or of mixing politics with their communal interests. They have a key role to play also in the secularization of law. The Muslims and Christians have been far more reluctant than Hindus to allow the state to secularize personal law. The strong plea by Christians for exemption from the 1961 legislation prohibiting the dowry system, which is as onerous a burden to Christians as to Hindus, is an illustration of this negative attitude. Instead of taking such reactionary measures, the Christians should give a lead to other religious communities. In the secularization of education and social welfare the Christian contribution is important. But here too Christians have been far too slow in giving a secular character to their educational and welfare institutions, although there has been a definite change in their attitude in recent years. The Christian community has also failed to take much interest in Indian art, literature, music, dance, architecture and so forth. At the same time they accepted as Christian many western cultural forms. But here too a definite change of attitude is evident. Efforts are being made to indigenize Christian forms of worship, patterns of community life, and ways of thought. However, this is not enough. The Christian community must make a contribution to the reconstruction and renewal of Indian cultural media.

In the development of common national values and a common ethos, the main task of the Christian community is to express solidarity with their fellow countrymen in their common quest. They must grow out of their theological and cultural exclusivism, and their intolerant attitude toward other religions and people. The Christian church in India must rediscover the universality of the

---

[18] DONALD EUGENE SMITH: *India as a Secular State,* Princeton, 1963, pp. 41–44.

gospel and the common humanity of man. It must believe that all men are created by God; that all live by his providence and all are in the state of sin; that the redemption God has wrought in Christ is for all; and that it is his purpose to direct all history to its consummation in his kingdom. Such belief should issue forth in an attitude of solidarity with all men, without any feeling of moral or spiritual superiority over non-Christians. The Christian community in India must claim the Indian cultural heritage as its own, and offer its own unique Christian tradition as part of the composite national culture.

The gospel is the good news of the God-given community: the concept of "Koinonia" is at the heart of the Christian faith, and, by and large, the church has fostered a sense of community across social, national and linguistic barriers. If this theological insight and tradition were translated into secular terms and introduced in the society at large, it would contribute to the future of Indian society which is at present engaged in a search for new patterns of community and new forms of social life. The church, which believes in the solidarity of all men, and which has the experience of being a universal community, should help the developing culture to avoid the temptation to become exclusive and aggressively nationalist. It should also emphasize that national unity and new patterns of community should not lead to monolithic structures that destroy human freedom and cultural pluralism.

> The reordering of the new society should be based on the principle of pluralism. Both the study of society and the Christian doctrine of man convince us that man in society is in fact a many-sided person and that he has a number of different needs. Any attempt to satisfy these needs with one rigid social pattern, such as a communal or Communist society, results sooner or later in the suppression of individuality and the frustration of creative aspects of human nature.[19]

A new understanding of secularization has emerged in recent years as one of the most important ecumenical insights. The Christian community in India must be engaged in the current debate

---

[19] P. D. Devanandan and M. M. Thomas: *Christian Participation in Nation Building,* Bangalore, 1960, p. 159.

among both Christians and others. They may not agree with those theologians who speak of secularization as the continuation of Christianization or as the first priority in the mission of the church. Still they should listen to men like Bonhoeffer who challenge us to think in terms of a "religionless Christianity" and a new style of life in the secularized world. They need to recognize that secularization is a legitimate protest against religious control of society, and that it is rooted in the Christian faith. The autonomy of the civil society cannot be understood without reference to its responsibility to the laws and purpose of God. Without such a spiritual foundation secularization may become a new yoke rather than a new freedom.

20

COMMUNITY—CHRISTIAN AND SECULAR

by Charles C. West (U. S. A.)

What is the basis of human community? This question is not raised by people who are secure in their stable cultures and philosophies. Ideologists out to transform the world into the image of their ideal put it only as a foil for a certain answer. But the characteristic of our time is that this question is being asked, searchingly, sincerely, not only by the Christian contributors to this volume, but by secular and religious men, by politicians, scientists and philosophers in every part of the world, in a tone which shows that none feels that he knows the answer.

The question is not new to the ecumenical movement. The experience of ecumenism has in fact been the questioning, the breaking and the experimental renewal of the communities of the church, as they face, in missions, the work of God with a non-Christian world; in ethics and evangelism, the destructive impact of the word of God on traditional Christendom; and even in "faith and order" the force of a biblical rediscovery of the church over against the existing churches. The World Council of Churches indeed lives by the grace which comes to Christians when they honestly face the uncertainty, the problematic nature, of their own communities or ideologies.

What is new in our time is that during the past generation a large part of the world has begun to take part in a secular form of this experience. Ancient cultures are seeking in their national independence, a self-identity they once thought they had. Ideological movements (notably communism, but also the humanist secularism of the western world) find that the social realities with which they must cope call their basic assumptions more and more in question. Religions of all kinds are being forced by events into that self-questioning which Jews and Christians have faced from the beginning because of the God they serve. The behavioral sciences underline the experience of all of us that the very communities in which our being takes shape—family, neighborhood, parish, class—are shifting, relative units made and broken by larger social forces, not structures of a permanent order. Communities, cultures and ideologies, even where we cling to them or try to make them anew, are no longer the source of our certainty and security. They have become tasks in an uncertain world.

This process, and our recognition of it, we know as secularization. It moves toward a state of human relations in which no religion or ideology dominates, and where no common sense of the timeless order of reality prevails. Is this a real possibility for modern man? Does this condition inevitably give rise to a flight toward religion, or a philosophy of secularism which imposes a humanist world view and an unlimited confidence in man on the world? Is it possible for man to live with the relativity which a fully secular society brings with it?

This writer believes in this possibility. He does so because he is a Christian, and finds the secular attitude to be required by a faithful response to God's revelation in history. But he hopes to demonstrate also to non-Christians that secularization is not the practice of self-deception by unstable men and cultures, but the real state of affairs in society today, a state which is full both of dangers and promises for the future, and within which our responsibility for our fellow human beings is given to us.

The Process

We start with a historical definition. The word "secular," with its variations "secularism" and "secularization," is relatively new as a general term in our western languages. Derived from the Latin word "seculum," meaning "age" or by derivation "this age or generation," its meaning until the nineteenth century was highly specific. Today, in the vocabulary of the natural sciences, it still refers to a long, indefinite period of time which is, however, not recurrent or periodical, as for example "the secular cooling of the earth." In cultural history it was used for centuries to designate those clergy whose ministry was in the "world" as distinct from those who were part of monastic orders. The implication was clearly that the structure and order of the church itself, expressed especially in its monastic life, was not temporal but eternal, whereas the secular realm would pass away. The structure of the medieval synthesis, brought to completion in Thomas Aquinas but deep-rooted in the popular consciousness as well, was not, however, dualistic, but hierarchical. The secular realm was not evil. It was given a certain value and autonomy at its level. It was the realm of temporal political power, of labor and trade, of the appetites in their place, of the natural virtues and the natural law. It was the realm where man seeks his proper ends with the help of his unaided reason controlling his passions. But it was, in principle, a lower realm, the realm of nature not of grace, the realm where reason demands its completion by revelation and where goodness is subordinate to the higher virtues of faith with their structure in the church.

Into this relatively stable world view broke the dynamic process of secularization. The word seems first to have come into use when church lands were turned over to secular princes in the Treaty of Westphalia in 1648. The reality however was already at work, as not only property, but positions of political power, expressions of art and culture, fields of knowledge, and even human ideals and values were gradually removed from the dominance of the church and the sacred structure of ideas and culture it represented. Its expressions were manifold. Already in the late Middle Ages William of Ockham attacked the concepts of substance, being, and first mover as categories for understanding nature, and opened the way for later natural science's tendency to think in terms of functional operations. Galileo, himself a believing Christian, sought the right to declare as true a theory of the movement of the earth which his observations suggested and his imagination conceived, even though the entire religious as well as physical world view of his time, was threatened by this breakthrough.[1] The artists of the Renaissance broke through their religious subject matter to express increasingly the vitalities of secular existence in all its variety. Machiavelli, sometimes called the first social scientist, analyzed the political forces of his day to give advice to his prince without regard for any larger structures of philosophy, ethics or religion or for any goal save the unification of Italy. Hugo Grotius, spurred on by the terrible example of the wars of religion, felt it his proper service of God to develop a system of natural law in ethics which would be valid *etsi, per impossibile, Deus non daretur,* for it would be evidently true to all reasonable men, whatever their dogmatic persuasion.

All these examples have one common feature. They did not represent efforts to combat Catholic Christianity with another world view. They were simply movements toward autonomy in various spheres of thought and life. In most instances Christian faith accompanied, if it did not inspire, them. They were not aware of leading revolution, nor of setting up great new systems of truth. They were trying to solve the relative problems of thought and life which they saw before them, to express the reality they knew. The inherent dynamic of this process is to call in question not only the world view of medieval Christendom, or other forms of Christianized culture, but any sweeping ideology from any source, which

---

1 Galileo was, as VON WEISZÄCKER points out, fighting for a theory which he could not yet prove (*The Relevance of Science,* pp. 104–107). His theory, however, was not a new world view, but an explanation of a certain sequence of natural events. Galileo took no responsibility for the philosophical, religious and social consequences of his scientific theory. He demanded the right to be free as a scientist not to do so.

tries to organize all of life and thought into one system of meaning and order. This is the process we are a part of today.

The Ideology

In religious circles resistance to this process has been continuous, subtle and varied. Our entire understanding has been clouded however, and our very reaction to the word "secular" misled, by the rise of a massive wave of humanistic ideology which in recent years has taken to itself the very name "secularism."

Secularism differs fundamentally from the process of secularization. It is, in fact, one form of resistance to it. As a specific philosophy it is associated with the nineteenth-century free-thinker, G. J. Holyoake. Holyoake described his philosophy as a system of ethical principles based on four foundations: (a) primary emphasis on the material and cultural improvement of man; (b) respect for and search for all truth, from whatever source, which can be tested in experience as leading to human betterment (Holyoake believed that theological dogmas were both irrelevant and dangerous for this search for truth, since they were proclaimed *a priori* and limited freedom of investigation and expression); (c) concern for this world and its improvement and not with another (investigation of a possible kingdom of God or eternal realm could be left to those interested); (d) an independent, rational morality which did not base itself on faith in divine commandments.

This is a typical rather than a unique expression of principles. Holyoake was reacting, like many other humanists, against the church of his time. He was sharing that strange combination of radical epistemological relativism with complete optimism about the goodness and rationality of human nature which characterized the utilitarianism of Bentham and Mill. He was echoing Auguste Comte's positivism without the latter's elaborate religion of humanity. He was reflecting, in short, a world view which has pervaded recent centuries and has presented itself as a living alternative, and successor, to the Christian faith. It has many names of which secularism is only one. But its beliefs can be roughly described, on the lines of Romano Guardini,[2] under three heads:

1. Belief in the objective reality and normative value of nature, "the immediately given, the wholeness of things before man does anything about it, the embodiment of all energy, matter, essence and law—the binding norm for all perceiving and creating, of that which is right, healthy and perfect."

2. Belief in man, his reason, his feelings, his individual freedom, his unlimited development and power. Humanism has its antecedents in the secularizing process; there too the shift takes place from God and his order to man and his experience as the natural starting point and testing ground for human thought and action. Nicholas Berdyaev for example maintains that the spirit of the Renaissance showed a natural tendency to humanist faith:

> This divorce from the spiritual depth in which man's forces had been stored and to which they had been inwardly bound, is accompanied not only by their liberation but their passage from the depth to the periphery and the surface of human life, from medieval religious to secular culture; and it implies the transference of the centre of gravity from the divine depth to purely human creation.[3]

3. Belief in culture, that is, belief in the process whereby man creates the values and conditions by which he lives. "In regarding the world as 'nature'," writes Guardini, "man posits it in himself; in understanding himself as 'personality' he makes himself lord over his own existence; in the will to 'culture', he undertakes to build its form (*Dasein*) as his own creation." [4] Culture then, like

---

[2] *Das Ende der Neuzeit,* Würzburg, Werkbund Verlag, 1950. Eng. Tr. *The End of Our Time* (Buras, Oates). Guardini is not responsible for all the use we make of his categories.

[3] *The Meaning of History,* p. 131. EMIL BRUNNER: *Christianity and Civilization,* and PAUL TILLICH: "The World Situation" in *The Christian Answer,* H. P. van Dusen, ed., support this general conviction that the movement away from the medieval religious world view must be understood in terms of an alternative faith—in man and his possibilities—and that secularization, in the sense of this essay, does not exist. HENDRIK KRAEMER: *World Cultures and World Religions,* also inclines to this view.

[4] *Op. cit.,* p. 50.

nature and personality, becomes something mysterious and indefinable, a religious symbol of secularism.

Anglo-Saxon secularism has expressed the same faith somewhat differently. Adam Smith and the nineteenth-century utilitarians who followed him phrased it in terms of a view of history. The private efforts of individual human beings, each to enlarge his own happiness and profit, would lead to an ever greater development of the welfare of the human race, for the desires which lead toward harmony and cooperation predominate in human nature. Even the chilling evolutionary theory of the survival of the fittest through conflict was adapted to this optimism. Pragmatism, indeed, provided a better vehicle for this faith than did idealism, as John Dewey has demonstrated, because it placed fewer preconceived limits on what man would discover and create by his cultural experimentation. Man was free to affirm his individual ambition, for the natural checks and balances of his own nature and society would mold them to the good of the whole. He need no longer ask the question of the good in itself, for in his own self-assertion in interaction with others he would create the values which constitute this good. Similarly man was free to be a specialist and an empiricist in his investigation of the world. He need no longer ask the question of truth in itself, because all that he would discover would be a portion of this truth. Faith in man's cultural creativity and the reality it would bring forth replaced faith in God's providence and redemption of the world.

Hence the ideology of secularism, which the Jerusalem meeting of the International Missionary Council in 1928 rightly placed alongside Buddhism, Hinduism and Islam as one of the world's great religions. It deserves the epithet "secular" only in the sense which Holyoake defines: It is concerned with this world and not with another. It is, in the Quaker philosopher Rufus Jones' words at Jerusalem, "a way and an interpretation of life that include only the natural order of things and that do not find God or a realm of spiritual reality essential for life or thought." But it is also a structure of belief about nature, man and history in this world which says far more than this. It is a faith about the processes of nature and the possibilities of man which glorifies them both. It endows this world, the *seculum* in its historical development, with absolute and self-evident meaning and value.

Within the context of this faith, secularism is not inherently hostile to religion as such. As the expression of the human spirit reaching beyond itself toward wider and more complete structures of meaning, religion can have its due place in the secularist's view of life. The secularist objects to man's being confronted by a reality which enters his history from outside human capacities. He objects to dogmas other than his own. But religion, and even God, understood as the depth of human reason and experience or a predicate of the human consciousness, and as affirmation of the world in terms of it, is quite possible for him.

The curious result has been, in the postwar world, the growth of an alliance between secularism and religion; it would be more accurate to say, perhaps, a resurgence of religion, both Christian and non-Christian, on secularist premises. This resurgence has been long in preparation. Its roots are in the eighteenth-century enlightenment's concept of "natural religion," as reverence for and consciousness of God, nature, morality and human goodness common to all men, and expressed differently in different ages and cultures. David Hume annihilated the enlightenment's form of this religion, in his *Dialogue,* but he left the nineteenth century with the question: Where, then is religion based in the human consciousness? This question became the basis of the philosophy of religion from Kant and Schleiermacher to the present day. Many such philosophers have been subtle apologists for a Christian world view. Schleiermacher, for one, demonstrated the superiority of Christianity as the highest religion and developed a whole trinitarian dogmatics from the logic of the human feeling of "absolute dependence." They were all concerned to combat the secularist ideology with a reasoned philosophy which would give more place to specifically Christian values. But in their argument they accepted the basic secularist premise from the beginning: That man is the measure, through his capacity for religious experience and understanding, and that any truths asserted about God must be verified by reference to this capacity. Theology, then, was enclosed in religion, and religion was understood as one department of human life, one expression of human consciousness.

It was one step from here to the advocacy of religion, not because its propositions or beliefs are true, but because they are useful, and even necessary, for the stability of the social order and the flowering of culture. But secularist religion is not limited to Christendom today. It expresses the essential ambiguity of the resurgence of non-Christian religions as well. The late Professor K. M. Panikkar spoke for a large number of his fellow Indians when he analyzed the radical reforms which are needed in legislation and social custom in order to humanize his society and then asked, "What would remain to identify the Hindus as a race? Surely the Hindu religion and the samskaras associated with it, a purified and invigorated social order based on religion.[5] It was foolish, he argued in another book,[6] for Christian missionaries to imagine that they could change the religion of Indians or of any other Asians, for religion is precisely that which distinguishes a culture, which is its root and the basic expression of its self-consciousness. The relation of a nation to its eternal ground and meaning is expressed there. Religion is, in short, for Panikkar, the servant of the nation's and the culture's self-assertion. It is measured by its social usefulness to this end.

Once again, this illustration is typical, not exceptional. The principle, worldwide, is clear. There is no inherent opposition between religion, as such, and secularism, because religion can easily be explained and professed in a secularist framework.

The Uncertain Trumpet

In the long run secularism is a conservative force. It did not seem so in the beginning, for secularists made themselves the

---

[5] *Hindu Society at the Crossroads,* Asian Publishing House, London, 1961, 3rd Ed.

[6] *Asia and Western Dominance,* Oxford, 1957. Only the first edition contains the analysis of Christian missions in detail which for Christians is the chief value of the book.

spokesmen of the laws of nature and of the emancipation of man. It was secularist ideology which seemed to find the new discoveries in science and the new horizons of society meaningful and hopeful, when church and theology appeared to be holding the floodgates closed. But appearances are deceiving. The floodgates of change were opened by forces beyond the control and comprehension of either churchman or humanist. The world view we have described above took the form of many different philosophies as new problems arose in the secular world. But always these were efforts to control the flood of events, to bring order out of chaotic phenomena, to see meaning in the whole on the basis of faith in the goodness and the unlimited capacities of man. They did not follow knowledge wherever it led; they were forever setting up dikes to redirect the flow of its possibly dangerous conclusions. They did not allow secular events to take their course: they tried to form them into one great historical channel of human development toward harmonious community, and to banish from reality what did not fit.

Nowhere is this more clear than in the way in which both the idea and the reality of revolution developed. The reality is older in modern times than the idea. The prototype of all our later understanding is the "Copernican revolution" in science; a total reversal of perspective on the external world and on the place of man in it. Machiavelli initiated a revolution in political and ethical thought in similar fashion. Revolution takes place when men break fundamentally with the values and perspectives of the past, when they no longer feel themselves to be within that reality or indeed whenever they are in fact outside it regardless of their feelings. Revolution is the seeking of truth and standards for action in the future, not in the past, which results from this break.

The curious fact, however, which has attended revolutionary change is that its most radical agents have been unaware of their own agency. Copernicus was a profound conservative in spirit who propounded his theory of the heliocentric movement of the planets as an interesting mathematical hypothesis. Machiavelli dreamed of a united Italy which might one day recover the civic discipline of the ancient Roman Republic. The first modern use of the term "revolution" designated the restoration of the Stuart monarchy in England in 1660. The "glorious revolution" of 1688 was understood as completing what had at the earlier restoration been incompletely done. Life had been turned back to its preordained order.

It was the secularist philosophy of the French enlightenment which first grasped the reality of revolutionary change with an idea: the idea of progress toward the perfectibility of man, of the liberation of human reason from the fetters which bound it so that it might reach out toward the unbounded horizons of human achievement. The architects of the French revolution were not afraid of destroying the order of the past because they believed in the imminent dawning of a new age whose name would be freedom and whose laws would be the eternal laws of nature, the Supreme Being and the divinely rational heart of man.

It is a matter of history that this ideology could not contain the revolution it had itself promoted. Its own believers instituted the reign of terror. Some of its fondest ideas—Rousseau's general will, for example, or Helvetius' view that characters could be made by education—turned out to have demonic implications which dismayed the faithful and sometimes the philosophers themselves. The French revolution became a *torrent revolutionnaire* which moved with a force of its own, sweeping actors and victims with it. History became a problem in itself. In the words of Hannah Arendt: "The point of the matter is that all those who throughout the nineteenth century and deep into the twentieth followed in the footsteps of the French revolution, saw themselves not merely as successors of the men of the French revolution but as agents of history and historical necessity, with the obvious and yet paradoxical result that instead of freedom necessity became the chief category of political and revolutionary thought.[7]

The philosophy of history, then—the discernment of a meaningful pattern in historical necessity—became the last device of secularist ideology for bringing revolution under control. Hegel is

[7] *On Revolution,* Viking Press, New York, 1963, p. 46.

known to us as the philosopher whose massive *tour de force* put together a philosophy of being and history, of reason, fact and value, after the philosophy of David Hume and the events of the French revolution would seem to have separated them forever. It was he who explained the forces of historical necessity in such a way that they were made to contribute after all to the good of the whole society, just as the human spirit was shown its relation to the world spirit even in the midst of apparent alienation. He did this, however, at the cost of one basic step beyond secularism, which was to prove the downfall of conservative religious metaphysics: He embodied a continuing revolution in his very concept of knowledge and being. For Hegel, man can know the truth only as he struggles to realize himself against obstacles. The same is true of nations and cultures. "Spiritualization"—the conquest of every object and its absorption into the self—is the destiny of men and nations. Through it the world spirit, or God, realizes himself in our human spirits and the alienation between them is overcome. This means in practice that truth is a function of struggle, and being is the relation established as its outcome.

Karl Marx was in this latter sense a Hegelian, who destroyed Hegel's secularism with Hegel's own methodology. Marx inscribed on his banner that neither truth nor morality exists except as a reflection of the class struggle through which man expresses his relation to the forces of production. Marx and the Communists are in this sense the most genuinely secular, and therefore anti-secularist, of social scientists. They glory in their adherence to a revolutionary cause the relation of which to any system of truth or goodness outside its own strategy is meaningless and irrelevant. They deny any doctrine of man or any concept of nature in order to concentrate on the way in which they intend to remake both. They challenge all other ideologies, not in order to argue theory but to prove themselves in practice as more effective in forming the events of human history.

Yet Marxism is still, as everyone knows, an ideology based on a faith. It believes in the unlimited capacities of postrevolutionary man as a collective or generic being. It reckons with the dialectic movements of history as Christians reckon with God. Its concept of science and of the scientific method clothe it in the jargon of empirical objectivity. In many societies of great social injustice its analysis seems closest to human need and hope. But wherever the question of strategy and tactics arises, to achieve the revolution or to maintain it, the basic secularism of this faith reveals itself. Not the laws of history of the movement of the proletariat, but the program and power of the Communist party become the absolute. Not man as he emerges in the new society, but man as he will be molded by controlled social conditions is the object of adoration. Not reality with its revolutionary dynamic, but an ideal essentially achieved and waiting only to be realized progressively in practice, becomes the object of "scientific" understanding. Marxism, which began as a summons away from mystifying ideas to real social existence and which promised to follow the revolution wherever it would lead, has become one more structure of ideas by which men seek to impose their own meaning on history and to keep the revolution from getting out of hand.

This is the fate of secularism in all its forms, religious or atheistic. Beginning as a philosophical rationale of change, it ends by being itself a bulwark against changes the complexity of which its theory can no longer understand. Beginning as an emancipation of man from dogma, it ends by trying to bind man by an ever more futile repetition of its own dogmas. Lest the point be missed: this is just as true of Catholic Christian democracy, of British utilitarian common sense, of the American way of life, of Pan-African nationalism, of resurgent Islam, Buddhism or Hinduism as it is of Marxism. Human events themselves render philosophies of culture and history obsolete. The variety of human knowledge casts doubt on the theories which would knit it all together. A more acute sense of the human situation itself explodes our various doctrines of man. This is a process of which we are all a part, however much we may resist it.

Secularization

An earlier ecumenical study has defined this process as "the withdrawal of areas of life and thought from religious—and finally also from metaphysical—control, and the attempt to understand and live in these areas in the terms which they alone offer." [8] Such a definition has the advantage of coupling religious and secular world views and defining secularization as a movement away from both. But it hardly catches the drama which the word "life" implies, as familiar certainties are blotted out in the hurricane of events which has blown up in the last generation. It is the human crisis which concerns us mainly here. Let us look at it more closely.

1. Secularization is a process whereby men and societies have lost the sense of living in a totally coherent world the basic elements of which can be grasped by the human mind or by religious beliefs and practices. The word "empirical" suggests itself to describe this attitude, but it is deceptive. The spoiling of a beautiful theory by a single recalcitrant fact does not describe the way in which scientific investigation operates. Rather, it is in the realm of theory itself that total coherence has been lost. In the field of physics this has been dramatically illustrated by the disappearance of the mechanical model of the universe in favor of mathematical formulae of which no model can be made. But it is equally the case in economics, where the integrated theories which once undergirded capitalism or predicted its destruction have been replaced by a variety of functional models; in sociology, and not least in politics, where the great ideologies which at the end of the Second

[8] This definition was first offered as a tentative working proposition in a background paper for a consultation on "The Meaning of the Secular" for university teachers at the Ecumenical Institute, Bossey, Sept., 1959. It was again reflected in the report of this consultation, which is available from the Ecumenical Institute (Château de Bossey, Céligny, Switzerland). The discussion on the subject was continued in a European conference of the World's Student Christian Federation in Graz, Austria, 1962, and in its staff meeting in Jan., 1963. The papers from these meetings are published in *The Student World* (13, rue Calvin, Geneva, Switzerland), No. 1, 1963. See especially STEVEN MACKIE: "European Christians and the Secular Debate," pp. 4ff.

World War competed for the task of rebuilding the world have one and all lost their power to convince even the people under their influence of the power and truth of their basic ideas. Doubt about a coherent world has eroded not only religious institutions, but Communist, Social Democratic and Christian Democratic parties, labor movements, patriotic associations and countless other movements as well.

2. This in itself could be a healthy reaction, a return to concrete human realities from the abstractions which have bedeviled them. But beneath it lies a crisis, the crisis of being itself. Secularization is the process whereby men and societies have learned, more sharply than ever before, the relativity of human knowledge and ethics to the standpoint of the knower and the conditions of his investigation, or the character of his action. This was the insight of Hegel and Marx, though it goes back to David Hume. The world is known only by interaction with a collective or individual agent; and the resulting knowledge, or value, is never detachable from that relation. Once again physics offers the most dramatic illustration: as the objective reality of physical substance dissolves in sometimes contradictory pictures (the wave and quantum theories of light) and the experimenter finds it less and less possible to discover that which the conditions of his experiment themselves do not help to create, the physicist magnifies human control over an unknowable reality to frightening and exhilarating proportions. The ontology of physics becomes ever more problematical; its functionality increases every day. So also with social existence. Ancient structures of the common life, cultural, economic, political and familial in one, often rooted in a profound and ageless sense of relation to divinity, suddenly lose their power to give security and meaning to human community. As industry moves in, trade moves more rapidly and persons are forced to work, often alone, with those of other cultures, the ontological question loses its relevance also in the social sphere, and the question of function takes its place. Nature and society alike become, in the words of Guardini, "a complex interaction of relations and functions which can only be grasped by mathematical symbols, and which are based

on something which can no longer be given a name." [9] Secularization is the experience—the critical experience—of losing contact with being, of no longer being able to grasp the structure of reality as it is in itself, and at the same time being caught up in a changing network of relations and functions wherein lies greater power for good and evil than was dreamed of by our ancestors.

3. Secularization involves, as a by-product of this functional direction, a movement toward specialization, in thought and life. By a curious paradox the organ of universalism in man's spirit—his ideology and religion, his sense of continuity with the being of all things—has been rendered obsolete by the reality of universal history into which mankind has been swept. It is demanded of modern man not that he explore some realm of being, but that he master a field which has a functional value. The language of this field is related to its functionality; the psychologist, the sociologist, the physiologist and the neurologist all study some function of man, but none feels it necessary to have a doctrine of man as a whole. Functional collaboration among them may be wise at times, but no overall theory need embrace them. But what works well in the realm of thought becomes a crisis for human existence. For secularized man is himself a bundle of specializations—that of his place of work, of his family life, of his circle of friends and perhaps of his church or other group which claims a portion of his loyalty and time. The relevant confrontations with reality other than himself take place in those local, particular contexts, in the persons and conditions he meets there.

4. Secularized man, then, is integrated not by the structures of the world in which he lives but—if at all—by his sense of what it means to be a person in this network of relationship, and what it means to be responsible for the function and the power which lie in his hands. His is a terrifying freedom from which there is no escape in shifting the burden of his responsibility into some god or nation or philosophy of nature and history. As a nuclear physicist or a biochemist, he cannot beguile himself with confi-

[9] *Op. cit.*, p. 77.

dence in the inevitable beneficence of scientific discoveries for man. As an industrialist amid automation he cannot escape with theories of economic progress his responsibility for the growing mass of unemployed semiskilled workers which his policies help produce. As an African politician he cannot draw comfort in private from his public ideology of a developing nation catching up with Europe and America. As an American politician he becomes dangerous to his country and the world when he sincerely believes in "total victory" over the enemies of his way of life.

The list could be extended indefinitely. Responsibility for the control of the power he himself has produced, for the fateful consequences of his own accomplishments in a world where metaphysical dreams no longer convince and where no superior power makes things right, is the hallmark of secularized man.

This is a dangerous and exposed position. Many of the greatest thinkers of our time regard it as an unstable one, a stage in the dramatic process of social decay which seeks to exclude the divine structure of reality which gave it birth only to end by setting up sacred absolutes of its own which are all the more rigid for being unrecognized as such. Mircea Eliade speaks of "raw religion," that urge to divinize portions of the world that is present in every man and culture. Paul Tillich speaks optimistically of extreme autonomy of man preparing the way for a new breakthrough of theonomy. But Roger Mehl describes the trend more ominously:

> We discover in the midst of secularized society a process of resacralization. Some turn back to the church as a sacred structure, some turn to secular religions. . . . They make no clear distinction between the sacred and the profane. They bring the sacred down to earth in a false incarnation which results in a self-deification of man.[10]

The flight to secular religion is furthermore only one of the dangers which beset us in this condition. Nihilism in its various forms threatens equally from the other side. Technology can become an

[10] Summary of Professor Mehl's remarks in the report of the conference of the Ecumenical Institute on *The Meaning of the Secular, op. cit.,* Appendix, p. 7. See also "La sécularisation de la cité" in *Le problème de la civilisation chrétienne,* Presses Universitaires de France, 1958.

end in itself for those fascinated by its processes, regardless of its human effects. The Sophists of ancient Greece who sold the art of argument to the highest bidder have their counterparts today in the physicists, chemists, biologists and engineers who limit their horizon by the project in which they are engaged; in the economists and financiers whose ideas or policies are at the disposal of the particular interest that hires them; and in the technicians of politics and of advertising who manipulate the human mind for their clients. Power can be its own rationale in a world where "realists" reckon with no universal power which limits and judges their own. Human beings can be misused and their humanness destroyed not only by fanatic idealists, but also by cynics who recognize no objective values in society or structure to human nature. If Orwell's *1984* symbolizes the one type, Skinner's *Walden II* might stand for the other.

This is the demonology of secularization. But there remains one descriptive word to be said. Man without religion and metaphysics, man the problem solver alone with his responsibility for a world which he has made, remains a human being. There is implicit in the secular attitude an open reciprocal relation of man with man in the pursuit of truth and the solution of problems. There is an acceptance of the relativity of every man's point of view and interest and therefore of the inevitability of conflict and compromise. There is a search for the form of humanity not in an ideal or a doctrine, but in the give-and-take of human relations. He may say with sober relativism, "We need not hope in order to act, nor need we succeed in order to persevere," [11] but he is seeking nevertheless the substance of a reality which will claim his allegiance, and to which the future belongs, in the business of daily human life.

Christians in the Seculum

We have described secularization as a movement away from religious world views in theory and away from the dominance of

[11] CARL J. FRIEDRICH: *Transcendent Justice,* Duke University Press, Durham, N.C., 1964, p. 116.

religious institutions in practice. This means, in large parts of the world, a movement away from Christianity and the authority of the church. Those historians have been largely right who have described it as a drama of Christendom, imported in an advanced state of development into cultures which had never known the dichotomy of religious and secular before. But now we must say more than this. Theologically perceived, the proclamation of the Christian gospel is responsible for the dynamic of secularization, and is its first agent. This is so, even when those who carry it have no idea of producing these consequences, because the process begins with the history of the Hebrew people—with the calling of Moses and the revelation at Sinai—and is fulfilled in the incarnation of Jesus Christ and is expressed by the sanctifying work of the Holy Spirit in the church. To put it bluntly, the secularized state of human mind and society can be creative and is full of hope because it is the state into which God calls his people through their relation with him, and in which he sustains them by his grace. It is the attitude toward structures of thought and the common life which is most appropriate to the history and promise of that relationship. It is a quality of faith in believers and, where faith is not present, it is a condition in which, precisely for lack of any social and metaphysical obstructions, the word of God can be heard most clearly. Let us examine this thesis more closely.

Secularization begins with biblical history. The Dutch philosopher Cornelis van Peursen suggests two forms of man's relation to objective reality which precede it: (a) the mythical, wherein man feels himself continuous with the nature and society around him, deriving his very sense of self from his participation in their forms; (b) the ontological, in which being is objective and accessible in its timeless substance to the human reason.[12] Arend van Leeuwen combines them both, on the basis of a comparative study of Hindu, Chinese and early Mesopotamian civilization, into what he calls the "ontocratic pattern."[13] It is pre-biblical, but it is also modern, a

[12] "Man and Reality—The History of Human Thought" in *The Student World,* No. 1, 1963, pp. 13f.

[13] Arend van Leeuwen: *Christianity in World History,* Edinburgh House Press, London, 1964, Chap. IV.

temptation and a tendency in primitive culture and modern social science.

From this baseline the biblical history departed, toward a totally new orientation to reality. The story of this is now familiar to biblical scholars and cannot be told here in full.[14] We can only indicate its direction.

1. Man's efforts to lay hold of a structure of being which he himself would control, by grasping it with his mind (metaphysics) or by securing it with ceremonies and experiences (religion) were overturned by the way God revealed himself. One could illustrate almost at random from the Bible. When God first spoke to Abram there was no evidence of mystic illumination or of rational insight into eternal order; rather the content of the address was command, "Go out from your kindred, from your father's house, to the land which I will show you," and promise, "And I will make of you a great nation—and in you shall all the families of the earth be blessed" (Genesis 12 : 1–2). The God who made himself known to Moses introduced himself historically: "I am the God of your father . . ." and specifically refused to answer the question about his name, except in historical terms (Exodus 3 : 14–17).

2. As with the being of God, so also with nature and history, reflected in the human activities of economics and science, politics and culture. The biblical basis of human knowledge and action in all these spheres is the relation which God establishes with his people, known as covenant. The biblical covenant is first a personal relation. The reality it reflects is that of the personal claim of another on us as free and responsible agents. But it is also a relation between God and a community of believers through which his relation to the whole human world is expressed; and it is a dynamic, active relation which expresses itself in events to which structures of society and the stuff of the material world are instrumental.

Once again the biblical history is the story of human attempts

---

[14] See, for example, MARTIN BUBER: *The Prophetic Faith;* J. PEDERSEN: *Israel;* G. ERNEST WRIGHT: *The Old Testament Against Its Environment,* et al. A good summary of the argument is found in VAN LEEUWEN: *op. cit.* Chaps. 2 & 3.

to capture this relationship in sacred structures of political or natural order, and of God's judgment on the structures which re-establish the community of faith in a properly secularized world. We take three examples which still play a role in our life today.

(a) It is well known that the basic principles and prescriptions of human behavior known as the law play a large part in biblical, as in later Jewish and Christian, history. The laws in the Old Testament, as the prescriptions for Christian behavior in the Pauline letters of the New Testament, are of various kinds. They have borrowed heavily from the codes of surrounding peoples. In some cases they represent improvements on those codes, in others they reinforce the best available morality of the time. In any event they were modified and even reversed from time to time as historical conditions in the covenant relation beteween God and his people changed the response required. Ceremonial laws commanded at the time of the Exodus became an offense to the eighth century prophets, as did commandments in modified form for the postexilic Jews. The Ten Commandments were drastically modified by Jesus; in some cases, as with the law against killing, adultery and covetousness they were given a new dimension; in others, as with the Sabbath commandment and that on honoring parents, they were sharply corrected. The moral law, in the Bible, was basically those teachings (*torah*) which expressed for a time and place, the quality of relation which God had given with his covenant and which is made finally clear in Jesus Christ.

In short, biblical history secularizes the law. It also records revolts against this secularization. The Book of Deuteronomy records a legal reform whereby the people of Judah hoped to make themselves acceptable to God, only to be told by Jeremiah, "They have healed the hurt of my people slightly saying 'peace, peace,' when there is no peace" (6 : 14). The law which Paul rejected was of the same character. His "All things are lawful for me, but not all things are expedient" (I Corinthians 5 : 12) expresses exactly the congruence of biblical and modern secular attitudes. Law is, and should be, the servant of expediency.

(b) The biblical story also secularizes nature. It places creation—the physical world—in the context of the covenant relation and does not try to understand it apart from that relation. The history of God with his people has a setting, and this setting is created nature. But the movement of history, not the structure of the setting, is central to reality. Physical creation even participates in this history; its timeless or cyclical character, so far as it exists, is unimportant. The physical world, in other words, does not have its meaning in itself. There are no spirits at work in it which can help or harm mankind. It is the creation of God alone and is the object of his manipulation.

(c) The biblical history secularizes the forms of the community of believers itself. This has been the hardest lesson of all for believers to learn. The people of Israel did not believe the prophets who prophesied the victory of their enemies because God, in their minds, was bound to his temple and to the prosperity and security of the people he had chosen. Even the disciples throughout the life of Jesus were thinking in terms of the kingdom of God as a sacred order which he would bring in: "grant us to sit, one at your right hand and one at your left, in your glory" (Mark 10 : 37). And Paul was at constant odds with the sacralists to whom he himself brought the gospel: "already you are filled! Already you have become kings! And would that you did reign, so that we might share the rule with you!" (I Corinthians 4 : 8). Over against all this the covenant shows itself to be an ever-changing relation, the constancy of which lies in the character of God and not in the structure of the community.

The church is the community which cannot escape knowing all this, and which is called first to apply it to its own life. It lives by its participation in the death and resurrection of Christ in the Lord's Supper (Holy Communion, Eucharist). Its worship is a hearing and a responding to the word of God preached in its midst. These two acts give to the church itself a functional, secular existence. Because of them the church lives by rediscovering itself as judged and renewed by the work of Christ, by the transformation—potentially the transformation of the world—which goes on in its midst.

Secular Theology

This sets the terms of the theological task in modern society. We close with some suggestions on its content and direction.

1. We are left by the whole history we have described with the question of the reality of God. We say "reality" rather than "being," "essence" or "nature" in a deliberate effort to avoid the kind of thinking we have hitherto called metaphysical. We mean by it that long tradition of deductive system building based on the first principles of thought and being, which is associated with the names of Aristotle and Plato, with the Greek Church Fathers and with Thomas Aquinas, with Descartes, Spinoza and Leibniz, and subjected to basic criticism by Kant. The secular mind and biblical revelation are at one in rejecting the way of thinking which this system building requires, and the understanding of reality which is associated with it. Neither God nor his creation reveal to the human mind the structure of their essential being, for the very idea of such a structure or essence is a product of the human mind and therefore the instrument of man's desire to make his own ways sacred or absolute. The metaphysical task in the secular context then must be differently conceived—as the task of clarifying and relating ideas about man's situation within the limits of a particular position and bias in human history. Its point of reference will not be an ultimate structure of being but the dynamic relations of this history and the responses it brings forth.[15]

We know the reality of God only in and through his acts in history, his covenant relation with man, his calling, judging, forgiving, reconciling and saving acts toward society, centrally expressed in the life, death, resurrection and coming again of Jesus Christ. Through these acts and in this relation we know him to be free sovereign Lord over creation, man and history. The words we use to describe him—just, merciful, loving and the like—are not definitions, but themselves expressions of our relation, and

[15] I am grateful to Mr. Ian Ramsey for the reminder that such a metaphysical task is possible. Cf. also S. N. HAMPSHIRE: "Metaphysical Systems" in *The Nature of Metaphysics,* D. F. Pears, ed., London, 1958.

pointers to a reality which transcends our comprehension. Nevertheless, we know God as truly and wholly present with us, not partially removed into a mystical absolute. "God is who he is in the deed of his revelation," writes Karl Barth.[16]

This reality is differently perceived from most objects of human knowledge. He who acknowledges it lives within it. It lays claim on his actions; he understands himself and his world as part of this history. It is not a doctrine the truth of which he demonstrates, but a relation which he explores with his mind and expresses with his responsible life. For him "the will of God is what God does in all that nature and men do. It is the universal that contains, transforms, includes and fashions every particular." [17] He does not comprehend it or control it fom God's perspective. He reckons with and depends on it as God's gift.

This is conventionally known as the response of faith. It is not, however, optional for secular man. In his specialized fields of activity, in the variety of his human relations, in the use of the power in his hands and in his free responsibility the question cannot be avoided: What is the character of the reality with which I will reckon here? It is first a practical question. It is answered in the way money is spent—in families or in the budgets of nations. It is answered in the way machines are built and handled, and in the direction of research. It is answered in the way of a man with a woman, in lifelong marriage or passing relation. It may well be that most of us at this level are practical polytheists. Our realities clash and jostle, and we acknowledge them all. But it is the most responsible secular man whom this satisfies least, for he is left with the question of the integrity of his human responsibility itself.

> There is a law in me or in my mind, the law of my integrity; and there are many laws in my members, the laws of response to many systems of action about me. In my responsiveness and responsibility to the many I am irresponsible to the One beyond the many; I am irresponsible as a self, however responsible the natural, the political,

---

16 KARL BARTH: *Kirchliche Dogmatik*, II/i, p. 203.

17 H. R. NIEBUHR: *The Responsible Self*, Harper & Row, New York, 1963, p. 164.

the domestic, the biological complexes in me may be in relation to the systems of nature, or to the closed societies of nation, church, family or profession, or to the closed society of life itself.[18]

The problem of reality in secular terms is the problem of the one Other to whom I as a whole human being am responsible, in and through the actions I perform and the other responsibilities I bear.

2. We are left with the question, then, of the secular reality of man. Toward this the whole foregoing discussion points. "The being of man is the history," writes Karl Barth, "in which one of God's creatures is elected and called by God, is included in his self-responsibility before God, and in which he shows himself qualified for this call and task." [19] The reference is of course to Jesus Christ. It would be incomprehensible were we to think of God, Christ or man as substances with attributes. In fact, however, it expresses the heart of the dynamic relation of all three. Christ, says Bonhoeffer, is "the man-for-other-men." This is his character. It describes the innermost quality which his acts and relations revealed. As such he revealed also the decision of God to be for man, epitomized the meaning of all the full-bodied terms—holiness, righteousness, mercy, loving-kindness—with which the Old Testament had tried to express this relation. Man then is defined —given his existence, calling and destiny—by his relation to the action of this God in Christ. In this action the whole world is included in its secularity and man is turned toward it as servant and witness by virtue of being "in Christ."

Man exists, then, as Christian faith sees it, in a field of personal relationships at the center of which is Jesus Christ. He is constituted in his very being by his actions and responses in that field. From him we derive our power to be human and our ever-changing understanding, in specific relations, of what it means. Through his work God negates the power of our inhumanity, releases us from fear of ourselves and frees us to shoulder responsibility and take

[18] *Ibid.*, p. 138.
[19] *Op. cit.*, III/2, p. 64.

action which serves our neighbor, even when we incur guilt thereby. Because Christ is there, man is not an individual, nor part of the masses, nor the creature of a race or culture, nor the citizen of a nation, but a person in these various contexts, free for the responsibilities they carry because he is free from defining himself in terms of them.

3. The question of an authentically secular society receives thereby a theological answer. Society—the political and economic structures of the common life and the cultural habits and values which give it a sense of unity—is a creative task given to man, not a structure to be received. It is a Christian responsibility to help the secular world to remain truly secular when it itself is tempted to lose confidence in itself and to give way to new ideologies or myths.

The church participates with every secular society in its search for justice and freedom for all its people. As this involves social analysis, political action and formulation of the particular hope of that people, it may mean many an ideological risk. But the church and its theology have the task of reminding such a society that its focus is the true need of man, that its function is the cultivation and development of personal relations among its members in free and experimental interaction. They have the task of warning the commonwealth whenever human beings are in danger of being sacrificed to institutions, projects or ideas. They have the task of confronting such a society through the church's own life and thought with the vision of what man is, the purpose for which he lives, in Jesus Christ, and with the continual self-criticism and reform which this involves. The final point will attempt to spell out one illustration of what this implies.

4. In no area of society are the problems of responsible action more baffling or the situation more dangerous than in the sphere of national and international politics. This is partly because power which can destroy the world is located here, but also because it has been so incompletely secularized. Many political ideologies have lost their convincing power; indeed we owe the precarious peace of coexistence to the fact that this is so. But mythology, especially of

the secular religion of nationalism, persists even among those who no longer believe it, and political decisions are made which reflect illusions more than reality. The present writer is an American. What he says will inevitably reflect that country's experience. But it may still be of some more general value to pose the question from one setting: What is a Christian's responsibility for his country's policy?

First, he is called to act as a solvent of the nation's remaining ideological illusions. When several years ago George F. Kennan propounded the thesis that foreign policy must be based frankly on a nation's self-interest, and not on moral principle, he was speaking as a responsible Christian. When a nation sets up its own national morality—even its concepts of freedom, justice and peace—as a universal standard by which to measure others, this self-justification becomes the heart of disobedience to God. In fact, a nation is, like its citizens, a self-interested body, whose insight into the truth about world order and whose morals in working for it, are highly relative. It lives in a world of other such nations with which it must interact. The Christian is called to prepare the nation to see the judgment and calling of God in the give-and-take of world affairs, in the defeats as well as the victories of its policies. As a secular institution the nation is not absolute. Loyalty to it must be critical and qualified, in order that it may better serve its proper limited purposes, as one expression of responsible community among men.

Second, the Christian is deeply involved in the responsibility which his nation has for using what power is at its command to serve human need. From this responsibility there is no withdrawal without unfaithfulness to God and to one's fellowman. Having said this, however, let us be clear that there is a radical difference between a nation's self-interested use of power and the use of it which God intends. The power of foreign aid and trade is a major example. Christians are in the position therefore of continually seeking to help the nation to reinterpret its self-interest in terms more inclusive of the needs and interests of others, and at the same time holding up the mirror of Christ to all self-interest as a judgment and a stimulus to the imagination. The nation will always argue that its most creative and altruistic policies are consistent with its self-interest. The church lives from the conquest of its self-interest by the power of Christ, on which the peace of the world depends. By the continual operation of this tension the policies of the nation are made fruitful.

Third, the Christian, fully involved with his nation's capacity to make war—in this case possibly nuclear war—bears witness to the nation of the relativity of all conflict to the purpose of reconciliation. No nation is righteous enough to seek an unconditional surrender. No cause is just enough to excuse any means of conflict to fight it. Because Christ has brought peace to all men there are no absolute conflicts or enmities. There are also no absolute governments. It may be that a nation must fight at times for people—its own or others. But then the welfare of the people must be the test of the battle and of the terms on which it ends.

Finally, the Christian recognizes that political power, like all power, has its limits. It can coerce, but rarely heal. It can set limits to human behavior, but rarely win people's allegiance. It can put down rebellions, but it cannot—at least American power cannot—produce a social revolution. Secular reality in politics includes the moment when the most creative political action is to renounce power and to bear witness in defenseless service to the human relations one seeks to establish. There are times—and there are nations which have lived through them—when the only wise political act is to suffer injustice and oppression not in hate but in forgiveness and inner freedom, out of which a new relationship may grow. Here also the pattern of secular reality is the pattern of the Man-for-other-men. Secular men in any situation can see the human logic of this. But that this pattern contains hope, that the future belongs to the reality we find in this man, is a truth for which there is no proof, there is only witness. This is perhaps the irreducible Christian contribution to the integrity of the secular community—to live within it ourselves, in all its incoherent functionality, in all its appalling responsibility for power and for powerlessness, in all its search for particular forms of humanness, as men who see by faith a promise here which is based on analyses of social trends, but which comes to all of us from without. If we live by the reality of this future we shall be secular men but we shall not be conformed to "the world," for we shall be looking at it from the angle of its meaning and direction given by that acting reality whom we call God. By the never-ceasing operation of this tension in all who believe, the secular life of the world is made fruitful.

21

SECULAR SOCIETY OR PLURALISTIC COMMUNITY?

by PAUL VERGHESE (INDIA)

THE *secularization* of society in which many Christian thinkers have shown an approving interest should be clearly distinguished from the ideology of *secularism*. Christian advocates of the former roundly repudiate the latter, although the two have this in common: they are both concerned only with this world and not with any other. Ideological secularism confers on the *seculum* an absolute meaning and value, which can be discovered by rational means. For the Christian advocate of secularization, *seculum* must be understood in reference to a reality which is not human; for the secularist, "man is the measure of all things."

Secularization is a process, continuing and dynamic, which has been described as "the withdrawal of areas of life and thought from religious—and finally also from metaphysical—control, and the attempt to understand and live in these areas in the terms which they alone offer." But here is its dilemma: the secularist and the Christian may agree on both the definition and the positive response to secularization, and yet differ in their basic assumptions, and in their evaluation and expectations of man, nature and history.

The secularist is basically optimistic about man, his reason, his destiny and his nature. The Christian advocate of secularization cannot be described as a pessimist: he would rather call himself a realist. He has no illusions about the perfectibility of man, no preconceived notions of what is or what to expect. He is agile and plastic, willing to adjust to new circumstances, never surprised by the turn of events, ready to reconsider earlier judgments in the light of subsequent experience. All but crushed by the realization of the complexity of the relationships within which he lives, he yet seeks valiantly to retain his freedom as a person and not to be crushed by the leveling forces of mass society. He seeks with great skill and some success to identify the new gods of the secularist—whether they be an idolized technology, an absolutized scientism, the worship of power. a fanatic nationalism or even a secular-cultural religion—and to expose them as vain idols. Even cynicism, which recognizes no absolutes and is in this sense dangerously close to this type of Christian position, is exposed as making self-interest the ultimate view. The Christian secularists do not belong to any of the philosophical schools, though they learn from them all. They have close affinities wtih the existentialists but disagree with their view of history.

Existentialism can hardly be termed a philosophy so much as a philosophical approach. Its cardinal principle, in its most over-simplified form, is the assertion that in man, as opposed to nature, existence precedes essence. Unlike a cow or a tree or a machine, man is not determined before he is born. He is free—or rather, to be a true man means to be free to shape one's own destiny. There is no rejection of law and order, but a sharp protest against law and order dominating man rather than serving him. The opposition to ontology and metaphysics is more resolute. Terms like "being" and "nature" are rejected in favor of others like "function," "reality" and "relation."

In theology, the Christian advocate of secularization draws his inspiration from the three great Bs of twentieth-century Reformed [1] thought—Buber, Barth and Bonhoeffer—with a liberal inhalation from that postliberal genius of American social thought, Reinhold Niebuhr. In the background lie the contributions of biblical scholarship, especially the new Old Testament theology which sees the

[1] I include within this term the Reformed Jew and the neo-Lutherans.

prophetic as the main stream of the experience of Israel, and the demythologized New Testament theology of that other great B, Rudolf Bultmann, and his school.

There is even a Christian secularizationist "missiology" best exemplified in Dr. van Leeuwen's brilliant treatise, *Christianity in World History,* which sees secularization as the main thrust of God's saving activity from the time of the calling of Israel out of Egypt. From van Leeuwen, salvation consists in the liberation of man from the dominance of civilizations and religions with an "ontocratic" pattern for genuine and creative freedom in a secular society. The liberation of man is the central thrust of the mission of the church, transforming societies even when they reject the gospel in explicit terms. The spread of urban-technological-industrial culture to all continents is itself an integral, though ambiguous, part of this process of desacralization and secularization. The Christian gospel is, for van Leeuwen, the gospel of secularization. Christ himself has won the victory over the principalities and powers, and the gospel continues throughout history to expose and overthrow the powers that dominate and enslave man. Van Leeuwen argues passionately in his concluding chapter that both western and nonwestern churches "ought to focus their theological reflection on the encounter with secularization" for any other central concern can lead the church totally astray. He maintains that the true progress of the gospel will not be manifested in the baptizing of more Gentiles to become members of the Christian church, but rather in "the renewal of society in the direction of a truly secular and man-made order of life." [2]

"In this age of ours, 'christianization' can only mean that peoples become involved in the onward movement of Christian history." As Hendrik Kraemer rightly asks in his foreword to the book, what does that mean? Or to put it another way, can there be a "genuinely secular society" from the Christian perspective? It depends very much on the meaning given to the word "secular." If it means time-existence, then there is no debate: all societies exist in time.

[2] *Christianity in World History*, p. 420.

The current definitions of secular society all seem to agree that it is a state of human relations in which no religion or world view (ideology) dominates. But this is not a practical possibility. We do not know of the existence of any such society at any time, including the present. Even modern science and technology have their origin in a "religion" or "world view," as Edwin A. Burtt demonstrates in *The Metaphysical Foundations of Modern Science* or C. F. von Weizsäcker in *Zum Weltbild der Physik*. Man can refuse to formulate his "metaphysical" world view, but he cannot live, think or act without consciously or unconsciously holding such presuppositions. All he can hope for, within the limits of the human mind and its time-existence, is that he will be aware of the tentative and hypothetical character of his world view, and be constantly on the alert to revise it in the light of experience and experiment.

Even if "religion" were to be banished by the concerted efforts of the secularizers, some world views would still dominate. Not only the Marxists, but even Christian secularizers have a world view. It may not be articulately or consciously held, but it is there. They may not hold their world view as a final absolute, but they would like to see it dominate. This is not the place in which to discuss these implicit world views, but we have no choice but to reject the first part of the definition of a secular society as practically impossible.

Some theologians also tend to argue that the concept of the secular implies the absence of a common understanding of the timeless order of reality. But what is the "timeless order of reality"? Those religious schools, like Vedanta or Zen Buddhism, which seem to know, insist that it be beyond human conception, without quality or extension. Christians can think only of the creator God as belonging to the timeless order, since time belongs to creation and God is not part of it. We ought not to speak of the "reality of God" as a secular reality since God is not simply a reality within the *seculum,* though our knowledge of that reality is secular, or acquired in time-existence. And if that is so, then it is impossible for Christians to "believe in one God the Father Almighty, maker of heaven and earth, and of all things visible and invisible" and not to have faith in some order of reality that transcends time and space.

The problem of adequately defining "secular" has led the present writer to be skeptical of the efforts not only of his Christian friends in the West, but even of his own country's non-Christian government. The anomalies of Indian "secular" society have been adequately lampooned by critics both within and without the country. Yet it remains true that we are all groping toward a certain type of society for which we have yet neither an adequate name nor an articulate theoretical conception. If we were to speak of an "authentic" rather than a "secular" society, we would soon discover that Greek *authentia* means *absolute sway* or *absolute authority* (from *autoentes*—one who does something with his own hand), which may mean that the "authentic" society recognizes no norms outside itself. This cannot be what the secularizationist seeks, for he wants "to understand and live in these areas in the terms which they alone offer," but does not want to invest those terms with any degree of finality. Is it possible for a Christian to conceive of a society which has no norms outside itself? Would not the "declaration of human rights" of the UN come into the category of something which transcends the terms which society normally offers? On what secular basis do we assert the dignity of man or the principle of equity—on the basis of social experience?

We need, at least for our own use among Christians, a slightly different vocabulary. It is not easy to find a surrogate term for the "Kingdom of God manifesting itself in history," which is what we are groping for. This kingdom could not be "secular" in any "authentic" sense. Its very roots would be in the transcendent *eschaton*, in that "timeless order of reality" whence it has entered into the order of time-space. A happier term may be "pluralistic human community," provided "pluralistic" and "human" are precisely defined. Pluralism means more than mere variety. Without some unity within the diversity, we should simply have a chaotic or anarchic rather than a pluralistic society. That element of unity should be spelled out as the definition of the term "human."

But this society cannot constantly be working out its own terms from within itself. It will need the presence within it of a transcendent unit which will constantly challenge its attempts to become "autonormic." This unit will normally be a small prophetic group within the Christian church of the country, though they may be joined by men of good will who are not Christians. They will not make this challenge on the grounds of any temporal authority vested in them. They may use all the normal channels provided within the structure of "law and order." But it will be for them to decide in conscience when the challenge must assume extralegal forms. This will mean the acceptance of suffering and of opposition from the majority in society, and, if necessary, of death. But this cannot be undertaken by a group of people who have no transcendent loyalty, though radicalism often goes with professed atheism. It would be strange indeed if a constitution were to provide for the "right of conscience" to violate the constitution. That right in the final analysis will have to remain something which transcends the constitution itself—the right of appeal to the deepest elements of freedom in the human person.

The yearning for a purely "secular" society among some western thinkers seems to be a reaction to the history of ecclesiastical and ideological domination in the western past. As a "reaction ideology" it may be creative in challenging the entrenched positions of the old order. It may even be aware of the danger of becoming itself an "ideology." However, it can never claim to become an adequate substitute for the traditional Christian pattern of social thinking.

The Elements of a Pluralistic Community

What then are the elements of a "pluralistic human community" as a Christian conceives it? The concept of "pluralism" comes, for the Christian, not from social experience, but rather from the doctrine of the Holy Spirit. Similarly, the concept of "human" has its roots, not in the tradition of secular western or eastern humanism, but in the fact of the Incarnation itself. It is methodologically important to start our Christian social thinking from these two fundamental realities of the Christian faith, rather than from the Old Testament doctrines of the call of Abraham, or the "history of salvation." Underlying these twin doctrines of the Incarnation [3] and the Holy Spirit is the fundamental concept of "freedom in love."

Freedom is by definition not open to definition, since what is defined is no longer free. Yet certain statements can be made about freedom, including that already made in the previous sentence. "Freedom" is both a relational or functional concept and an "ontological" or "being" concept. The being of God is a "free" being, and therefore does not lend itself to exhaustive definition or even exhaustive revelation. The revealed God is also a *deus absconditus*. He is Yahweh, God who will be what he is or is what he will be (*"ehyeh asher" ehveh*). This is an ontological and not a functional or relational statement about the being of God; but not about a static being, who can be defined even by this statement. When we say that God is "free," we do not mean to define God. We mean primarily that God's being is not determined by anything outside it, but by his own will. And that will is free—free not only *from* external constraint or bondage, but free *to* fulfill that which it wills. That is the twin meaning of freedom—the absence of heteronomy and the presence of infinite power to accomplish what is willed.

"God is love" is also a biblical statement, though the converse, "Love is God" is not.[4] Love exists only in a context of freedom in a community of persons. Love also defies definition. But some statements could be made about it. It is nothing less than beneficent intersubjectivity in freedom, the principle of interpersonal relationships within the Holy Trinity and therefore of human relationships within society. This twin principle has, as far as we can see, an enduring validity for all societies. And therefore we need

[3] The Incarnation as a theological term in eastern Christian thought denotes the whole *oikonomia,* which begins with the Annunciation and ends with Pentecost and the coming into being of the Christian church. The doctrine of the Holy Spirit is thus integral to the doctrine of the Incarnation.

[4] See BISHOP ROBINSON's *Honest to God,* SCM Press, 1963, pp. 52ff.

to consider it in connection with the Incarnation of our Lord Jesus Christ.

Man is made in the image of God, and Jesus Christ is the image or *eikon* of God. An icon is not a representation of someone who is absent (as is often the case of a photograph or a statue) but the mark of a presence. The presence of man in the creation is thus a concrete presence of God within it. Jesus Christ is the *présence par excellence* of God, not only within history, but in physical nature. "God became flesh" is not simply a historical statement, but is related equally to physical reality or nature. "Became" refers to history, "flesh" relates to matter or nature. Any separation of history and "nature" seems therefore contrary to the Incarnation. The Incarnation is both "ontic" and historical. It is also an act of "love in freedom." God could have saved the world by *fiat,* since he is free and his will is unbounded. But precisely because he is free, and man is made to be his *eikon* in love and freedom, he chose the means of incarnate involvement rather than imperious *fiat.*

The tragedy of the *Corpus Christianum* lies in its forgetting of this fundamental principle. The "two-edged sword" of the medieval papacy and the *cuius regio eius religio* principle of the Lutheran Reformation both militated against this principle of the Incarnation. In a genuinely pluralistic human society there can be no imposition of religious or political views by *fiat,* instead of loving persuasion. But this immediately raises the related question of the role of authority, law and punishment in such a society.

Incarnation does not effect a radical break with the past. Automatic righteousness which needed no law was often associated with the hopes of a messianic age. But in practice the tension between the external authority of the law and the loving and wise actions of freedom continued to manifest itself even in the apostolic community. The "royal law"—"Love thy neighbor as thyself"—comprehends statutory law but, until society achieves maturity, statutory law will be the form in which most of the negative and some of the positive requirements of the royal law will be met. For example, statutory law can regulate murder but not hatred; it can give structure to service to the needy (through social security or other forms of taxation) but not to compassion as a free expression of intersubjectivity. In the pluralistic human society authority and law have to be constituted as frameworks which can be finally dispensed with, when voluntary love, or beneficent intersubjectivity in freedom, can progressively grow to fruition. This is why neither law nor authority can be ultimate in society. Education, through family, school or "mass media," should be seen as a tool in the progressive elimination of authoritarian legal structures and the introduction of higher degrees of voluntary beneficence. Punishment yields to correctional education, no longer seen as a deterrent based on fear, but as a means of redeeming the culprit himself.

Law and order thus become relative to the ultimate objective—the production of creative intersubjectivity in freedom. Revolution becomes a necessary corrective to outmoded structures of law and order rather than a threat to security and well-being. The transition from a law-and-order state to a welfare state can thus be seen as a progressive step toward the kingdom; yet the welfare state itself stands under the judgment of the principle of creative and beneficent intersubjectivity in freedom. Insofar as it stifles freedom and promotes lazy parasitism, it must itself be restructured and remodeled.

The growth of democracy can also be seen in the favorable light of this principle. What was wrong with the notion of kingship? Not the "ontocratic pattern" which it represented, but its failure to develop creative and responsible freedom in all members of society. The "ontocratic pattern" was part of the framework used by royal societies to bolster the authority of kingship, which it considered essential to a stable and viable social structure. In democracy, greater demands are made on the freedom of persons in society, but democracy itself is less an ultimate value than part of a necessary structure for the current stage of the development of society. The establishment of democracy itself, however, requires that people shall have arrived at a stage where personal responsibility has attained some maturity. The premature imposition of democracy can come only from a false absolutizing of a structural principle without historical perspective and can endanger the true development of personal freedom.

This can be illustrated by the problem that some African countries faced on attaining independence. Adult franchise was extended to all. But the structure of tribal authority had not yet been broken down, and the tribal chief often decided for whom the members of his tribe should vote. The authority of the chief had been abolished by law, but a tribal people had not yet been educated to assume responsibility for national decisions. The end result was that those elected to government were defenders of the interests of the tribal chiefs, and national democracy was denied.

The progress of "secularization" provides another example. The abolition of ecclesiastical domination requires the development of personal freedom. In Soviet Russia, the authority of the church and of the feudal lords was ruthlessly abolished, only to be replaced by the equally arbitrary authority of what Milovan Djilas called the "new class" of bureaucratic party and government officials. The creative and responsible freedom of persons in society has thus been slow in developing. It is not simply the "ontocratic" ideology of Marxism-Leninism that is to be blamed here, but rather the failure to come to grips with the fundamental principle of "love in freedom."

The Place of the Church in a Pluralistic Human Society

The destruction of the Temple (A.D. 70) is often adduced as an argument for desacralization and secularization. Nothing could be more misleading. The cleansing of the Temple at the beginning of Christ's ministry was symbolic of the destruction of the temple that was to follow the establishment of the church. To conceive of the Temple as a symbol of the "ontocratic" pattern is to misunderstand it completely. For the Jews it was the *eikon* of the "presence" of Yahweh in the midst of his covenant people. The *shekinah*-presence in the temple and in the person of Christ[5] are serially

[5] John 1 : 14.

related to each other. Equally important is the Old Testament figure of the ladder which reaches up to heaven in Jacob's dream, which van Leeuwen would too easily interpret in terms of the "ontocratic pattern" rather than in terms of the more biblical scheme of antetype and fulfillment. In the Fourth Gospel Christ is the true ladder (John 1 : 51); and the true temple (John 2). He boldly calls the temple "my father's house" (*ho oikos tou patros mou*), and goes on to identify it with the "temple of his body" (*ho naos tou so matos mou*).[6] The first phrase is repeated in Chapter 14, with reference to the place which he is going to prepare for his disciples.

The destruction of the temple is thus to be seen as the result of its replacement by a living temple. "We (plural) are the temple of the living God." [7] The temple is the new community. God is now to be encountered by Jews and Gentiles, not at Jerusalem, but wherever the community is. There is no "desacralization" or "secularization," but the fulfillment of the antetype of the temple by its archtype, Christ, and his body the church. The new temple, not made with hands, remains in the midst of the world as the organism of the new community, Jesus Christ himself being the chief cornerstone. This is a recurring theme in the New Testament,[8] which we overlook at great peril to the very core of our faith.

The church, as the great new community in heaven and earth and not merely as an institution, has this function to fulfill as long as the *seculum* lasts. In Revelation 21, the seer saw the heavenly Jerusalem seen descending from God, but he "saw no temple in the city": the presence of God is manifest, and there is no longer any need for the community to be the veiled presence of God. But the total removal of the temple happens in the *eschaton,* not in time. And, in another sense, the holy city itself is the temple where God is present.

The church therefore has to be the "sacred temple" of God in

---

[6] John 2 : 16–21.

[7] II Cor. 6 : 16; cf. I Cor. 3 : 16ff, 6 : 19.

[8] See I Cor. 3 : 9–16, 17; 6 : 19, II Cor. 5 : 1; 6 : 16; Eph. 2 : 19ff.; I Peter 2 : 4ff.; Heb. 5 : 6.

the *seculum.* The *seculum* without the church is not in God's plan, and we must see the establishment of the Christian church in nearly all countries of the world in the light of its special role within the *seculum.* We should not despise the church for its smallness and insignificance, and respect only the *Mündigkeit* of the world simply because the latter's achievements and significance seem more impressive.

The church can be called a secular reality only insofar as it manifests itself in time. But the church certainly transcends the *seculum.* If it is truly the risen and ascended Body of Christ, then its limits are not set by the curvature of the time-space cosmos. Its foundation is in Jesus Christ, who is seated at the right hand of the Father. He was present in the time-space world at a certain point—Palestine in the first century. But that is not where we encounter him today.

The Ascension is an integral part of the Incarnation. Jesus told his disciples that it was necessary for him to ascend to the Father. Only so could he prepare an abiding place for them. The very existence of the church was a consequence of Ascension and Pentecost, both of which events link time with the transtemporal.

The presence of this transtemporal "secular" society within human society alone gives the latter meaning and purpose. The church serves the society in which it is placed in a threefold sense: (a) as the Temple of God in the midst of time-space existence; (b) as the royal priesthood within that temple; (c) as the model and pattern for the human commonwealth. The idea that the church is placed in time-space only to preach the gospel constitutes a major misconception of Reformed ecclesiology. The church does exist to proclaim the gospel and to speak the prophetic word about the will of God for the world, but the very performance of that function depends on the fulfillment of its threefold vocation in the Holy Spirit:

a. *The temple of God.* The theologian claims that modern secular man is so desacralized that he no longer has any use for temples. On the contrary, he needs and desperately longs for a temple —a place where he can encounter the living God. Modern literature is full of veiled or explicit references to this deep hunger in the secular man's consciousness. Both those who proclaim that "God is dead" and those who are either seeking to be "honest to God" or "waiting for Godot" express this need.

The tragedy of modern man's secular existence is that when he asks for bread he is given a stone. When he looks for the living God in the church, he finds the stone of the theologian's concept of God. If there were a Christian community which truly served as a living temple of the living God, secular man would have encountered God there. In the past half-dozen centuries we have so conceptualized our theology that God also has become merely a concept, perhaps necessary to close the gap in our structure of thought.

Whenever secular man encounters a Christian community which expresses in its worship and life the authentic presence of God, he is drawn to it. He may complain of archaic forms which are difficult for him to accept. But the accommodation of forms and language to those familiar to modern man will not in itself make the encounter any less problematic. In fact such accommodation, indiscriminately pursued, can fall into the trap of bringing God once more within secular man's understanding, in such a way that he is no longer a challenge to erroneous and self-sufficient conceptual structures.

The church exists in the midst of secular society as something that does not easily fit in. That is its vocation. It cannot be the temple of God, if it becomes merely a lecture room or a "gospel hall." If God is totally other, and has to be encountered, the time and place of that theophany have to be distinct from the time-space of ordinary existence. The church need not set out to be archaic, obscure, irrelevant and peculiar, but if it is the community of the Holy Spirit, it will express itself in forms that do not fit in to the "secularized" world. We shall discuss below how the community is to become such a temple.

b. *The royal priesthood*. The models offered by the New Testament for the nature of Christian existence must baffle the philosophers of logical analysis. The community is both the temple (house of the Spirit) and the corps of priests (I Peter 2 : 5). We need to make clear that when we speak of the "church," we speak neither of the building nor of the structures of ecclesiastical authority, but of the whole Christian community in time-space and beyond. This community, only one aspect of which appears at the present moment in time, has as its primary and everlasting vocation the exercise of its priesthood. Christ is the priest of creation who, on behalf of the created order, offers himself perpetually to God the Father. In the life and death of Christ, the creation said the "Yes" of freedom and love to its creator. The church has no greater vocation than to continue to manifest this "Yes" in its worship. Worship is neither ancillary nor subsidiary to mission: it is the characteristic act of the church, participating in the characteristic act of Christ its head. Without the recovery of authentic worship the church can be neither the temple of God nor the proclaimer of the Word. But we do not recover authentic worship in order better to proclaim the word of God. True worship in itself is sufficient *raison d'être* for the existence of the church.

No secular society can be authentic without the presence within it of the Christian community as temple of God and royal priesthood. But to be the royal priesthood also means to exercise a perpetual ministry of self-offering and intercession. The church's continuous worship and prayer in the midst of the secular community preserves, transforms and sanctifies that community, often without its knowledge, sometimes against its will.

Worship is an act of freedom and love, not subsidiary to anything else; and yet worship and prayer become instrumental in the transformation of society itself. Christ was a man of action. So were the apostles—or at least some of them. But Christ and his apostles spent much more time in prayer than in action. Our perennial temptation is to put our trust mainly in our words and action. Claiming to be prophets, we can miss the secret of the prophets and the true mark of the royal priesthood—sustained and disciplined prayer. The secular society for which we are struggling is then in peril of becoming anything but authentic.

c. *The model and pattern for the human commonwealth.* It is perhaps only an idle dream or a pious wish. But the church is called to be the manifestation of the kingdom of God in history. And that kingdom has three fundamental interrelated principles: love, freedom and wisdom. The Spirit is the bearer of all three. He is the spirit of love (Romans 5 : 5, 9 : 30; I Corinthians 4 : 21; Colossians 1 : 8), the spirit of freedom (Romans 8 : 15; II Corinthians 3 : 17) and the spirit of wisdom (I Corinthians 2 : 10ff; Ephesians 1 : 17). In II Timothy 1 : 7 these concepts are brought together: "God has not given us the spirit of fear; but of power and of love and of a sound mind." The Spirit works with God in Christ for the fulfillment of his purposes for the whole of creation.

Three things should be said about the nature of the Holy Spirit before we speak of love, freedom and wisdom as the three principles of a genuine "pluralistic human community." First, the Holy Spirit dwells in the community of the church, but works in the whole of creation. Second, the Holy Spirit works in the individual, but always relating him to God and to other human persons. Third, the Holy Spirit works in the openness of freedom. The Spirit becomes active in a person or in society without abolishing the subjectivity of the personal or social agent in whom he operates. The church, which knows the Holy Spirit, opens a channel for his work within both the church and human society as a whole. The church, as a true community of the Holy Spirit, is open at both ends, to God and to the world.

The church does its work in the world, not through ecclesiastical domination, but by identifying with the world in such a way that it continues to be a true agent and is not reduced to a passive listener or recipient. It is in this sense that the church becomes a model for the human commonwealth.

The Three Principles

The three principles of a "pluralistic human community"—love, freedom and wisdom—have their origin in the very being of God and, as the church manifests these, it becomes a theophany or the temple of God.

a. *Freedom.* There is no definition for freedom—nor for love nor wisdom: all three have their origin in God. One of the few things we can say about God is that he is free, loving and wise. In fact he *is* freedom, love and wisdom. We should be careful about making "is-statements" about God. He is. But to put a "subjective complement" to the verb can be dangerous, for that is to try to define God. And yet neither freedom nor love nor wisdom is a definitive concept. They derive their meaning from the "being" or "is-ness" of God, which is itself beyond definition and constantly free.

Freedom is more than the liberty of choice, or the absence of external constraint. Freedom means the possibility of achieving what one wills, unhindered by external constraint or lack of power. Power in this sense is synonymous with freedom: lack of power is lack of freedom. God alone is free. He wills, and it is done. Nothing "outside" him limits his freedom, except that which he has willed to create. But even the creation does not exist "outside" God. It is always in him and therefore under his power. Man is made "in the image" of God and therefore made for freedom. In Christ, man is adopted as the Son of God. "The sons are free," says our Lord in Matthew 17 : 26. We have been called "into the freedom of the glory of the children of God" (Romans 8 : 21).

Stemming from St. Augustine, there exists, especially in the western tradition, what Eric Fromm calls "the fear of freedom." There is a spiritual grandeur in Augustine's *Da quod jubes, et jube quod vis* (Give what thou commandest and command what thou wilt). Pelagius, the pragmatic Englishman, certainly misunderstood it. But the tradition of western theology which makes God the sole agent and man the passive recipient also misunderstands the delicate work of the Holy Spirit, who refuses to storm the citadel of man's resistance, but acts through inner prompting without abolishing subjectivity and freedom. In the lives of both St. Paul and St. Augustine, the Holy Spirit activated the free seeking and acceptance of God's will without suppressing the agency of man. It should not be forgotten that in this petition Augustine was referring specifically to continence and purity. He made and asked for that choice. It is theologically dangerous to assert that God gives and man simply receives, or that God commands and man obeys. That kind of obedience does not lead to maturity in freedom. The adulthood of man requires the development not only of dependence but of freedom. Pelagius called man's peculiar "freedom in either direction" "the glory of our rational nature." [9] He and Augustine both erred, however, in treating freedom in terms of the *ability* to sin or not to sin, and in conceiving of sin primarily in individualistic and moralistic terms. John Cassian, whose eastern heritage helped him to see that both sides erred, was, however, unable to point out the locus of the error. He thus lapsed into the equally unsatisfactory compromise of semi-pelagianism and synergism. The Council of Orange simply ratified the error of St. Augustine in less profound but more precise terms.

The fear of freedom, which denies freedom to err, too easily assumes the possession of articulate truth. The church thus sought to guard the truth both by temporal power and by exact formulation. Ever since the Reformation we have been witnessing the effective revolt against both the false claim and the human attempt to defend the truth. That very revolt, however, has led to new errors which made individual judgment the arbiter of truth and developed a new *corpus* of pseudo-biblical truth. The present secular revolt asserts the freedom of man over against the dogmatic formulations on both sides of the sixteenth-century controversy. It has its roots in the freedom of man rather than in Christianity as van Leeuwen claims. Confronted by the apparently contradictory authority of "church" and "Bible," modern man slowly discovered the experimental or pragmatic notion of truth which bases itself neither on dogmatic authority nor on individual judgment, but on repeatable, demonstrable, public experiments and eventually on the laws of mathematics.

Technology also has its roots in the freedom of man. Man belongs to the biological continuum of evolution and has been car-

[9] PELAGIUS: *Epistula ad Demetriadem,* Migne, P.L. 33 : 1100.

ried along by it. The evolution of his consciousness has also resulted in his emancipation from the blind movement of evolution. He has become aware of himself and of his environment. Instead of being transmuted by the forces of the cosmos, he seeks to understand them and to transmute them and himself. Even primitive man's patterns of social organization and methods of forming tools are part of this evolution of human freedom. The Greeks held that *technè* and *politike* were the gifts of the gods to men. Modern science and technology belong to this continuum which has its origin in pre-Christian and extra-Hebraic society. Whenever men learned through experience and devised tools, there were science and technology. They belonged to the freedom of man to emancipate himself from the cosmic forces and to gain control of them.

In recent times, however, there has been an unprecedented acceleration of the development of science and technology. But this must not be attributed too hastily to the theocratic spirit of western Christianity. Many thinkers would hold that the technocratic revolution also has its roots in the steady inflow of raw materials from the colonies and in the ready market the colonies provided for the products of western European industry.

Our purpose here, however, is not to debate the origins of science and technology, but to place them in relation to power and freedom. Christians in the past have always tended to look upon power as neutral, if not evil. This springs from a basic misunderstanding. The ability to transcend the evolutionary process through self-awareness and through understanding of the environment, and then to redirect the evolutionary process itself by changes in the self and in the environment is an integral part of human freedom. Insofar as they help to create that ability, science and technology—and the power derived from them—are good, not evil or neutral.

One must welcome freedom, even when its emergence is accompanied by acute suffering. For example, the liberation of the Congolese people from the Belgian yoke may not seem to be an unmitigated good. It is accompanied by savage and brutal acts of inhuman cruelty. Is it not destroying the dignity of man? Would it not have been better if Belgium had kept the Congolese under tutelage for another thirty or sixty years as they had originally intended? The answer is an unequivocal No. Freedom could not have emerged in western Europe if the primary concern had been for nonviolence, law and order. Some lessons have to be learned by experience. If Europe, after centuries of "civilization," has not yet learned to avoid war and to respect the dignity of men, we should give the Congolese at least half a generation in which to come to terms with their own situation. Freedom should be welcomed by the Christian, even when it is freedom from forces favorable to Christianity and the church. Freedom should also be granted to error, since the truth cannot fear error. Every advancement in the knowledge and power for mankind should be heartily welcomed by the church.

There are areas, however, where freedom does not so easily emerge. The New Testament speaks of freedom as being free from sin, law and death (Romans 6 : 8). Man's bondage to evil and guilt, to dependence on heteronomous structures and to fear of death, as well as to the disintegration of personality and society, must also be broken, if a genuinely human society is to emerge.

The greatest problem of freedom, however, is the possibility of its dissociation from love and wisdom.

b. *Love and justice.* To say that "justice" is an approximation of love can be misleading. Both justice and love are social realities. But justice, understood in the traditional Roman sense, seems to be opposed to love rather than to approximate it. Underlying the concept of justice is the notion of rights and duties, which do not properly belong to love. This is the crisis of western society. It has proceeded on the assumption that "social justice" is the highest attainable value and has often failed to see the great gap between it and love. The end result is that while western societies are incomparably more "just" than societies in eastern Europe or in Asia, Africa and Latin America, genuine intersubjectivity is becoming increasingly problematic in the West.

Here we come to the delicate question of structures and persons. Can "love" be built into structures? Justice certainly can. But justice operates primarily in the areas of external actions and cannot deal directly with the "inner" man.[10] However, even the maintenance of justice cannot be assured by the structures. Where men are willing to sacrifice their freedom for the sake of some lesser good, justice always succumbs despite all structures. To think therefore of the "principalities and powers" as resident primarily in the power structures is a gross oversimplification. The demonic cannot be kept out by structures of any kind. Only the vigilance of human freedom and love combined with divine wisdom can struggle successfully against the principalities and powers. Social injustice is indeed demonic, and the demons must be unseated from the control-chambers of society. Yet even within the most just social structures the most demonic of all forces—the denial of freedom and love—can persist.

But what is this love that we oppose to justice? It is the greatest gift of the Spirit, greater than the power of miracles or of speaking in tongues. It is the one gift that is bestowed on all and without which all other gifts of the Spirit are of no avail (I Corinthians 13 : 1–3). All social action and all acts of sacrifice are without value if they are not accompanied by love. Even faith, without love, is nothing.

Although love should never be identified with the merely sentimental and emotional, it does involve sentiments and emotions as well as the will and the mind. Paul begins his famous exhortation on love by describing it in the concepts of generosity (*makrothumia*) and kindness (*chrèstotès*). Our own traditional understanding of love includes two characteristics which are contradictory to the Pauline understanding—*limitation* and *possession*. We love someone *more than* we love others. We have to exclude others, in order to love one. We choose the person whom we love. Family

---

[10] BONHOEFFER denies the existence of any distinction between inner and outer man in the Bible: *Letters and Papers from Prison,* Fontana, ed., 1963, p. 118. This is surprising in a man who knew his Bible rather well and must often have read Romans 7 : 22; II Cor. 4 : 16 and Eph. 3 : 16.

love is limited to those who are related to us by blood or marriage. The objective of romantic love is the possession of the beloved.

The range of Christian love is as wide as humanity. Whoever the man is whom I confront, I am to love him. Samaritan, Jew and Gentile are alike: humanity is the limit. And *com-passion* rather than possession is the motivation. We enter into the other's being, feel, think and act with him and in his best interests. We allow him to enter into ours as well. This is true *com-passion,* true kindness, true intersubjectivity. It is not simply dialogue or communication, but rather communion, or *koinonia,* the word we often translate as "fellowship." This ability to enter into all men, and openness to all men that they may enter into us, is the precondition of love and its primary expression. It can hardly be built into structures of social justice, though these structures are necessary for its expression. A truly pluralistic human community is one where love exists. A just society does not guarantee love. Love can exist even where there is social injustice. But without love even the just society perishes.

c. *Wisdom.* Knowledge is not wisdom. Knowledge can assist wisdom, but the two can exist apart from each other. The foundation of wisdom is truth itself, not the knowledge of truth.

The Spirit is always the spirit of truth. Our Lord promised the "spirit of truth" (John 14 : 17) who leads us into truth itself (John 16 : 13), not merely to a knowledge of it. Wisdom is a "being" rather than a functional category. One has to be *in* the truth in order to be wise (John 8 : 44). To "know the truth" (John 8 : 32) is to participate in it, to stand in it (John 8 : 44). True freedom and true love require this being in the truth. The movement from falsehood to truth is faith (the fear of the Lord) and the beginning of wisdom.

Time-space existence can be false existence. To be *ek tou kosmou* is to have a false existence. If the ground of our existence is the time-space world, that existence is founded on that which is not true. The true is that which abides: the world passes away.

The *seculum* is a flow, a passing away. We find true existence in the evanescent course of time-existence only if our foundations are in something that transcends that course and abides "forever."

The only absolute truth within the *seculum* is the presence of God within it. The Incarnation is not so much a "revelation" as a presence. Christ can therefore say that he is the truth, and the Johannine prologue can say, "We beheld his glory, full of grace and truth." The precondition of wisdom is less "knowledge" (in the sense of cognition) of this truth, than "knowledge" (in the Hebrew sense) by participation in him.

Unless our objectives and foundation of our life go beyond the *seculum,* we contine in the folly of human wisdom. Our decisions, our purposes, our science and technology cannot provide an adequate and abiding foundation for our life. These can be properly utilized only when this foundation is in the truth. Wisdom comes by the hearing of the gospel, by faith in Christ and by baptism into his Body, which alone abides. When we are in the Body of Christ, and not in our own bodies, the Spirit helps us to grow in wisdom.

Can there, then, be wisdom outside the church, in a "pluralistic human community"? This question is wrongly formulated, for the church and the world cannot be seen as two mutually exclusive spheres. The church penetrates the world, as the "soul" does the body, to borrow a rather archaic analogy. The church exists with the world in identification with it. This is not to claim that whatever good there is in the world belongs to the church by right. The spirit of truth operates in the whole of creation. Even where there is no conscious faith in Christ, no sacramental baptism into the Body of Christ, "the Spirit bloweth where it listeth."

Nor is this a question of the church appropriating the wisdom in the world and offering it to God. As Etienne Gilson once said, it would be too easy if the scientists and technicians were to do all the work and the lazy Christians to pick it up and offer it to God. Pluralism is a true precondition of wisdom: the church has no monopoly on it.

It seems to be God's purpose that the pursuit of knowledge should take place largely outside the church. But this does not mean that the church can too lightly appropriate this knowledge and transmute it into wisdom. It appears to be God's will that the church will depend on the experience of the whole world for its own wisdom, which gives us a good reason for our "dialogue" not only with "secular" man but also with "religious" men of all faiths. But neither is the church selfishly to seek wisdom for itself, profiting from the experience of the whole world.

The wisdom that the Spirit gives is for the whole world, that it may know how to use its freedom to live. The church works in identification with the world, open to the Spirit, that the way of wisdom may be opened to all mankind. It has the advantage that it knows it has been liberated from anxiety, from guilt and from the search for false security and self-justification, the two great enemies of wisdom. It can therefore act as a catalyst in liberating groups in the world from the folly of seeking false security and self-justification.

The wisdom of history teaches us that the church needs opposition and external criticism in order to be faithful to its calling; and God seems, therefore, to have decreed that the church can find true wisdom only in a pluralistic society. The tragedy of western theology is precisely its development in an essentially homogeneous society. It is to be hoped that as pluralism develops in the West and the western church is thrown into a pluralistic world community, it will clarify its wisdom thus to the benefit of the whole world. Only thus can it have a more balanced understanding of its own contribution to wisdom, which though great, is often exaggerated.

Conclusion

Man finds himself in a pluralistic society; it is his task to make it more human and more free. The church's role in history has been ambiguous. In large measure, it has been used of God to humanize and liberate society. But in no small measure has it strode in the way of freedom.

The growth of freedom by itself does not assure that society will be more human. The dynamic interaction and growth of power, love, and wisdom alone can make a pluralistic community more human and therefore more divine.